To and from Gigs

To and from Gigs
Challenges, Choices, Chances, Changes

HERB HICKS

iUniverse LLC
Bloomington

To and from Gigs
Challenges, Choices, Chances, Changes

Copyright © 2013 by Herb Hicks.

Cover Photo of Author: Donna Kroeger
Back Photo of Author: Karen Ohno

All rights reserved. No part of this book may be used or reproduced by any means, graphic, electronic, or mechanical, including photocopying, recording, taping or by any information storage retrieval system without the written permission of the publisher except in the case of brief quotations embodied in critical articles and reviews.

iUniverse books may be ordered through booksellers or by contacting:

iUniverse LLC
1663 Liberty Drive
Bloomington, IN 47403
www.iuniverse.com
1-800-Authors (1-800-288-4677)

Because of the dynamic nature of the Internet, any web addresses or links contained in this book may have changed since publication and may no longer be valid. The views expressed in this work are solely those of the author and do not necessarily reflect the views of the publisher, and the publisher hereby disclaims any responsibility for them.

Any people depicted in stock imagery provided by Thinkstock are models, and such images are being used for illustrative purposes only.
Certain stock imagery © Thinkstock.

ISBN: 978-1-4759-9864-1 (sc)
ISBN: 978-1-4759-9863-4 (hc)
ISBN: 978-1-4759-9862-7 (ebk)

Library of Congress Control Number: 2013912931

Printed in the United States of America

iUniverse rev. date: 08/08/2013

For my children,
Joanne, Allan, and Janine

Contents

Prologue ix

Chapter 1: Beginning Time Remembered 1
Chapter 2: Swing Music and Brown Gas 9
Chapter 3: On the Road 22
Chapter 4: Air Force 34
Chapter 5: The Big Apple and a Slow Boat 44
Chapter 6: The French-Swiss Connection 54
Chapter 7: Back in the Good Old USA 68
Chapter 8: Into the Sunset to the American Riviera 78
Chapter 9: The Minneapolis School of Art 93
Chapter 10: Minneapolis to Mexico to Maine 100
Chapter 11: Return to Paradise 109
Chapter 12: Ice Cream Delight 122
Chapter 13: LA North 135
Chapter 14: Sixties' Shrapnel, Seventies' Splendor 150
Chapter 15: Transitions 163
Chapter 16: Road to Recovery 176
Chapter 17: New Millennium of Discoveries and Losses 189
Chapter 18: Frightening, Surprising, Thrilling 203

Afterword 215

Prologue

Alone Together

"Hey, Bob! We should be going back the other way."

"Why?" he asked.

"Look!" I answered. "Look at those tracks beside the creek. Let's go back."

My brother, Bob, and I were struggling through the dense underbrush beside a mountain stream in the Canadian Rocky Mountains near Westcastle, Alberta. With fly rods in hand, creels and hip waders snagging on the thick bushes, we were determined to go upstream to find that elusive trout habitat where we could catch cutthroat on every cast.

Bob looked along the bank of the stream and saw what had made me decide to turn back. Going the same direction as us were fresh, enormous bear paw tracks.

"Definitely grizzly bear," Bob said reflectively. "Let's go back."

I agreed. Traveling the same direction as a grizzly canceled any thoughts of going farther upstream.

The day before, we had watched a grizzly from afar through our binoculars and seen a display of awesome brute force. The bear, tossing fallen dead trees about as though he was playing pick-up sticks, was foraging for grubs and bugs. We certainly didn't want to be on his menu. Going back downstream was easier and faster (probably because we wanted to put a lot of distance between ourselves and the bear tracks).

Walking back to our camper, we hardly said a word. We were by nature quiet, preferring the subtle sounds of the forest to verbose chitchat. Our communication in those outings was more by sight and gestures that expressed our moods and emotions. Our actions together spoke louder than words. We were enjoying our moment of being alone together in this beautiful mountain environment in the late summer of the mid-1970s.

The sun, sinking behind the mountains, cast long cerulean-blue shadows across the pine-treed hillsides. We could feel the coolness of the pending fall season. We had followed the mountain stream since early morning, stopping only once for a small sandwich and cola we had packed. Now we were feeling weary and hungry. Our fishing activity of catch and release had netted us some nice cutthroat trout, and we had saved a couple for our evening meal. It was time to relax and cook our supper.

After our fill of fresh trout sautéed in beer, we hit the sack early and almost immediately were fast asleep in our comfortable camper. It was still dusk when we were suddenly awakened by a scraping noise and felt the camper rocking back and forth. Our first thought was that the smell of the fish we had cooked for supper had attracted a bear. We wondered if it could be the grizzly whose tracks we had seen earlier that day. Cautiously we pulled back a curtain and peered out the window into the evening dimness. We burst out laughing at what we saw; there in the twilight were some rancher's cattle. One scruffy steer was rubbing against the camper to scratch his backside.

My first thoughts in writing these memoirs were of the times I'd spent with my brother, enjoying an outing in nature or playing the piano with Bob on his bass. These events were numerous throughout my life and are some of my most cherished remembrances.

Our partnership as pianist and bassist began in 1960 when Bob and I shared an apartment in Minneapolis. Bob was working for the Minneapolis/St. Paul radio station KSTP, and I had just enrolled in the Minneapolis School of Art. We had a second-floor apartment on Twenty-Sixth Street, just a few blocks from the school. The street had low-rent apartments, and a number of art students lived in the area. Our apartment had a huge kitchen, two small bedrooms, and a large front room. We turned the large front room into an art studio where

I would paint and Bob would sculpt. The large kitchen, we decided, would be our music room.

We bought an old upright piano and proceeded to move it up the back stairs to the second floor. Those stairs were steep, but being young (and foolish), we were determined to move that archaic piano into our music room. We were damn lucky that piano didn't break free and roll over one of us. After much grunting, groaning, cursing, and sweating, we rolled the monster keyboard into our huge kitchen. There was enough room in that kitchen to have Count Basie's band do a gig there (or so it seemed). We enjoyed many jams (the cuisine kind and the musical kind) in our Twenty-Sixth Street music kitchen.

Bob was playing alto sax at this time, and we'd spend hours playing the standard jazz tunes and listening to recordings by the jazz giants. Bob told me he wasn't sure if the alto was the instrument for him. He couldn't find what he wanted to sound like. He said he only knew that he wanted to sound like himself—whatever that was—and he'd have to explore the music realm to discover what that meant.

He did find out what he wanted to sound like. One day after school when I was climbing the stairs to our apartment, I heard a low-pitched boom coming from our place. I opened the door, went into the kitchen, and saw Bob embracing a huge double bass violin, plucking away and grimacing.

Looking at me over the top of his glasses—and still plucking the bass strings—he said, "I traded my sax in on it. I got a good deal."

To my knowledge, Bob had never shown an interest in the bass violin until then. Bob taking up the bass delighted me as it crossed my mind that not only had he found *his* sound, but he had also found *our* sound. We were a united music entity, a piano-bass duo.

We began playing gigs as a duo, then as a trio (adding a drummer), and finally adding horn players to form quartets and quintets. Our journey as partners in music continued for more than forty years of exciting travels going to and from gigs.

I've done self-portraits in pencil, charcoal, etching, oils, and acrylic paints, and music compositions reflecting my aural penchants. Why not try words? The more I thought about it, the more intriguing the idea became.

Writing, I soon discovered, was analogous to creating a painting or playing an improvised music solo. Doing a self-portrait is somewhat scary, no matter what media you use, as you strip away disguises and expose yourself. Candidly recounting the events of my life was an emotional catharsis. I felt as though I was standing naked in front of God and everyone.

I chose to write about my personal experiences, the events that encompassed my life, and the historic events that influenced my philosophical perspectives. This, I hope, will give my readers an insight into my views that were formed during my journey and my response to history. My views are a manifestation of what I thought, what I said, and what I did.

Chapter 1

Beginning Time Remembered

*R*ecollections of past events are, at best, subjective, and those images I remember become distorted by time, experiences, and attitudes acquired, giving me a biased view of a scene related to my past history. As that may be, I have been as candid as possible in presenting my reminiscences as I recall them.

There is the theory that everything you have experienced is recorded in your brain. Total recall, known as *eidetic memory* (the ability to recall all sensory experiences), would be fantastic. Being able to recall in detail any pain, pleasure, or event that had happened to you would give you a perspective on life different than the fragmented, subjective view your memory gives you now.

My memory works in mysterious ways. Sometimes a past event will just pop into my mind, as though it had bubbled up from the bottom of my memory milieu, and I have a dialogue with myself about a remembered past.

The beginning of my remembered time starts in a small town in North Dakota. That was over three-quarters of a century ago. My first day on this earth was May 7, 1934. The place was Williston, a town in the northwestern part of North Dakota near the confluence of the Yellowstone and Missouri Rivers. The town, surrounded by flat prairies and vast acres of wheat fields, is today the center of one of the largest oil fields in the United States. Oil was discovered forty miles northeast of Williston in 1951, and in 2010 a new oil boom in the northwestern part of North Dakota (in a formation known as Bakken) has put Williston on the map as a leading economic oil center in the United States.

My mom and dad were hardworking, conservative parents; although they believed in traditional ideas and behavior, they were always open-minded. They always listened to what my brother and I had to say about what we wanted to do with our lives. Since there were no television or computer games to amuse me, my entertainment was made-up games that were limited only by my imagination. Books, radio, and movies were the influences that prompted my play acting. I was an extremely shy child, easily embarrassed by the slightest mishap, but my shyness didn't limit my curiosity. I was curious about every natural and man-made object and investigated them with scrutinizing detail as long as I could do it on my own terms—alone. I was an incorrigible introvert.

My parents gave me clear guidelines about work and play. The chores I was to perform were well defined.

When I was young, one of my responsibilities was to make sure the drip basin under our ice chest was emptied before water overflowed onto the kitchen floor. Our ice chest was a handsomely crafted, ornate wooden cabinet about as high as I was at six years old. A block of ice would fit in the top compartment to cool off the interior of the cabinet where food was stored. As cool air descended from the block of melting ice, water would drip down a drain pipe into a basin placed under the chest.

One day, I was forgetful in my duties, and water overflowed the basin and spilled onto the kitchen floor. Mom was too late in noticing the flooded kitchen floor as she came up the stairs from the basement with a load of laundry. She stepped onto the kitchen floor, slipped on the wet linoleum, and landed on her back. She had really hurt herself. I had just come into the kitchen to witness this. Realizing my negligence was the cause of this accident, I was embarrassed and started to cry as I tried to help her up off the floor. I wasn't punished for my neglect, but I was given a lecture on the obligation to one's duties. Not fulfilling my duty, consequences were to be paid. I've constantly carried that lesson with me.

Our first electric refrigerator towered above me like a huge smooth, white monolithic icon. My most vivid memory of our fridge was not the appliance itself—it was the cardboard container the fridge came in.

The refrigerator's corrugated container was gigantic—the *Titanic* of cardboard boxes. That carton provided me with weeks of entertainment. It was magically transformed into a fort, a tank, a pirate ship, and a B-25 bomber. Last, but not least, the cardboard container was cut, bent, shaped, and taped into the image of a stagecoach, which was mounted on my little red wagon. Painted on the sides in beautiful script (lettering by my dad) were the words "Overland Stage Coach." I would give neighborhood kids rides across my imaginary untamed prairie full of Indians, outlaws, and wild animals. That stage traveled many miles through my fantasy world (around my neighborhood).

In many of my childhood's invented games I would emulate the roles of my cowboy heroes. Riding my imaginary horse, wearing my *real* bearskin cowboy chaps, I'd fire my Red Ryder BB gun at imaginary desperadoes. Sometimes, to the disapproval of my mother, I'd shoot blossoms from their stalks in her beautiful flower garden. I was a crack shot with my air rifle.

I was always bumping, falling, scraping, cutting, or bruising some part of me. It wasn't as if I was reckless or clumsy or did not have good parental supervision; I was just always super active and had an inquisitiveness that threw caution to the wind (I guess in a sense that was being reckless).

Considering all my catastrophes, I was fortunate to survive my juvenile years.

It was a macho thing to have a jackknife when I was young and even manlier to play dangerous games with it. One of our favorite pocketknife games was a version of mumbly-peg, a knife-throwing game popular in the thirties and forties. A more dangerous game was just called the Knife Game, also sometimes known as the FFF (five-finger fillets). This game challenged your coordination as you tried to stab a knife between your outstretched fingers while holding your palm down on the ground or on a table. Whoever could do that the fastest in an allotted time was the winner. The loser was the slowest—or the one who stabbed his hand or finger. I was the big loser one time, stabbing my left hand between the ring and middle finger. I think I was more surprised to see the knife sticking in my hand with blood oozing from the wound than I was mindful of the oncoming pain. It left an obvious scar; I wear it—with a number of others—like a badge of courage displaying validation of rituals confirming manhood.

A large part of my childhood was spent at my grandparents' house. I loved to go there in the winter to dig in the damp fresh soil of their greenhouse. It was a chance to get away from the humdrum of a long North Dakota winter. During the autumns in the forties, I would help my grandparents harvest their large vegetable garden. My Overland Stage had traveled off into the sunset, and my red wagon became a vegetable cart. My dad and I made wooden sides for the wagon so I could carry an assortment of potatoes, corn, tomatoes, beans, and carrots for sale around town. My vegetable cart also doubled as a junk wagon to collect scrap metal, boxes, rags, paper, and bottles that I could sell as part of the war effort (copper metal was the premium prize in finding junk). I was hustling to earn money to buy a bicycle.

Once while trying to make a sale of my vegetables, a cantankerous lady customer accused me of stealing the vegetables from someone's garden. She said she was going to call the police. I told her the vegetables were from my grandparent's garden, but she wanted to know their names so she could call them. She scared the hell out of me, and I took off down the street, spilling a large portion of my produce cart. My grandmother chastised the suspicious lady for accusing her grandson of being dishonest. I looked up to my grandparents and my parents as heroes and my guardians against the forces of evil in the world.

My grandparents (Greutman) on my mom's side emigrated from Switzerland to the United States in the early 1900s. My grandfather (Emil) was a baker in San Francisco, and my grandmother (Bertha Barbara) looked after a family who lived on Nob Hill. When the 1906 earthquake hit San Francisco, Grandma and Grandpa lost almost everything. Grandfather fell ill and died of what was suspected as "baker's lungs." My grandmother was a strong person, both physically and emotionally, and she was pregnant with her first child (my mother). Grandmother moved to Seattle where my mother, Bertha, was born in 1907.

Grandmother met her late husband's brother (Herman) who had also emigrated from Switzerland, and they were married. Herman, whom I came to know as my grandfather, was actually my step-grandfather. They moved to North Dakota around 1911. In

1913, my uncle (Herman Jr.) was born in Williston. Around 1919, the Greutmans decided to move back to Switzerland, and my mom and my uncle attended school there. In 1924, they returned to North Dakota. They bought a house in west Williston and started a greenhouse.

My mother was a petite woman. She was full of vim and vigor, and most people would have had a hard time keeping up with her work. She had this vitality until later in life when diabetes took its toll. During World War II, my mom, grandmother, and my aunt Ceil picked potatoes on large farms in the Missouri River bottoms. It was backbreaking work, but it meant extra income for all of us. At nine or ten, I would work the potato fields with them from dawn until sundown.

Looking down those long, long rows of freshly dug potatoes, I'd anticipate the day's work, but I would always be up for it and the serious money I could make.

A dozen or so years later, when I became interested in art, I saw some reproductions of paintings and drawings by Van Gogh of peasants planting and digging potatoes. I marveled at the way he captured the gesture of the stooped figures at work in the fields. I could feel the ache in my back just looking at those images and remembering my own experiences. As often happens, art imitates life as life imitates art. Oscar Wilde once said, "Life imitates art *far more* than art imitates life." I disagree. I think it's a tie. Sorry, Oscar.

My father, Melvin (Mel), was born in 1899 in Idlewood, Illinois. My father never knew who his father was and was raised by his mother, Mata, his aunt Vernie, and his grandfather, Oliver Zeller Hicks. O. Z. Hicks was a minister of the Church of the Brethren and he, his daughter Vernie, and my father moved to North Dakota in 1911. What became of Dad's mother, Mata, I have no record. Aunt Vernie was Dad's principal guardian, but she died in 1919 from injuries received while trying to start a car by cranking when the car slipped into gear and ran over her.

Dad was a true gentleman, cut from the same fabric as the strong, silent type. He worked at a variety of jobs in Chicago to finance his education at Chicago Coin Electric College. In the early 1920s, he worked for the Southern Illinois Light and Power Company. After Chicago, Dad was employed by the United States Reclamation Service at its Williston Power Plant. In 1926, the plant was purchased by

Montana Dakota Utilities, and Dad worked the rest of his career for MDU.

In June 1927, Melvin Hicks and Bertha Greutman were married. That year, on a stormy summer night, the power plant was struck by lightning. Dad, working the night shift, was inside the plant when it went up in flames. He came through the fire without any injuries, but the power plant was destroyed. A power station at Fairview, Montana, was put on standby power; Dad worked there for a couple of years until a new powerhouse was built in Williston.

The Williston Power Plant was an enchanted place for me. It was hot, noisy, and full of interesting levers, switches, dials, gadgets, gauges, pipes, cables, and wiring. I spent many hours there with my dad, and he explained the workings of a power plant. The boilers containing water were fired with natural gas furnaces to create steam to turn the turbines to generate electricity. Peering through the peepholes into those huge roaring furnaces was like looking into Hades itself. The noise was deafening, and you had to shout to one another to be heard. Working in that noisy environment for forty years affected my father's hearing.

In 1949, Dad became chief engineer for the Williston Power Plant. It was a very important position and was stressful at times. Whenever there was an electrical outage, Dad would get irate phone calls from customers who couldn't turn their lights on. The outages were usually caused by lightning storms at night in the summer. The Williston area had some awesome midnight firework displays of "*Donner und Blitzen.*" My father was thoughtful and sensitive; I think he took every outage personally. He retired on December 31, 1964, as superintendent of the Montana Dakota Utilities Williston Power Plant.

When I was in the fourth grade at Williston Webster Grade School, my friend Dan reached in his pocket to pull out his handkerchief—and a handful of marbles went flying. When those marbles hit the hardwood floor, they bounced in every direction and were as loud as ricocheting bullets. Our teacher was on him like a hawk. Grabbing him by one ear, she started dragging him, like a wounded animal, into the coat room. We all knew that meant a strapping. She said, "Spare the rod and spoil the child." She never had spoiled children in her class.

Poor Dan's yelps with every whack of the strap made us all shudder. It was like a scene from a pirate novel where a shipmate was being flogged. Was walking the gangplank next?

In the 1940s, it was permissible, and acceptable, for adults with any authority to spank children. Some people took advantage of this entitlement and went to extremes with this power. Our fourth-grade teacher was such a person. She was an absolute authoritarian in all matters in that classroom. I believe she really thought the way to teach was to beat the student into submission. Rule by fear. There are humans, and deities, who have wielded their power by this edict, but I can truthfully say I did learn something from my fourth-grade teacher.

- I learned to keep my desk in a straight row.
- I learned to obey orders. Do exactly what I was told to do.
- I learned not to ask questions or question anything.
- I learned to be very quiet and make myself as inconspicuous as possible.

That was my fourth-grade education.

We were an outdoors family of campers, hunters, and fishing people. I would walk the Dakota coulees, hunting pheasants and grouse and through the stubble wheat fields looking for prairie chickens and partridge. Dad taught my brother and me the proper rules about firearm safety and good sportsmanship in hunting.

The wild game we harvested always showed up on our dinner table. Pheasant was my favorite, and we always had plenty of game birds for our Thanksgiving and Christmas dinners. Upland game bird-hunting became a way of life for me when I was growing up. Getting ready in the early mornings to go hunting stirred some primitive instinct as I felt excited in anticipation of the outdoor adventures.

The art of fishing, for me, is summed up in a quote by Sir Isaac Walton. "Angling (is) like the virtue of humility, which has a calmness of spirit and a world of other blessings attending upon it. It is an art worthy the knowledge and patience of a wise man."

From the time I was a toddler to manhood I spent myriad hours fishing the Muddy and the Missouri Rivers. Walleye pike fishing was the favorite sport-fishing activity for my family. Although we had walleye in North Dakota lakes and rivers, the best fishing was in Canada. Dad would take us on numerous trips to the Fort Qu'Appelle Lakes in Saskatchewan. Walleye were the prize fish because of their succulent sweet taste; some of the best meat came from their cheeks. Their meat was white and flakey like halibut. We called them *the prairie fisherman's halibut.*

To this day, fishing and hunting still stir a primitive response in my psyche that makes me feel a basic empathy with nature. The DNA imprints that define us as Homo sapiens have been passed down over two hundred thousand years of evolution from the time when we were basically hunters and gatherers. It may be deeply buried subconsciously, but one cannot deny genetics.

I've always looked at life like it was a fishing outing. If you have patience, you'll catch something—first you have to have your line, hook, and bait in the stream. I keep a little sign on my fridge that reminds me of one of my passions: *Time is a stream that one goes fishing in.*

Chapter 2

Swing Music and Brown Gas

When I was twelve, I would play country-and-western songs, picking out the melodies on the piano, accordion, and violin. I was a big fan of the singing cowboy balladeers and western swing bands like the Sons of the Pioneers, and Bob Wills and the Texas Playboys. I'd strum away on an old four-string (tenor) guitar that had been my dad's. This old guitar had been stored in a barn for years; no matter how much soapy scrubbing I did on its body, I couldn't get rid of the mice pee smell that had permeated the wood. I finally chucked it—throwing it on a pile of burning leaves. I remember thinking it made the finest musical sound it ever had, popping and crackling as it went up in flames.

In my teens, I discovered the big bands. The sound of horns playing swing music really appealed to me. From there, I began to dig the jazz horn soloists playing in a small group setting. I loved the rhythms and the melodic and harmonic structure. I dug the idea of the soloist having the freedom to express his or her own musical ideas according to the tune's rhythmic and harmonic form. I was intrigued by the musical acrobats of the bebop players with their superb techniques and the unique sense they had for fast, unexpected twists and turns of a melodic line. They took my ears to new tonal adventures. I heard jazz players performing on their instruments the instant expression of their emotions by means of the art of improvisation. Adding jazz to my list of music genres, I joined that distinct minority group of true jazz fans.

Enthralled by the sounds of swing music's dynamic pulsating rhythms, lush harmonies, and melodic phrases, two of my friends and I formed a little combo to try to play this music. Wayne Hagge (alto sax), Bob Miller (drums), and I (piano and clarinet) were excited about applying our musical knowledge to playing dance music. Our music teachers were not very keen on the dance music genre, and we were more or less on our own.

My experience taking piano lessons varied from being thrilled to being tortured. I started music lessons in grade school with teachers who made playing music fun. In junior high, I had a music teacher who was a strict disciplinarian (my fourth-grade teacher reincarnated). She taught piano by a method that was very perfunctory and more related to mechanics than as an art form. When I missed one fingering, I would get a ruler across the knuckles or a stab in the head with a pencil. Then I'd be sent to her outer waiting room to practice my fingering technique on a cardboard keyboard and wait for my turn while the next student had their lesson.

She had no time or love for any of that "jazzy" music that interested me. I was beginning to play popular sheet music on my own and noticed little symbols above the written notes. Showing this to my piano teacher, I asked what these meant.

"You don't have to worry about those," she said. "You'll never use them."

How wrong she was. For contemporary pianists, those little chord symbols are important basic codes of information for the harmonic structure of a tune.

Climbing the stairs to her music studio every Saturday was mental anguish as I anticipated my tortuous piano lesson. It is ironic that I spent the rest of my life pursuing the *joy* of playing the piano.

I didn't continue with piano lessons after the eighth grade, but I did continue with our trio, practicing dance tunes and establishing a library of songs that were standards by the Tin Pan Alley composers, some waltzes, polkas, and pop tunes of the day. The first gig for our trio was a formal dance for the Rainbow Girls.

The Rainbow Girls were part of the Masonic Lodge Order. I was in the Order of DeMolay, which is the boys' order of the Masonic Lodge. I'd joined the DeMolay with a friend of mine, mainly because the lodge had a pool table we could use. These organizations were open to kids from eleven to twenty-one. I have many friends who are Masons, but I never knew of any who had mystical abilities. I also didn't know of any Masonic phrases that had the power to unlock ancient wisdom and bring about worldwide enlightenment as Dan Brown alludes to in *The Lost Symbol*. But it is a fascinating allusion.

A friend of our family was the head of the Rainbow Girls, and she had heard we had formed a music trio. She wanted to know if we could play for a dance. I told her we could and that we had a selection of tunes of different dance styles from fox-trots to waltzes and polkas.

"Would fifteen dollars for the band be a fair price to pay you?" she asked.

"Oh, yes," I answered. *Wow! 5 bucks apiece—great.*

She wanted to know if we could play something for the grand march. I told her we could, but I had no idea what a grand march was. I'd played enough marches in the school band and figured I should be able to cut it.

I did some research on what a grand march was and found it to be a parade of dancers marching to a tune like "Pomp and Circumstance," displaying the dancing couples to the audience.

The evening of the dance, we didn't play a marching tune; instead, I thought we would take a standard tune and turn it into a march. We chose "Over the Rainbow," fitting for a Rainbow Girls Ball. We gave the tune a marching beat and played it very staccato; it seemed to work. People complimented us on our innovativeness in using that song for the grand march rather than a traditional marching tune.

Our first gig was a success. We had fun, we were paid, and we were hooked on that multifaceted vocation called "the music biz."

Our trio expanded into a quartet. We added a trumpet player. Gene Hamann and I were in the high school band together. We had known each other since grade school, and both of us had an interest in amateur ham radio.

We played for school dances and began to travel to local country and small-town dance halls. The more country dances we played, the more I could see that we needed to add instruments that the local people could relate to. Dad had a small accordion, and I thought I could double on piano and accordion. We added a guitar player, and he said a friend of his who played "very good" accordion would love to play with us. I immediately hired him before I could become an embarrassment playing a squeeze box.

Some of the halls we played had pianos that were only distant relatives to musical instruments. One place with the "world's worst piano" was Indian Hill Hall. I might as well have played the gig on my piano teacher's cardboard keyboard.

Indian Hill was a little dance hall of rough-cut timber that had been built by early 1900s' settlers. It was across the Missouri River, south of Williston. We had to cross the Missouri over a rickety old one-way bridge that always give me a fright, but it was in better shape than the piano I was about to play on.

The piano was dirty and smelled of mice pee; the worn-out old grimy keyboard was scarred with cigarette burns. It had strings missing, hammers and felts missing, keys missing, and it was so out of tune the horns could barely tune to it. After playing on the Indian Hill piano, someone in the band suggested that I only get half my pay for the gig because I only played half the notes required for the job.

As time went on, I decided to change the composition of the band. I dropped the guitar and accordion. We formed a band that was composed of alto sax, tenor sax, trumpet, piano, and drums. I wanted to add a bass player, but we couldn't find one. I filled in that part by playing a bass line on the piano. From 1950 to 1952, we played almost every high school graduation and prom in western North Dakota and eastern Montana.

One of our favorite places to play was the Sherman Hotel in Wolf Point, Montana, which booked us often. The hotel had a large ballroom; when we played there, the sign said, "Dance to the Herb Hicks Orchestra: The Youngest Band in the Land." We were all around sixteen or seventeen. Wolf Point was a hundred miles from Williston on a narrow highway. My dad would usually let me use his 1949 Chevrolet as a band vehicle. We were able to cram five musicians, two saxophones, a trumpet, a set of drums, music fronts, and our small PA into that vehicle.

The band was booked to play the Sherman Hotel for a Christmas dance. The Wolf Point gig paid about twenty-five dollars each and ten dollars for travel. In those days, our Montana gigs were usually paid in silver dollars, and our pockets would be weighed down with silver coins. After the gig we packed our gear, bought some snacks for the trip home and were on the road at around three in the morning.

It was beginning to snow, but the roads were in pretty good shape for winter driving. I was feeling tired and asked if anyone wanted to drive. Bob Miller felt wide awake and didn't mind driving. We took off down the Montana highway toward North Dakota. The snow was beginning to come down thick and fast. The warm car and its gentle movement lulled me to sleep in the front passenger seat.

Wham! The jarring woke me abruptly.

"What happened?" I asked.

"I think we hit a horse," Miller said.

We stopped by the side of the highway, our headlights illuminating the snow-covered road. We opened the doors to a blast of wind-driven snow. When we got out, we could see that the front right fender and right side of the car had been damaged. There was blood on the side of the car, and horse hair caught in the door handle. We had hit a white horse in a snowstorm!

Luckily the car wasn't damaged enough that it couldn't be driven. We couldn't see a horse anywhere and climbed back into the car to continue toward home. I found out later that Montana had an open-range law that stated that livestock had the right of way in crossing highways; anyone hitting livestock on the roads was responsible for damages to the animal. *Did the animal have any responsibility for damages to the vehicle?*

I was wide awake and drove the rest of the way to Williston. When we arrived at 5:30, Mom and Dad were up waiting for me.

I hesitated in telling Dad what had happened to his car, but then I blurted out, "We hit a horse."

"You did what?" Dad asked.

"We hit a white horse in a snowstorm," I said.

"Anyone hurt?"

"No. No one injured except the horse. Come outside and take a look at the car."

Dad hurriedly put on his coat, and we went out to inspect the Chevy. He saw the damage to the side of the car—and the blood and horse hair.

I started apologizing to Dad for damaging his car.

He said, "It was an accident, something none of you did on purpose. The car is just an object that is insured and can be fixed. Objects are not important; *people* are."

In my senior year of high school, the composition of the band changed again. Wayne and Gene had enlisted in the armed services, and Cliff, our tenor sax player, had moved. I needed an alto sax, tenor sax, and trumpet player. We tried a number of combinations. Finally I hired a young high school student to play trumpet and a recent high school graduate to play alto.

A high school friend, Gary Jorgenson (everyone called him Jerk—with nothing demeaning attached to the nickname), had just started studying the tenor sax, and he was becoming a fine player. Jerk was a jazz fan like me, and we had begun an extensive record collection of jazz. We were interested in learning to improvise; since there were very few theory books on the subject in the fifties, we would listen to jazz recordings over and over in an attempt to learn this skill. We'd jam a lot together, and we convinced a friend of ours to take up the bass violin. Our friend, Dick Forness, bought an old upright bass and began to study, rehearse, and jam with us. Jerk and Dick both became members of the band.

Having a band with three horns and three rhythm instruments was the combination I'd been looking for. I was trying to figure out how to play those chord symbols, and it opened a whole new piano technique for me. We expanded the band's library and began to get more bookings.

Most bands in the area were country or rock and roll. There was only one other band in the area that had horns and played the type of swing music we were playing. That band was run by an excellent clarinet player, Bill McFarland. My band was playing at a dance where Bill was in the audience. After listening to us, he approached me and asked if I would like to play some gigs with his group since their band was losing its piano player. I was very flattered by the offer, but I told him my loyalty was to my band. He understood but asked if I would consider playing with him whenever I could make a gig.

"I'd be delighted to," I said.

"Great. I will teach you how to read and voice chord symbols—as that is what my piano parts are, just a lead line with chord symbols."

Besides being a clarinetist, Bill was a good pianist and organ player. I was thrilled by this offer and couldn't wait to get started with my lessons in "comping."

It was the end of the big band era, but there were a number of name bands still on the road. The State Line Nightclub, on the border of North Dakota and Montana, was one venue that booked top name bands. I was able to see and hear Duke Ellington, Count Basie, Charlie Barnet, Tony Pastor, and others. For young musicians from North Dakota, who were so isolated from the mainstream of contemporary music, it was an absolute thrill to see and hear them.

Some of the clubs had jam sessions on weekends, and I would make as many as possible. One place in particular for sessions was the Blue Moon in Plentywood, Montana. A band from Regina, Saskatchewan, had a number of good jazz players and would be at the jam sessions in Plentywood quite often. I got to know some of the guys in the band; the drummer, in particular, was very good. His name was "Tihs," or rather that was the nickname his fellow musicians gave him since he had a habit of always saying "shit." Another good jazz player with the band was the guitar man whose name is lost to my recollection.

Years later, when my brother and I were traveling through Las Vegas, we stopped at a club to hear the Red Norvo Quartet and the guitarist, Tal Farlow. As we entered the bar, someone shouted my name. I saw Tihs, the guitar player, and another musician from the Regina band sitting at the bar. Bob and I grabbed a couple of stools beside the Canadians. They told us that their band had a gig for a week in Las Vegas. The guitar player was very excited about having the opportunity to see and hear Tal Farlow play. They'd been waiting about an hour for Red Norvo's Quartet to come on stage. The bandstand was directly behind the bar, at eye level, and we would have a great view of the quartet when they came on.

The Canadian guys had been drinking heavily for a while, and they were more than a little sloshed. They bought us drinks, and the quartet started to come onto the stage to set up. All of a sudden, the barstool with the guitar player flipped backward, sending a table of drinks flying—and the guitar man fell to the floor.

Norvo said, "We haven't even started, and we're knockin' 'em out."

A bouncer appeared, grabbed the guitar player's arm, and pulled him up off the floor. "Okay, you drunk. You're outta here."

A punch from the guitar player missed, but the bouncer put a neck hold on the guitar man and shuffled the mumbling Canadian guitarist out the door.

The Canadians decided to get the guitar man back to their motel to sober up. The guitar man never did get to see his idol. Bob and I stayed to catch Norvo's Quartet, and we marveled at Farlow's smooth guitar and Norvo's agile vibe solos. What a shame that the Canadians missed this first-class jazz act.

"Brown gas or red gas?" asked the gas station attendant.

"Brown gas," I replied. I was traveling with three of my buddies through Weyburn, Saskatchewan, and filling up my 1948 Willys Jeep station wagon. The station wagon got good gas mileage, but it had a small gas tank, and I'd fill up whenever I had the opportunity. Traveling through Canada, I had a choice of red gas (high octane) or brown gas (lower octane and cheaper). I always chose the lower-priced gas. Every time I got gas, I'd say, "Fill it up with brown gas." Thus, my nickname became "Brown Gas."

We were on our way to a jazz concert in Regina, featuring the George Shearing Quintet and the Billy Eckstine Orchestra. I was a big fan of Shearing's piano style and would copy his "five-block-chords" style. I was looking forward to seeing and hearing him in person. As anticipated, it was a great concert. Both groups were tremendous, but as a devoted fan of smaller combos, I was blown away by Shearing's Quintet, especially their improvised soloing.

The summer of my sophomore year, I meet my first love. Linda was a cute, blonde-haired, blue-eyed Norwegian girl. We went steady for my junior and senior years in high school. I was in love. I was, and continued to be for many years, an incurable romantic. A popular song in the forties and fifties was a tune called "Linda." I learned how to play the tune on the piano and could sing every word of the song, which I did for Linda every chance I could get. Singing might be an exaggeration of what I did to that song; my horrid voice was not able to match the words to the right pitch of the melody. But it was my attempt at being romantic.

The ages of my group of friends ranged from seventeen to early twenties, and we had a number of common interests outside of school. We were looking for a forum where we could express and exchange ideas, meet socially over a good meal, and have a brotherhood of good fellowship. We formed a club and called it "Kloober's Klub." Kloober was a word derivative of words that meant clumsy, clodhopper, and uncoordinated. Although it was a word with negative connotations, we meant it as a term of endearment—in a satirical way. We would meet monthly at a restaurant for a fantastic meal, discussions, and companionship. It satisfied our need for a creative voice.

When I'd come home for lunch from high school, I'd always turn on the radio to the Canadian Broadcasting Corporation from Regina. They had a program recorded from Toronto called the "Happy Gang," which featured some excellent musicians. On one broadcast, they featured a guest pianist who caught my undivided attention. He had a technique like Art Tatum. They announced his name and had an interview with him. The pianist's name was Oscar Peterson.

Williston was a Scandinavian community and had a lot of Petersons; many were named Oscar. *Wow,* I thought, *that Norwegian can really play the piano.* Later I learned that the fantastic pianist I heard was the black jazz pianist from Montreal. Oscar Peterson, the prodigious Canadian jazz pianist, became my idol.

I began a quest to see and hear every jazz musician I possibly could. There were jazz concerts in Regina, which was somewhat accessible (two hundred miles), and Minneapolis, which was a little harder to reach (seven hundred miles). Jerk and I had read in *Downbeat* that the Stan Getz Quartet was going to play at a hotel restaurant in Minneapolis. Jerk was a huge Getz fan, and so was I. We really wanted to see that quartet. Both of us had saved some money to cover the trip. Only one big obstacle stood in our way; we were both juniors in high school and had classes on the dates that Getz would play in Minneapolis.

One of my grandmother's friends had taught high school for many years and was in charge of study hall in our high school. When my grandmother heard that I was trying to figure out a way to get out of classes to go Minneapolis to see this music event, she said she would see if Miss Moe could help us. Miss Moe was one of the most liberal teachers I'd ever met. She knew me well and always complimented me for starting my dance band. She had an enormous interest in the fine arts and had a lot of pull with the high school administration. She spent her summers in Minneapolis and was a regular guest at the

Radisson Hotel. She loved the Minneapolis Symphony and the many fine art galleries in that city.

When she heard what Jerk and I wanted to do, she said she would help us. She made arrangements for us to make up the studies we would miss and told the high school administration that we were going on a "cultural field trip." She also wrote the Radisson Hotel, booked us there, and told them to take good care of her boys, which they did.

After an overnight train trip from Williston, we arrived at the Minneapolis station. Making our way up the stairs with our luggage, we hustled out of the main entrance to a noisy, bustling, crowded city. We spotted a cab stand and started to make our way there to get a ride to the hotel. Two men approached us from either side; they both flashed badges and identified themselves as FBI. They asked us for some identification and wanted to know where we had just come from. We sat our luggage down and showed them our driver's licenses. We told them where we had arrived from and where we were going. We wondered what we had done to warrant being stopped by the FBI. I showed them a letter I had from Miss Moe, introducing us to the Radisson Hotel. After a couple more questions, they apologized for detaining us and told us they were looking for two young guys who fit our descriptions. We continued on our way, got a cab, and—even though taken back by our detainment—we joked about the unusual welcoming committee of G-men in Minneapolis.

That evening, we were seated in front of the Stan Getz Quartet. The quartet consisted of Getz (tenor), Tommy Potter (bass), Tiny Kahn (drums), and a new young piano player by the name of Horace Silver. We were all eyes and ears as we took in every nuance of sight and sound. Horace Silver played some great bluesy solos. Tommy Potter kept putting talcum powder on his sweaty hands to help keep them dry on the bass fingerboard. After seeing that, Jerk and I referred to Potter as "Tommy Powder." Getz's incredible solos ranged from beautiful ethereal ballads to fiery up-tempos.

Hearing and seeing a jazz musician in person is quite different then hearing a recording. At a live performance, you can see and hear all the subtleties of the music. In person, you are more aware of the exchange between the individual musicians and the dynamics of the group as a whole.

After returning to Williston, I read an article in *Downbeat* about a music school in Los Angeles. Westlake College of Music in Hollywood was one of a few schools in the fifties that had a curriculum consisting primarily of contemporary music. In May 1951, I wrote for an application and set up an appointment date for an entrance audition.

My appointment was for August, and I began to make plans to go to California. Jerk said he would like to go with me, and a very good friend of ours, Larry Gaudreau, said he'd also like to go. My dad said my Willys Jeep wagon would never make the trip, and he offered to swap cars with me for the two weeks we'd be gone. I thanked him for the use of his '49 Chevy, knowing that we could travel in comfort and wouldn't have to stop at every town to fill up the little gas tank.

After finishing my junior year the end of May, I took a job for a couple of months with a construction company that was renovating the power plant for an addition of new gas turbines.

In August, Jerk, Larry, and I headed out through the southeast corner of Montana toward Wyoming and the amazing works of nature at Yellowstone. We stopped overnight in Salt Lake and took in a state fair. Looking around the fairgrounds, we meet up with a guy who befriended us and began to follow us around the exhibits. Suddenly we were confronted by the Utah State Police, and all of us (including our newfound acquaintance) were hauled in for questioning. After producing our identification and convincing the police we were three guys from North Dakota, we were released. As for our new acquaintance, the police told us that they had been looking for a fugitive—and had found him with us. They assumed we were his associates. Jerk and I kidded each other about having features that police officers and FBI agents thought somehow identified us as being fugitives.

The next day, we drove across the Nevada desert to Reno and on to San Francisco. Driving across the Golden Gate Bridge, the smell of the salty sea air of the Pacific Ocean and the skyline of the city brought back memories of when I had first visited San Francisco with my parents for the 1939 World's Fair.

We planned on staying one night in San Francisco before heading down to LA the next day. However, due to circumstances, we ended up staying in San Francisco for a couple more days.

A traffic cop was yelling his head off at us to get moving. I gunned the engine, but the Chevy just sat there. We were in the middle of

Market Street, at the peak of rush hour, when the Chevy's driveshaft U-joint went out. We had traffic backed up, and people were honking their horns and yelling at the car with North Dakota license plates to get off the road and go back to the farm. Californians are a generally congenial people—except when some get behind a steering wheel. Then a metamorphosis takes place, and they become driving demons. We got out of the car, embarrassed by our situation, and heeded directions from the cursing traffic officer. As we pushed the car to the side of the street, the officer called a tow truck—and we were towed to a garage.

Other than the U-joint incident, I enjoyed San Francisco. One place we planned to go was the Blackhawk Jazz Club. We were underage and wondered if we could get in to hear the Cal Tjader Quartet. At the club, there was a screened-off area where those under drinking age could pay a cover charge, get a soft drink or a sandwich, and sit and listen. The club was dark, smoky, crowded, and noisy, but when the quartet walked onto the stage, everyone was quiet; the patrons were there to listen. *Now this is the way to run a jazz club.*

Leaving San Francisco, we headed south along the California coast on the old winding Highway 1. The scenery along the Pacific Ocean coastline through Monterey and Big Sur was something out of this world to us wide-eyed prairie dwellers. We arrived in LA eight hours later, and the salty ocean air mixed with an intoxicatingly sweet smell of smog and orange blossoms had a poignant fragrance. The freeways were like a gigantic racetrack; vehicles jockeyed for an open position to take the lead; even little old ladies were zooming past us. On the Hollywood Freeway, we turned onto Hollywood Boulevard and headed for Vine Street. Westlake was located on the corner of Vine, just a block north of Hollywood Boulevard. In 1951, the building was an old recording studio that the school had taken over for music studios.

As I walked through the school's front door, I noticed a sign above my head: *See music with your ears, and hear music with your eyes.*

I introduced myself to the man behind the desk. Alvin Learned was the school's director. He immediately made me feel at ease, and we set up an appointment for the next day for my audition and registration. The day after the interview and audition, I found out I'd been accepted to the program. I was overjoyed to realize I'd be going to a music school that had teachers and alumni who were some of the country's great music innovators.

I was ready for my long trip back to North Dakota—to my senior year, graduation, and the independence to search for myself. At seventeen, I hadn't lost myself—I just hadn't yet found myself.

Chapter 3

On the Road

I loved traveling by train in the 1950s, especially on the Great Northern Empire Builder. The repetition of the *clickety-clack* of the wheels on the rail tracks was music to my ears and could lull me to sleep in no time. The dome car was my favorite place to ride. As the landscape rushed by, the train would flush pheasants from along the cut of the rail tracks. I'd track, lead, and fire my imaginary shotgun, bagging, figuratively, hundreds of birds.

On one train ride through Montana, I discovered that the club car had a piano. It was a little apartment-sized piano, and anyone wanting to play it could. I sat down to play and ended up playing that little piano for most of my trip. I was having fun entertaining myself and figured the travelers were so bored that they'd let anything entertain them. Some people must have dug it since free drinks kept being lined up on top of the piano. It was beyond my capacity to consume all those drinks, and I wished I could turn them in for refunds.

Another train trip was not as pleasant as the earlier ones. In June 2007, I traveled from Cut Bank, Montana, to Williston, North Dakota, to attend my fifty-fifth high school reunion. I had driven from Lethbridge, Alberta, where I was living, to Cut Bank to leave my car at a friend's house while I took the Amtrak to North Dakota.

My friend Carol Gordon drove me from her house in Cut Bank to the station, and we waited for the train. And we waited, and we waited. It was nearly three hours late. The train had to put on a couple of extra cars somewhere around Seattle because they were overbooked, but they were still overcrowded. When I boarded the train at Cut Bank, there wasn't a seat to be had; the only place I could put my luggage was in a little video game room that was stacked with other passengers' baggage.

A conductor told me I would have to stand until the next stop. Then he would see about getting me a seat—if someone got off.

"Okay, I'll hang on till then. You're really packing them in today."

"Yeah, this run has been a disaster."

"What a way to run a railroad," I said.

He didn't take my sarcastic comment as a joke. "Beats walking," he grumbled.

At the next stop, the conductor poked me and said, "I've got a seat for you, buddy. Follow me."

I followed him through two crowded coach cars to find my seat among a throng of noisy kids and bored people of all shapes and sizes. Some were sleeping, and others had contorted themselves into various positions to sleep. What an assorted collection of humanity. The scene reminded me of the French artist Honoré Daumier's painting, *The Third Class Coach*.

The conductor showed me to my seat, put my ticket stub in the clip over the seat, and said my baggage would stay in the game room until I got to Williston.

"Where are the restrooms?" I asked.

"The end of the car," he replied.

The restroom toilet was a mess, so I went to the next car to find a clean one. After finding a relatively clean restroom, I returned to my coach and dropped into my seat. The man next to me was drinking a beer and eating an assortment of sausages. I tried to sleep, but there was no *clickety-clack* of the train tracks to lull me to sleep; in 2007, the tracks were made of continuous rails.

What a way to run a railroad.

The return trip from Williston a week later was almost as crowded. I boarded the train and looked for a seat.

"Here's an empty seat." A beautiful young lady with a deep soft voice offered me the seat beside her.

What luck! I anticipated a pleasant trip through Montana.

She looked to be in her late twenties; I was seventy-three years young. We struck up a conversation and told each other stories about ourselves. She was traveling only as far as Havre, Montana. I offered to go to the club car to get us a drink.

She said her Mormon faith prohibited drinking alcohol. However, she asked for a drink of water. She was quite different than the Mormon girl I had married fifteen years earlier who consumed vodka in greater quantities than a Russian Cossack could have.

The club car was packed with people in various stages of inebriation. I ordered a bottle of water and a shot of rye with a coke on the side. Two Hutterite farmers were standing beside me. The stench of pig manure on their boots and clothes from their fields was appalling. I downed my shot of rye in one gulp and made a fast retreat back to the passenger coach, clutching my coke and the bottle of water for my velvet-voiced traveling companion.

My Mormon friend and I chatted, covering a variety of mundane subjects; she did most of the chatting while I pretended to be the perfect listener. True listening is an art that takes practice. I can be a good listener when I want to. When I listen with intent, I become very quiet and seem withdrawn or disinterested. Other times, my quietness is because I'm lost in my own thoughts. When I would get lost in thought, my kids used to say, "Dad's spaced out again."

After my companion left the train in Havre, we took on more passengers. A lady who could easily have passed for a Sumo wrestler, pound for pound, got on our coach and squeezed her way into the empty seat next to me. I never did figure out whether she altered her shape to be seated or altered the seat's shape.

What a way to run a railroad.

When I got to Cut Bank, Carol asked how the train ride was.

"It was the train from hell," I said, laughing.

The train ride I took on the Empire Builder at the end of May 1952 was my "Freedom Train." My parents and my girlfriend, Linda, were at the station to see me off. I would be traveling from Williston to Minot. The uncertainty of what was in store along this new road of travel was gripping me. I had graduated from high school a week before, and I felt a liberating sensation about my new life. It was spring, I was eighteen, and I had my high school diploma. I had just landed a job with a traveling territory orchestra. I was ready to take on the world, unaware of what a formidable opponent I had. Ah, the naïveté of youth.

I'd been hired by the Tony Williams Orchestra, which booked out of Minneapolis. I had gotten the job through Bill, the clarinet player who had taught me how to read chord symbols and voice chords on the piano. I got the job because the piano book for the Williams band was just chord symbols (something I would never have to worry about, according to my piano teacher). The first thing I had to do to join the band was get a musicians' union card. This could be done in Minot on Friday, and the band would pick me up on Saturday morning to travel to our first gig in Devils Lake, about a three-hour drive from Minot.

In Minot, I planned to visit with a friend, Dwayne, who played trumpet with a group in town. I checked into the hotel where Williams had made a reservation for me. I called my friend, and we had dinner together. After a pleasant visit with Dwayne, I retired to my hotel. As soon as I closed the door, there was a knock.

I opened the door and, to my complete surprise, Linda was there.

"Linda, what are you doing here?"

She told me she had to see me one more time before I left. She had caught a ride to Minot with some friends who were staying overnight.

We stood in the doorway for a minute.

"Well," she said, "are you going to invite me in?"

"Come in. Come in," I replied.

My first-time experiences in life are some of the most evocative events that are stored in my recollections. My first love, Linda, is one such memory.

The next morning, we had a huge breakfast. We giggled and laughed while playing games with our eggs and sausages like a couple of kids. After breakfast, she met her friends for a ride back to Williston. We said our good-byes, and I took a cab to the musicians' union to get my card.

On Saturday morning, the band picked me up in their sleeper bus to travel to our gig in Devils Lake. As I stepped aboard the bus, I became aware of a musty odor mixed with the aroma of cigarettes and alcohol.

"Welcome to the bus with square wheels," said one musician.

I was bombarded with numerous questions.

Someone said, "This one's yours," pointing to a bunk.

At first I felt somewhat intimidated, but the guys were all friendly and wanted me to feel right at home. All I had to do was prove I could play the charts—and I was in. We would see how I rated that evening.

Our nine-piece band consisted of an alto sax, two tenors, two trumpets, one trombone, drums, piano, and bass. The leader, Tony, played bass (or sort of played at it). He was a large Norwegian guy with a blond bass violin that matched his hair, and he manhandled that bass like it was a broom, sweeping and spinning it back and forth as he wrapped his huge hand around its fingerboard. Calling off the first number, Tony would stomp on the floor and bellow, "Ah, one, ah, two, ah, one, two, three, go." The first number, which was often repeated during the gig, was "The Dipsy Doodle," one of the leader's favorites. I came to detest that tune. The leader insisted we play the tune with a square two beat feeling and a syrupy sweet sound that would have made Guy Lombardo cringe. Bill had taught me how to read chord symbols well. I had no trouble cutting the book. I was in.

The band traveled the Midwest from Saskatchewan to Kansas—and Minnesota to Montana. We met other traveling bands on the road, and the older guys in the band always knew some of the musicians in these groups. They would reminisce about times they had played with the so-and-so band and about guys they knew who had played with Lawrence Welk's band or with Frankie Yankovic, "America's Polka King," or "Whoopee John" Wilfahrt's polka band. I wasn't very interested in those groups; my heroes were Ellington, Basie, Kenton, and the contemporary bands.

Most of our gigs were one-night stands, but we also played at resort dance halls where we would be booked for a weekend. We were booked to play a resort at Detroit Lakes, Minnesota, which was the hometown of one of the saxophone players. Elmo was a heavy drinker who could drink anyone under the table. He said we should have seen him when he was really drinking; he had cut down to a fifth a day.

Elmo had a new Hudson parked at his house in Detroit Lakes. He was always boasting about what a great car it was. He claimed it was the smoothest-riding car ever made—and one of the fastest. He offered to take some of us for a ride one evening, and we accepted like fools. I sat in the front passenger seat, and three other guys rode in back. We took off for parts unknown.

Elmo had a drink in one hand; a cigarette and the steering wheel were in the other. "Boys, I'm going to show you something amazing. Hang on. You won't believe this." He sat the full glass of whiskey in the middle of the floor. "I can take a sharp curve at a hundred miles an hour and not spill a drop of booze."

"We believe you," we said, almost in unison.

He had to prove it to us. We took off with the motor roaring, tires squealing, and his passengers jolted back in their seats. Apparently he had done this before and knew exactly where he was going to find this sharp curve. As we approached a hundred miles an hour, we were scared out of our wits. There were no seat belts, and no pleas could slow him down.

The tires screeched as we rounded a wicked curve.

"Look," Elmo shouted. "Didn't spill a drop!"

If he had spilled a drop, did he have to repeat the performance? Thank god we didn't spill a drop of booze—or a drop of blood.

All the guys in the band had quite a sense of humor, but Elmo was the biggest joker of all. We had a couple of days off in a little town in South Dakota and decided to take in a movie. There was a flick playing that was about werewolves. I wasn't keen on going because I'd had a reoccurring nightmare about being chased by wolves. However, I did decide to go. Sure enough—that night I did have a nightmare about werewolves. I woke up screaming and woke all the guys in the bus. They kidded me about my phobia and joked that they were all werewolves. They had me totally terrified.

A week or so later, my sound sleep was disturbed by a hand running through my hair. I awoke with a start, staring into the face of a wolf. I freaked out! After the guys had calmed me down, they explained what had happened. Somewhere, somehow, Elmo had bought a werewolf mask and had put it on to scare me. Scare me he did—and then some. For a number of years, I had wolf nightmares.

The personnel changed very little in the band, but we did lose a trumpet player and picked up a new one. To my surprise and delight, our new trumpet player was Dwayne from Minot.

Along the way, we also changed drummers. Our new drummer was a short—and short-tempered—Italian guy from Chicago. From the beginning, he and the leader disagreed on everything from tempos to neckties. We were on our way to Montana and had one gig left to play in North Dakota. That gig was at the Elks Club in Williston. I had written and called a number of people in Williston to tell them be sure to come see us. I was especially looking forward to seeing my folks and my girlfriend.

The Elks Club was packed with friends, relatives, musicians, and others who wanted to hear the band. The first set went really well, and the band sounded exceptional. At the start of the second set, the leader and the drummer had a disagreement over something. The second tune of the set ended up in an infuriating climax to that disagreement. Full of rage, the drummer hit his cymbal with a loud crash, threw his sticks at the leader, and shouted, "Fuck you, Tony Williams." He ranted on in Italian with a string of swear words. "I'm out of this fuckin' band. I quit."

Tony replied, "You are fired."

There was a tense silence in the ballroom—except for the slamming and crashing the drummer made while packing up his kit. I couldn't believe what was happening. Having this blowup happen in my hometown was a thorough embarrassment to me.

To make matters worse, Tony pointed to me and said, "Herb, you're from this burg. Do you know a drummer who can finish this job?"

I really didn't want to be recognized as a member of the band. I said I knew a drummer in the audience. He got his drums and was hired for the rest of the gig.

We finished the gig, but only about half the audience stayed till the end. Afterward, I apologized to my friends and relatives.

One of my friends said, "You weren't the cause of the ruckus—no need for you to apologize for the commotion temperamental musicians cause."

I took this as a backhanded compliment. After all, I was a musician—and could be temperamental at times.

After a brief tour through Montana, we headed back to Minnesota with a stop in Bismarck and one in Fargo. *Ya. You betcha!*

After the Fargo gig, we had some free time. When we had gone through Fargo a couple of weeks earlier, some of us had dropped off our laundry to be picked up later. We could get our laundry, have a couple of days off, and catch the bus for the road again.

Dwayne and I decided to get a hotel room near where we were to meet the bus in two days. It would be great to take a long hot shower, get a haircut, and spend some sack time in a nice hotel room. We spent part of the night in a little Fargo dive where the T-bones were humongous, and the country-and-western band was horrendous. After a couple of hours of people watching, eating, and drinking, we returned to the hotel. We picked up a fifth of bourbon for a nightcap and stumbled up to our room. After drinking shot after shot of bourbon, I don't remember exactly what happened. I remember something about being able to fly as we kept jumping on and off the bed in our room at four in the morning.

The knock on the door sobered us (just for a minute).

The hotel manager said, "Okay, you guys are out of here . . . now. Or I will call the cops."

Being underage, we didn't want to face the law in our intoxicated state. We packed our belongings, staggered down the stairs, and found our way out the front door into the warm August night.

We were just across the street from a park and thought we could spend the rest of the morning there until the bus showed up. Sleeping soundly, just as the sun was coming up, somebody started shaking me.

A police officer was standing over me. Dwayne was trying to explain to another officer that we were waiting for our bus driver to pick us up since we were part of a very famous traveling orchestra. Whatever Dwayne told the cops satisfied their curiosity, and they bid us good morning and left.

Man, did I ever have a hangover. I swore that would be the very last drop of booze that would ever touch my lips. Sad to say, it wasn't though. There must be an ingredient in booze that affects long-term memory; otherwise people would certainly stay away from ever having another harrowing hangover. The sleeper bus picked us up a couple of hours later, and we were on the road again.

The last gig I played with the band was in the middle of August 1952 at a little dance hall outside of Dickinson, North Dakota. I had packed my suitcase and was ready to take a bus back to Williston the next day. I was anxious to get home since I would be leaving for California the last week of August. All I had to do after the gig was turn in my stained, well-worn yellow orchestra jacket and tie, get my final paycheck from Tony, and hit the road home.

The gig that night was one of the country community dances where everyone brought lots of food and booze—and consumed a lot of both. The drunks put on a floor show of absurdity (another reason to stop drinking). There was a fight; thankfully, it was outside the dance hall. It seemed like the gig was the longest we had ever played, partly because I was anticipating leaving for home and partly because of the raucous crowd. When we played the last tune at two o'clock, the people hollered for more. It was the band's policy to play one encore if need be; in this case, it was. We were not going to say no to all those drunks. Of course, our encore was "The Dipsy Doodle," a fitting farewell to my tour with the band.

After the gig, we hustled our equipment out to the bus. The bus door was ajar, and it had been broken into.

"Hey, where's my suitcase?" said one of the band members.

Someone else said the same thing.

My suitcase was gone too. Man was I pissed off! I had just packed all my stuff for the trip home. The clothes weren't that important to me, but some of the music books I had acquired were treasures. I dislike thieves intensely. I could not comprehend the mind-set of someone who could stoop so low as to steal another's possessions.

We reported the theft the next day in Dickinson. About a week later, I received a call from the sheriff of a county near Dickinson. They had found my empty suitcase in a wheat field. I hoped the thieves made good use of my music manuscripts and appreciated my dirty laundry.

After my 1952 graduation from Williston High School and my summer tour with the Tony Williams Orchestra, I was ready to explore new horizons. I was excited about my plans to move to LA to go to school. The social, cultural, and climate differences between North Dakota and California would be like going to another planet.

With some money I'd saved—and some help from my father—I bought a 1950 Ford. It was a straight-six cylinder, beautiful black, and ran like a charm, using no oil and getting fantastic gas mileage.

Larry, and another friend, Wes, were going to California with me. Jerk had left to attend the University of North Dakota in Grand Forks.

Larry, Wes, and I made the sixteen-hundred-mile trip to California in a little over two days. Wes went to San Francisco, and Larry and

I went to LA. When we got to LA, Larry and I found an apartment just off Hollywood Boulevard, not far from school. I began to make arrangements to attend class, and Larry began looking for employment. He found work with a roofing company, and I started attending classes.

Our neighbor, looking very much like a Hollywood rhinestone cowboy in cowboy boots and ten-gallon hat, introduced himself as "Jog-along Jacobs." His claim to fame (most people in Hollywood had some claim to fame) was that he had ridden a horse from New Jersey to California. To back this up, he had an album of photographs and articles documenting his ride, which he showed us ad nauseam. He was trying to sell his story to a Hollywood screenwriter.

We tooled around LA in my Black Beauty; the city's attractions were astonishing and wonderfully new to two kids from the Midwest. The weather and the ocean were especially attractive to us. Every day was like a summer festival. Santa Monica Beach was the epitome of the California beach lifestyle, and people watching was the number-one activity. The art galleries, nightclubs, and theaters were all of interest to us. The Hollywood Palladium on Sunset Boulevard, not far from our apartment, was a favorite place.

During the years I spent in LA, I saw many famous big bands at the Palladium. The first big band concert I saw there was the Stan Kenton Orchestra. Kenton's band was known as "The Wall of Sound." The screaming high-note trumpets, huge sounds of the complex sax section figurations, hard-driving swinging rhythm section, and creative soloists made for a unique progressive jazz big band. They blew me away.

Los Angeles was full of beautiful customized automobiles (their head-turning recognition surpassed only by the beautiful girls). Larry suggested that my car would be a great candidate for a custom job. We talked about everything from chopping and channeling to frenching, decking, and doing multi-multi-coats of lacquer paint. Big ideas with a small budget were not a good mixture. We found a custom car shop in East LA and ended up getting the headlights frenched and the hood and trunk decked. It gave the car a streamlined look and my billfold a flat look. That was all I could afford. Black Beauty ended up with only a partial customized job, but it looked great. About three years later, a train did a total "customized job" on it and changed its look forever.

Mort Weiss was a clarinet player I met at Westlake School. He asked me to join a quartet he was forming. I joined, and we began a beautiful relationship as friends and musicians. He is an excellent clarinet player who was friends with the great clarinetist, Buddy DeFranco.

As the fall semester went by—and it was getting close to Christmas—I received word from my folks that my grandmother was very ill with stomach cancer. I decided to go back to North Dakota, and Larry said he would go as well. After spending Christmas with my folks, I made arrangements to return to Los Angeles. Larry had decided to stay in Williston, and I went back to school for the next semester.

I became a member of the musicians' union, Local 47 Los Angeles. Joining the union was a requirement for a gig we had on a variety TV show televised from NBC in Hollywood. We played a variety of gigs—from weddings to cocktail parties and nightclubs.

I found a nice apartment in Hollywood on Russell Avenue. Rows of palm trees stood ninety feet tall and framed gorgeous old homes with beautiful landscaped yards.

In Hollywood, I had a chance to see and meet a number of celebrities. Art Pepper (alto saxophonist with Kenton's band) sat in on a gig I was playing in Long Beach. Art's girlfriend at the time was singing with the band. Art was a fantastic alto player, and it was nothing short of a miracle that he lived to be fifty-seven (1925–82) because his life was full of troubles as a heroin addict.

Near the corner of Hollywood Boulevard and Western Avenue, just a few blocks from where I lived, there was a drug store that had a nice lunch counter where I'd get my stable noon meal of a hot beef sandwich with mashed potatoes, gravy, and a thick, creamy, malted milkshake. This was the right combination of food and price for a student on a limited budget.

One day at lunch, a couple sat down beside me. The guy turned to me and pointed at my sandwich. "That looks good. That's what I'll have."

The couple was Louie Bellson and Pearl Bailey. Having the top jazz drummer and female vocalist of the day eating lunch next to me was a real thrill. I don't remember our conversation other than they praised Westlake School and knew a number of people there. They were two of the nicest celebrities I met. I met Nat King Cole at NBC. I was a big fan; although he said he was mainly a piano player who just happened to sing, he was best known by the public as a vocalist. He was a very gracious person.

The list of celebrities with whom I crossed paths is quite long, as might be expected when you live, work, and frequent places that are an extension of their home base. Star musicians, entertainers, and movie people were always popping up at some gig or event we'd be attending. A unique opportunity was being able to see the great Charlie Parker in concert with Chet Baker on trumpet. I was in awe of Bird's and Chet's amazing abilities as improvisers. My chance to see and hear so many great jazz performers was a dream come true. At first, I was like anyone else meeting a famous person—I was starstruck. After a while, the experience became a little more common, but it was always a thrill to be in the presence of a great talent.

I was busy trying to satisfy my inquisitiveness of life. I was young, full of curiosity, learning new skills, gigging, exploring, contemplating the meaning of life, and drinking in—with all my senses—the marvels of the contemporary world.

It was toward the end of the Korean War, and I was worried about being drafted. A musician friend of mine in Williston, Rich Snyder, was also concerned about the draft. At Christmas, I returned to Williston to enlist for pilot training in the air force. Rich and I figured that joining the air force for four years would be better than being drafted by the army for two years and ending up in some foxhole in Korea.

The air force recruiter explained the procedures and obligations of becoming an air force pilot.

We agreed that signing up to become air force pilots was a lifetime commitment, too deep and too long to make. We opted for a four-year enlistment of active duty and four years in the reserve. The recruiting officer assured us we would serve together and could choose our careers. Somewhere near the top of my list, I chose music and aerial photography, which sounded interesting to me. Farther down on my list, I put radio operator, which I had a slight interest in. In January 1954, Rich and I signed our names to the enlistment papers, took a train to Fargo for the physical exam and enlistment oath, and headed to San Antonio.

Chapter 4

Air Force

We arrived by train in San Antonio and were bused to Lackland Air Force Base. We had eight weeks of basic training at the 737th Basic Military Training Group. When we arrived at the base, a training instructor (TI) had us assemble in some fashion of a formation and started yelling orders at us. He was like an animated cartoon character—puffed-up, chin back, chest out, strutting back and forth like a prairie chicken during a mating dance. He informed us that we were the lowest of the lowest creatures on earth. Within eight weeks, he would make or break us—making soldiers of us.

Thus began the first part of our basic military training. There were two components—psychological and physical. First we were given haircuts, stripping us of any hair on our heads. Then we exchanged our civvies for military clothing. This was a physical change in our appearances and the beginning of a psychological change in our attitudes. We were no longer individuals; we were small components of a larger unit. Some recruits were completely transformed by this idea. I was not, but I thought it was imperative to go along with this concept to stay out of trouble. Basic training was basically following orders beyond all questions. We discussed and philosophized about all of it.

We were sitting in our little pup tent in the middle of the Texas prairie. It was late at night after a long, hot, and dusty march. Removing our brogans and rubbing our tired feet, we shone our flashlight on our sleeping bags and looked for any little foreign creatures that wanted to spend the night with us. Rich was deadly afraid of spiders, and I didn't have much love for them. The TI had warned us that there were scorpions out there and told us to make sure we shook our boots out in the morning in case one had crawled in at night. We were very thorough in the inspection of our quarters.

We thought of ourselves as being lucky to know only about war secondhand. We had seen war movies and newsreels, met veterans of war, and seen army training films. We could only imagine the fear and the horrors of combat. We discussed the issue of killing another human being—looking him in the eyes and shooting or stabbing him to death. Without having any malice toward your adversary, this would seem impossible, but we were being trained to defend ourselves and protect our homeland, loved ones, and our way of life. We were conditioned to hate the enemy—whoever they were. In those terms, we agreed that that kind of killing was *justifiable homicide*. One can find a justifiable cause for anything in life, depending upon one's beliefs and conditioning. Murder has been justified by religion, race, politics, honor, insanity, superstition, revenge, defense, and any number of other conditions that put fear into human minds.

Our discussion had gone from the mundane to the morbid. Realizing the lateness of the hour, and knowing that reveille would come before dawn, we concluded our conversation with a midnight snack. Rich had brought a small pack of dry breakfast cereal from the chow hall. We relished those crispy little tidbits as though they were sautéed prawns, and we thought if the guys back home could see us, they would crack up. This was a long way from our Kloober's Klub dinner/conversation get-togethers.

The marching, the bivouacking, the firing range, the obstacle course under live fire, and the inspections came fairly easy for me. I'd had some experience as a hunter, scout, and had always looked for outdoor adventures. But there were some things I definitely did not like about basic training. One was KP; another was the training for poison gas warfare. The day of the gas-mask training exercise, we put on our gas masks and were told to go into a little building where there was gas being deployed so we could experience the smell of gas. On a command, we were to take off our masks, smell the gas, put our masks back on, and get outside quickly. I, like a fool, took a big deep breath and sucked in the gas fumes as hard as I could. Coughing, choking, and crying, I ran outside with my mask off. I ran blindly into other airmen in formation. The TI never let me forget my "gas attack." I could only imagine the horror of the poor GIs in the World War I trenches who were attacked with gas.

Wednesdays were the one day I would not eat at the mess hall because they served liver. Like the gas, liver made me gag. Generally the food wasn't that bad—and we had lots of it, which put many extra pounds on me. It was the most I've ever weighed. One of my favorite breakfasts was shit on a shingle (SOS). SOS was thick creamed beef on a slice of toast; it looked nasty, but tasted great.

Kitchen police (KP) was the one thing I dreaded most about basic training. Anyone who hates washing dishes can imagine the nightmare of doing thousands of dishes, scrubbing huge, dirty, greasy pots and pans, and swabbing miles of surfaces in the mess hall kitchen. Starting KP at three in the morning, the shifts lasted a couple of days. We were to check the bulletin board every day to see when we were scheduled for KP. Other policing duties, like cleaning the latrines or policing the area by picking up litter around the grounds, were a cinch compared to KP.

Rich and I saw a notice on the bulletin board for any airmen who had musical talent to audition for a variety show on the base. We immediately auditioned; Rich played drums, and I played piano. We made the audition, and a memo was sent to our TI saying that we were to be made available for all rehearsals and performances of the show. That meant we were freed from KP and policing duties—but not from our scheduled basic training exercises.

We began rehearsing for the show, which consisted of about twenty airmen and air force women (WAF). We did shows on the air base at the officers' club, enlisted men's club, and service clubs. A lieutenant who did the booking informed us that we were to do a show off base at the Elks Club in San Antonio. We were delighted to get a chance to get a look at civilian life again, which seemed like something we had left behind in the past.

We were scheduled to do the show on a Saturday night in San Antonio. On the bus ride into town, we were wondering what kind of audience we would have. Would the Texans be responsive to our entertainment group? We were definitely lacking country music. We had a number of New York musicians and musical theater performers. Rich and I were oriented toward the swing and jazz genres, but our thoughts about the audience's reaction to the music in our show were to be the least of our concerns.

We arrived at the Elks Club about two hours before performance time in order to unload our equipment and set up the show. Our director went up to the front door of the club, and someone told him to drive around to the back entrance. The bus pulled up to the back door, and we all climbed out and began unloading the equipment.

The rear door of the club opened and a couple of guys from inside came out and looked at us with puzzling stares.

"Y'all wait a damn minute," one guy hollered and pointed to some of the black guys in the show. "You boys know you're not allowed in this here club. This club is *white folks* only!"

My first encounter with racial discrimination was one of disbelief and bewilderment. This was followed by my revulsion at the angry scene that developed between the air force servicemen and the club's "white folks." Instead of starting a race riot, the servicemen decided to back off, get our equipment back on the bus, and head back to the base. Conversations during the trip back to the base were charged with emotional dissonance. I had never experienced a conflict between two different races before. I had worked with a number of black musicians in LA and never felt any racial tension. This was my first encounter with racial discrimination, but it wouldn't be my last.

The eight weeks basic training passed quickly, and we were issued orders to report to various tech school training centers. The recruiting officer had neglected to tell us that we would go through basic training together—and then we would be placed wherever the air force needed us. When the orders for tech schools were posted, Rich headed to a clerical school in Wyoming, and I went to Illinois for a radio mechanics and electronics school. We were given a brief furlough before tech school assignments. I picked up Black Beauty in Williston and drove it back to my new assignment at Scott Air Force Base in Illinois.

Scott Air Force Base is about twenty miles from St. Louis, near Belleville, Illinois. The only thing I knew about this part of the country was that I remembered the 1944 movie *Meet Me in St. Louis* starring Judy Garland. My only other affiliation with St. Louis was that I could bang out W. C. Handy's "St. Louis Blues" on the piano.

I arrived at Scott AFB in the early spring of 1954. Air force radio tech school was to prove to be an interesting education; if not for certain circumstances, electronics might have become my life's vocation. I enjoyed being stationed at Scott Air Base, and I was able to get into St. Louis quite often to take in the many music venues there. In St. Louis, I encountered another racial discrimination scene.

When I was living in Hollywood, I had been introduced to the Buddy DeFranco Quartet by Mort Weiss. The quartet consisted of Buddy on clarinet, Eugene Wright on bass, Art Blakey on drums, and Kenny Drew on piano. They were booked to play a club in St. Louis. I drove to St. Louis with a black friend from the air base to catch the act.

As we were about to pay the cover charge, the club's bouncer said, "Welcome to the club." Then he stopped us and said we couldn't get in.

I thought he might have meant we were underage.

The bouncer said to me, "You're okay, buddy, but *he* can't come in, *white folks* only."

This is ridiculous! Three of the quartet members playing tonight were black. I explained that I knew the band, and we were airmen from the base. I asked why black servicemen should be discriminated against.

The bouncer was sympathetic and said, "Wait outside, and I'll be right back."

We waited, and soon he appeared at the door. Apparently the code of "whites only" was not as strict at the Mason-Dixon Line as it was in Texas.

"You and your friend can go down the alley around to the back door, and you can listen to the band from the kitchen," he said, motioning to the side street.

We nodded and mumbled, "It's better than not hearing the band at all."

For the first time in my life, I felt like a member of a minority group and began to realize the stigma of discrimination. We sat in the kitchen like two naughty school kids being sent to the coatroom to be disciplined. We listened attentively to the quartet, tapping our feet in time with the music among the rattle of pots, pans, and dishes being shuffled about with food orders. It brought new meaning to "get out in that kitchen and rattle those pots and pans."

Finally having enough of this humiliating experience, we split for the air base without saying a word, our silence confirming our disappointment. Back in our barracks, we joked about our ordeal.

My friend said, "Hey, whitey, welcome to the club."

I said, "Yeah, right! Is it for black folks only?"

It didn't take me long to make connections with musicians on the base; we put together a trio with bass (Smitty), drums (Jay), and piano (me). We joined an entertainment group on the base—and I was again exempt from some KP duties.

That summer, Linda made a trip to St. Louis to visit me. We spent a lovely weekend together touring the town and listening to a jazz band on a paddlewheel steamboat trip on the Mississippi River. I was a fan of *The Adventures of Huckleberry Finn* and *Tom Sawyer* and could imagine that Samuel Clemens was the riverboat pilot at the helm. I expected that any moment someone would holler out, "Mark Twain!" Clemens took his pen name from the reading of the depths of the river that meant safe water, two fathoms.

That was the last time I saw Linda. By the time I was out of the air force (four years later), I heard she was married and raising a family. *C'est la vie.*

A friend at Scott Air Base, who knew I was a hunter, asked if I'd like to go goose hunting in the fall. Don could arrange it with another guy from our outfit that we knew as Tennessee Bob. TB was a tall lanky guy from Tennessee who had the demeanor of an Ozark hillbilly. He liked his booze, and he did make moonshine whiskey in Tennessee known as White Lightning, but he was no backwoods, uneducated hillbilly. He was amiable, always ready to give a helping hand, intelligent, and at the head of our class in radio electronics.

In October, we were set to go on our hunting trip. It was like reliving my childhood hunting days. With a three-day pass and the purchase of hunting licenses, Don, TB, and I took off into the misty night, heading for southern Illinois. We would meet up with some friends of TB's who would supply us with shotguns and ammo. They would take us to where the geese were feeding and set us up in the hunting blinds they had constructed.

It happened in the blink of an eye, but it seemed like the scene was in slow motion. There was screeching of wheels, a loud bang, the clash of metal against metal, grinding, and glass breaking as the force of the crash hit us on the right side of the car, right in the middle where the center post support was (luckily, I guess). The tremendous impact propelled my car sideways, and we spun off the railroad tracks into a ditch. I could hear the screeching of train wheels and the train engine in the distance. I felt a sharp pain in my right arm. The car's front and right side windows had exploded, and a long sharp shard of glass had shot like an arrow into my arm. Part of my shirt was soaked with blood.

My first concerns were for Don and TB. They were sitting on the right side of the car when the train hit us. Don was in the front seat, and TB was in the back.

I said, "Is everyone okay?"

It was obvious we weren't okay. We were all conscious, but we were banged up, bleeding, and in pain.

TB groaned and reached up behind the backseat and retrieved a bottle. "I don't want to be caught with this White Lightning." He flung it out the open window just as he passed out.

Good thing none of us had been drinking. I pushed my door open, and Don slid out on my side. The doors on the right side were smashed and wedged shut. Don was holding his right arm, and his hands were covered with blood.

TB was coming to, and we helped him crawl out of the car. Railroad workers came running to help us. We lay in the damp weeds while people milled around and asked how we were. Surrounded by the wet grasses and weeds of the ditch, I could feel their coolness and smell their musky odor—something that is vivid in my memory to this day. I heard sirens in the distance; the next thing I remember was the hospital.

Don and TB were taken into rooms to be x-rayed and treated, and a nurse bandaged my wounded arm. I met with the police to make out an accident report. We were lucky to survive a crash with a train. I was the luckiest of the three of us. My injuries were only the sliver of glass that cut my arm. All of us suffered from shock, but Don and TB also suffered some major physical injuries. Don was a Golden Gloves boxing champion; he'd broken every bone in his right wrist and fractured his right arm, and he never boxed again. TB broke his right arm and fractured three ribs. We stayed at the small-town hospital for two days until an ambulance from the air base came to transport us back to our squadron.

I phoned my dad to let him know what had happened and to give him a detailed report of the accident. I explained how we had approached the railroad crossings (there were three tracks) at 4:30 on the moonless, misty morning. The crossing did not have signal lights, was poorly marked, and had no flagman or lights on the back of the train as it backed up, switching boxcars. As we got to the third track, I saw, for just a moment, the shape of a boxcar to my right as it smashed into us. We were lucky the train was backing up and not going full steam ahead when it hit us.

Dad said, "It sounds like the railroad was clearly at fault for not having a flagman and no lights at the crossing." He knew a lawyer in Chicago and would contact him to bring a lawsuit on our behalf against the railroad company.

"Do you think we have a chance of getting a settlement from the railroad?" I asked.

About four months later, I got my answer. The railroad agreed to a cash settlement to replace my vehicle and a small amount for my injuries and inconvenience. Don and TB both received a larger cash settlement for the injuries they suffered. Through my lawyer, I found out there had been three accidents in the last five months at that railroad crossing. The month before our accident, a woman had been killed at that crossing.

I bought a 1952 Buick Riviera to replace my 1950 Ford. The Buick was a heavy tank of a car with more chrome on it than ten Fords. It had three portholes on each side of the hood. I kiddingly told my friends I was going to mount guns in them to fire at any trains that tried to ambush me.

After getting back into the routine of things at the base, one of the guys in my barracks told me he thought we had a thief among us. A couple of days later, it affected me personally. I had taken off my watch for a shower. I put it in the top tray of my footlocker and closed the cover, but I didn't lock it. My bunk was on the second floor of the barracks, and the showers were on the first floor. I used the shower, wrapped myself in a towel, and ran shivering back upstairs to my bunk.

Hurriedly opening my footlocker to get dressed against the chill of the barracks, I grabbed some clean socks, a T-shirt, and underwear, and I looked for my watch. It was gone. I thought it had fallen on the floor when I took my clean clothes out of my footlocker. I looked everywhere, but it was nowhere to be found. It was a situation where I couldn't really believe that it was missing. I kept looking at the spot where I put it as though it would somehow magically reappear. My folks had given me the expensive, Swiss-made Gruen timepiece as a high school graduation gift.

I was infuriated by this act of thievery. I hurriedly finished dressing and looked around the barracks to see who was there. There was no one but me in the barracks. It was Saturday afternoon, and everyone was off for the weekend. I was only there because I had just gotten off duty as barracks fire-stoker. The heat for our barracks was obtained by burning coal in a large furnace, and we had a duty roster that scheduled turns stoking the fire to keep it burning night and day.

Later that evening, I met up with the guy who had told me about suspected thievery in the barracks and told him what had happened.

He said, "We have to devise a plan to catch the thief." He had seen one guy hanging around other airmen's bunks and told me that person was his prime suspect, although he had never caught him in the act. Besides money, watches, rings, and bracelets were missing.

With four of my buddies, we decided to take turns keeping vigilance duty in the barracks. After a week, Don said he saw who the thief was. It was the earlier suspect. He was seen as he lifted something from another airman's locker and put it in his own.

We asked everyone in the barracks for a voluntary footlocker inspection. Everyone in the barracks agreed to the inspection—except for our suspect. He wouldn't open his footlocker, and we couldn't make him do so. I usually have a long fuse when it comes to losing my cool in tense situations, but I lost my cool. I grabbed him by the collar, pushed him out onto the fire-escape landing, and forced him up against the railing. I told him I was going to throw him over if he didn't consent to the inspection. Don was right behind me. We grabbed his legs, hoisted him up and over the railing, hung onto his legs, and dangled him upside down.

He yelled, "Don't drop me."

"Give us your lock combination—and we'll pull you up."

"Okay, okay. Pull me up."

He blurted out the combination, and Don and I pulled him back over the railing. My heart was pounding, and I was sweating and boiling with rage. Don held on to our suspect, and I went to open the footlocker. I got the combination to work and opened the trunk. Lifting the top tray, I could see the glint of jewelry. In the thief's little stash, I saw my watch. I cursed the thief as I slipped my watch on my wrist.

Everyone crowded around the trunk to see if any of their missing items were there.

Our thief tried to get free, but Don held him down while an airman went to phone the air police.

When the APs arrived, they took the names of any who would testify. As they hustled our thief out of the barracks, he hollered, "I'll get you, Hicks—you'd better be looking over your shoulder."

A few weeks later, a number of us testified at the trial. He was court-martialed and sentenced to serve time in Leavenworth Penitentiary.

I never looked over my shoulder—except for once or twice.

My time at Scott Air Base was getting short, and eight or ten of us thought we would have one last fling in town. We booked supper reservations at one of the high-class joints in St. Louis and planned on a long evening of eating, drinking, and entertainment. My choice of drink for the evening was a martini, which after two became "Martoonies," and after three, Martweenies. We all became pretty rowdy, and I vaguely remember sitting under the table shouting for more Martoonies. We were all singing "What Do You Do with a Drunken Airmen" as we were escorted out of the club by a couple of bouncers.

Outside we sang our version of "The St. Louis Blues."

Chapter 5

The Big Apple and a Slow Boat

At the beginning of 1955, I took a train to New York City. I had four days in New York before I had to report to Camp Kilmer in New Jersey, thirty miles south of New York. Camp Kilmer was a staging area to serve the port of New York for troops headed for duty in Europe.

I arrived at Pennsylvania Station and was excited to be on my first visit to the Big Apple. I was amazed by the tall buildings, people, and taxis going in every direction. Everyone was moving at a fast pace, seemingly knowing where they were going—except for me. I hailed a cab, gave the driver a piece of paper with the hotel's address, and said, "This is where I'm going."

The air force had booked hotel rooms for airmen waiting to go to Camp Kilmer.

He did an abrupt U-turn, and we were off.

"Here we are."

It was an expensive ride for only a couple of blocks, but I was glad to get to the hotel. I'd had a long, boring train ride, but things were moving at a faster pace. I checked in, rode the elevator to my room's floor, went to my room, and pulled up the window shade to check out the view. I looked into the side of the building next door. *New York, New York, it's a wonderful town.*

Before leaving for New York City, I had been given the phone number of a classmate from high school. She was attending a college in New York. I called her and set up a date for that evening. On my first night in New York City, I had a date with a pretty girl and dinner at a jazz club (Eddie Condon's in Greenwich Village). Having a taste of the Big Apple is like taking a bite of the forbidden fruit of paradise. I loved it—and I wanted more.

The next day I planned on sightseeing in the city. My first stop was the Empire State Building; in 1955, it was New York's tallest building at 102 stories. The World Trade Center at 110 stories superseded it in 1970. The Empire State Building regained its status as New York City's tallest building on September 11, 2001, when a horrific act by terrorists brought down the World Trade Center buildings.

Walking through the huge marble lobby of the Empire State Building was like being in a Gothic cathedral. I made my way to the elevators and took an express to the eighty-sixth floor. I felt a little lightheaded from the ascent and the view from the observation deck. Although I didn't like heights, I marveled at the spectacular sight of the city and spent quite a bit of time taking in the panoramic view. I mustered up the courage to venture up to the very top, the observatory on the top floor. When I got into the cramped, glassed-in observatory—1,450 feet above ground—my sphincter was as tight as my grip on the guardrail. I didn't stay long and descended back to ground level. What a trip. Back on the ground floor, I marveled at the engineering achievements in constructing this enormous building and decided it was our equivalent to the ancient pyramids.

Riding the subway back to my hotel, I planned my evening outing. A night at the Birdland Jazz Club would be the highlight of my New York visit. It was my good fortune that one of my favorite jazz groups, the Jazz Messengers, would be playing at Birdland.

Birdland was located on Broadway near West Fifty-Second Street. It was started in 1949 and was named in honor of the great jazz alto saxophonist Charlie Parker, whose nickname was Bird. Fifty-Second Street was the heart of jazz music, and many other jazz clubs could be found nearby. Thelonious Monk's "52nd Street Theme" celebrated that famous street. In 1949, George Shearing played with Buddy DeFranco at the Clique Club, which later that year became known as Birdland. Shearing was asked to write a theme song for radio broadcasts from Birdland. "Lullaby of Birdland" became a popular jazz hit.

As I descended the stairs into the somewhat small (I expected the place to be as large as its reputation) and dimly lit club, I could hear the Jazz Messengers. I'd heard the unmistakably solid sound of Art Blakey accentuating the second and fourth beats on his tireless steady hi-hat many times on record and in person.

The Jazz Messengers included Art Blakey (drums), Horace Silver (piano), Doug Watkins (bass), Lou Donaldson (sax), and Donald Byrd (trumpet). In 1954, they had released A *Night at Birdland*; although the group's personnel were somewhat different, they had the same sound.

I was being seated at a table as the band finished playing a tune, and Pee Wee Marquette came onto the stage. The master of ceremonies was barely four feet tall. He was small in size but large in enthusiasm and knowledge of jazz. Marquette was featured on the *Night at Birdland* album as the MC and introduced the band in his high-pitched, spirited voice. I was listening to that spiel as though I'd been magically transformed to the album's recording. I felt like a teenage groupie at a rock concert. I was swept away by the whole ambiance. I was completely attentive to every tune they performed and scrutinized every note. I stayed through two of their sets and then left to take a look at Fifty-Second Street. It was late, but the City That Never Sleeps was in full swing.

Taking in the sights along Fifty-Second Street, I noticed a GI in uniform ahead of me. I had a strange feeling about this guy; there was something familiar about his gait and posture. I noticed he was carrying a clarinet case. I quickened my pace and shouted, "Mort?"

Mort Weiss said, "Herb Hicks in New York City?"

"Still carrying that clarinet wherever you go?"

"Never leave home without it," he answered.

We gave each other a hug and we expressed our astonishment at finding one another on the streets of New York City. What were the odds of that? We had last seen each other in LA over two years earlier.

Mort was waiting to be shipped overseas and had a couple of days of leave. He'd been to Birdland the night before and found a little jazz club where there was an open jam session. He was on his way there and asked that I join him for a late night of music and reunion.

We spent a couple of hours listening and sitting in at the club. Mort sat in most of the time, but I played a couple of tunes. There was a line of piano players waiting to sit in; some very good, some so-so, and others just plain sucked. I figured I was somewhere between so-so and sucked.

After our fill, we shook hands and said good-bye. It wasn't until about ten years later that we saw one another again at a restaurant in Santa Barbara.

Two days later, I—and a couple thousand other airmen—boarded the USS *General W. G. Haan*, a military sea transportation service troopship at the New York Port of Embarkation. We would be sailing to Bremerhaven, Germany.

Lugging our duffel bags aboard and down into the hole of the ship, we found our assigned spaces, which consisted of bunks in a maze of hammocks. They were strung in tiers three or four high, leaving an aisle just big enough for a person to walk through. We were packed in like sardines with duffel bags.

Spending time on deck was required every day to get some sunshine and fresh air, which we badly needed after being in the "hammock jungle." After two or three days, many of the men got seasick. We ran into a storm and were forced to stay below deck for a couple of days. Almost everyone got seasick. Luckily, I didn't get hit too hard and only felt slightly nauseous. I was more than happy to get back on deck to some sun and salty air. The weather was overcast, and the enormous swells would gracefully rise and descend like a sixty-cycle sine wave, taking the ship up to the apex and down to start the cycle over—and over—and over. It was like a gentle giant roller-coaster ride. The horizon was nowhere to be seen; the sea and sky melted into one continuous bluish-gray backdrop. I sighted a point of reference; a ship in the distance was appearing, disappearing, and reappearing with the heaving ocean. All of a sudden, a nauseous seasick feeling overtook me like the giant swells I was watching. I lost my breakfast, lunch, and every other meal I'd had since leaving New York.

After getting over my seasickness and gaining my sea legs, the most unpleasant conditions were boredom and crowded quarters. I soon found a way around both situations. The ship published a daily news bulletin. I saw an advertisement for a variety show to be staged in the service club area. My music experience came to the rescue again. The service club area was littered with chairs, magazines, board games, and card tables. In the corner, a piano was lashed to the wall. I teamed up with a guitar player and a bass player/vocalist to put on a little act. We were joined by a number of vaudeville-type acts. None of us were very good, but that didn't matter since we had an appreciative and captive audience.

The troops crowded into the service club. They were ready for any relief from the monotonous voyage. The biggest hit was a song our vocalist had changed the words to the tune, "(I'd Love to Get You on a) Slow Boat to China." His adaptation of the song became "(We're Sailing the Atlantic on a) Troop Ship to Europe." The laughter, cheering, and applause were deafening. We felt like we had a number-one hit on Broadway. I spent the rest of my voyage at the piano and retreated only to the mess hall to eat, the deck for fresh air, and my hammock to sleep.

After two weeks at sea, we sailed into the Bremerhaven Port of Embarkation. My first steps down the gangplank were a little unsteady, and when I stepped on the solid ground of Germany, I wobbled like a drunken sailor. With every step I took, the ground swelled up to meet me. I was still riding the ocean waves. We were bused to an army barracks to be billeted overnight and sent to our assigned units.

The next day, I boarded a train bound for Munich. The train ride across Germany would give me a chance to catch up on reading my German-English dictionary. Having been in the air force for over a year, I wondered why I'd never been in a military aircraft. I'd traveled on buses, trains, ships, trucks, cars, and even an ambulance—but never by plane. My logging of air miles would come soon.

I was assigned to the Eighth Radio Relay Squadron at Furstenfeldbruck Airbase in Germany. It was the busiest military airfield in Europe. Fursty, as it was known to us airmen, was a training air field operated by the Twelfth USAF 7330 Flying Training Wing. The base was located in the Bavarian section of Germany, about twenty miles west of Munich. It was a Luftwaffe airfield during WWII—until the USAF took it over in 1947.

The air base today is infamous for being the site of the tragic conclusion to the Munich Massacre during the 1972 Summer Olympics when nine Israeli hostages, held by eight Black September terrorists, were killed on the tarmac of that airfield—a senseless act of murder by cowardly terrorists.

The radio site at Furstenfeldbruck was part of a network of microwave radio sites that the Eighth Radio Relay Squadron operated across Europe. My job was maintaining microwave radio equipment and making sure we were back in communication as soon as possible if we had an outage.

I was invited by some of the guys in my unit to spend an evening at a beer garden in Furstenfeldbruck. My first time off base in Germany was one of apprehension. I wondered how the German people would react to American GIs. My buddies assured me that the natives were very friendly, had put the war behind them, and most of them loved us—especially our Yankee dollars.

I found this all to be true and thoroughly enjoyed my time at the little beer hall. The food was excellent, and the beer was even better. I had more than my share of both. My buddies had warned me about eating and drinking too much, but the food tasted so good and the beer went down so easy.

My buddy said, "The German beer has a higher alcohol content than the beer we get on the base, and it'll sneak up on you, and so will the food, and then—"

"And then what?" I asked.

"Be near a latrine."

Around two in the morning, we had the barkeep call a taxi, and we were on our way. It was a short drive to the airbase, but just as we took off, I knew what my buddy had meant. The Bavarian beer and pickled foods began to battle in my guts, and I could feel the storm of diarrhea coming on with hurricane force.

I told the taxi driver to hurry. "*Schnell, Mach Schnell.*"

My buddies hollered at the cabbie as we sped through the night toward the air base. After what seemed to take forever to check in at the main gate, we pulled up in front of our quarters. Not waiting for the cab to make a full stop, I jumped out, ran into the barracks, down the hall, and around the corner to the latrine. Just as I went through the latrine door, the diarrhea tempest unleashed its fury. "Oh shit," I hollered. I could hear laughter coming from down the hallway.

Munich, the capital of Bavaria, was just a short train ride from Furstenfeldbruck; I would travel into the city every chance I'd get. Munich's fascinating history is glorious and sordid. The city was founded in 1158; it was a city four hundred years before the discovery of America. My European friends often reminded me that Americans have very little history. I would remind them that Europeans thought the world was flat before America was discovered.

Oktoberfest in Munich is the largest festival in the world. Started in October 1810, it celebrated the royal wedding of Crown Prince Ludwig I.

I found the spirit of Oktoberfest existed all year in Munich. Many Germans spoke English and had been schooled in a number of languages. I had heard my grandparents speak a little Swiss/German, but I only knew a few simple phrases in German.

In Munich, I found my way to the Lowenbrau Keller Beer Garden and the famous Hofbrauhaus beer hall, which was established in 1589. It was a great place to see traditional Deutsch entertainment with oompah bands and dances. Patrons would sing, *Oans, zwoa, g'suffa* (one, two, drink), and guzzle large steins of beer. Hitler gave speeches at the Hofbrauhaus in the twenties and thirties while organizing the Nazi Party.

Although I found the traditional German music interesting and rousing, I was more interested in the jazz music and jazz musicians of Germany. Whenever I had a chance, I would seek out some jazz club or *jazzkeller* in Munich. Jutta Hipp was a very creative German jazz pianist and a favorite of mine. She was also a painter and did some stunning portraits of famous jazz musicians.

At the air base, I formed a trio with other airmen: a drummer/vocalist, a bass player, and me on piano. We'd seen some advertisement about a talent contest to be held on the base; the winners would go to the Twelfth Air Force Germany-Austria contest. Winners at that level would go on to the US Air Force Europe (USAFE) level, and those winners would go to New York to be on the *Ed Sullivan Show*. We entered the contest and won first place at the base level. Orders were cut for us to continue on to the Twelfth Air Force level competition to be held at Ramstein Air Base in Kaiserslautern, Germany.

At Ramstein, we won first place again and were assigned to an entertainment group called "Tops in Twelfth Revue." We were to tour air force bases in Germany, the Netherlands, and France. After winning the competition in Ramstein, we had to disband our trio. The drummer and bass man were due to rotate back to the States so they were out of the tour. I was left alone as a contestant.

The Four Bits of Rhythm was a black vocal quartet comprised of guitar, trumpet, bass, and drums. They sang beautiful harmony in the style of the Four Freshmen. We had jammed together on the tour, and they asked me to join their group. I was delighted to join the group, and I played piano with them. We officially became the Five Bits of Rhythm, but we kidded among ourselves that we were the Four Bits of Rhythm—Plus One.

The first leg of our tour was a gig in Amsterdam. At last, I was scheduled to travel by air. My flights on military aircraft required that I wear a parachute. We had a quick lesson in how to bail out in case of an emergency. The sergeant checked our chutes. As he checked mine, he told me to tighten up the harness on my crotch or I would lose my family jewels when the chute opened. You can bet I pulled the straps so tight it felt like my scrotum had replaced my tonsils.

The aircrafts we flew in were WWII Douglas C-47s, sometimes referred to as "Dakotas" which was the acronym "DACoTA" for Douglas Aircraft Company Transport Aircraft. C-47s were affectionately nicknamed "Gooney Birds." This reference to a seabird, the Albatross, could have a number of meanings. It could be an omen for good or bad luck or a metaphor meaning a "wearisome burden" as alluded to in Samuel Coleridge's *The Rime of the Ancient Mariner*. An albatross follows a ship and is shot by one of the sailors. The sailor's mates, believing they will be cursed with bad luck, punished the seabird killer by making him wear the dead albatross around his neck. I don't believe the C-47's reference to the albatross means a burden, but the true reference is the fact that the bird, like the plane, takes a long runway to slowly get airborne. But once taking off and climbing, both have stability and ease of flight.

A couple of takeoffs were a little worrisome; on one long takeoff, I thought we were going to taxi all the way to our next gig. The aircraft had no passenger seats, but two rows of benches ran the length of the fuselage on either side of its interior. We sat on these benches shoulder to shoulder like paratroopers, rigid and silent, with chutes on our backs, readying ourselves for a jump. Once we were airborne—and the old Gooney Bird stopped quivering and wobbling—everybody relaxed and found something to keep occupied with.

Amsterdam is a unique city with its historic canals, museums, and coffee shops. Today many coffee shops offer legal cannabis for sale, and the city is famous for its red light district, where prostitutes, displaying their wares, beckon from behind large windows in houses facing the canal. The girls and the cannabis are controlled by the government. This makes a lot of sense for two of the problems plaguing mankind.

Amsterdam is a city of bicycles. Cyclists rule the streets and alleys. Driving a car in central Amsterdam is discouraged, but it is fairly easy to get around with buses and tram lines. If I have the chance to visit Amsterdam again, I want to visit two of its most famous museums; the Rijksmuseum (where there are splendid Rembrandt and Vermeer paintings) and the Van Gogh Museum. Opened in 1973, its collection consists of Impressionist and Post-Impressionist paintings and the largest collection in the world of Vincent Van Gogh's drawings and paintings.

After our performances, we were given a two-day pass in Amsterdam before flying to France to tour bases and to Germany to finish up our tour. The people of Amsterdam are outgoing and sociable, and we quickly made a number of Dutch friends. With some of my air force buddies, I spent part of the afternoon at a little bar and met a lovely Dutch girl. She told me she knew of a jazz club close by and wanted to know if I would like to go there with some of her friends; of course, I would love to go. Before we took off, people began smoking a joint. When it was passed to me, I took a big toke and held it in as long as I could. Coughing and sputtering, I was trying to be cool while people were laughing at me. I felt a state of euphoria that I had never experienced—not a drunken stupor, but a feeling of well-being and intense awareness. With everyone laughing, I smiled and laughed too, stoned out of my mind.

We took off to the jazz club and listened to a trio of piano, bass, and guitar. The Dutch girl asked if I would like to come to supper at her house. Her daughter and mother, who lived with her, would also be there. First we had to stop by the market to purchase a few items. I agreed—if she would let me buy the groceries. I had sensed that would be the deal, and I was ready to oblige. I paid for the groceries she had selected; it seemed like a large amount for just one meal, but I didn't mind. It was a home-cooked meal and a chance to spend some time with a pleasant lovely Dutch girl.

At her apartment, I met her shy young daughter. Remembering my own young years of shyness, I reached in my pocket, retrieved a package of gum, and offered it to her.

The little girl said, "Thank you, sir."

I was astonished by her perfect English; with that one little gesture, the barriers of bashfulness were lowered. The daughter and I became instant friends. She proudly showed me her crayon drawings, and we rummaged through them like we were old school chums. It is amazing what one little expression of kindness can accomplish.

My Dutch friend told me that her mother had had a very hard time during the war and had nearly starved to death, causing her to go into deep depression. Her mother knew very little English—hello, how are you, and I am good. They were all preceded by or ended with "yah."

After a nice meal, the girl proudly played some of her record collection. It consisted of Dixieland Jazz, which I was not particularly fond of. Not wanted to offend her, I pretended to enjoy the music and asked if she knew of any of the modern jazz musicians like Monk, Dizzy, or Miles. They were not part of her repertoire, but we got along very well. She was beautiful—and very sexy. One thing led to another, and when everyone else was fast asleep, we ended up in bed wrapped in an amorous embrace.

The next evening, I boarded our Gooney Bird for a short flight to Toul, France, and we continued our tour. I thought about the beautiful dream I'd had in Amsterdam, but reality hit me a couple of days later when I was urinating—and felt like I was peeing fire. A day later, at an air base in Germany, I stood in line with other airmen at the dispensary for a shot of penicillin. The clap was the price I paid for a night of carnal pleasure in Holland.

We continued our "Tops in Twelfth Revue" tour; although the Five Bits of Rhythm didn't win the trip to New York, we had a great time and I'd made many new friends. After touring with the show for another two weeks, I returned to my home base at Furstenfeldbruck. I was told that I was being transferred to an Eighth Radio Relay Site at a USAFBE at Chaumont, France.

Chapter 6

The French-Swiss Connection

In the 1950s, the USAFE had eleven major air bases in France. The bases were part of a commitment to the North Atlantic Treaty Organization (NATO). In the sixties, French President Charles De Gaulle's dislike of NATO led to the decision that France would withdraw from NATO's military unit, and he ordered NATO forces to leave France. One reason for this decision was that there were continental ballistic missiles in place and no need for fighter-bomber bases in Europe. Another reason was disagreements over issues of storage of atomic weapons within NATO. The Forty-Eighth Fighter-Bomber Wing at Chaumont, France, was a USAFE atomic-capable fighter-bomber unit. At the time, this was supposed to be a secret, but everyone knew of this situation—and it worried a lot of people that we had nuclear weapons on our air bases.

Chaumont Air Base was known as the "Statue of Liberty" Wing. The base was located near the studios of Frederic Bartholdi, the French architect who designed the Statue of Liberty. This honorary title was bestowed on the airbase by the mayor of Chaumont.

During WWII, Chaumont and the area around Luxembourg and Belgium saw bitter fighting between the German Panzer Army and the Fourteenth Armored Division of the Third US Army. The Battle of the Bulge, a horrendous battle in late 1944 and early 1945, was the largest battle of WWII.

Ten years after the war, the scars of the war were still remarkably visible. While stationed at Chaumont, I visited a number of battle sites and saw the ruins of bunkers and shell-pocked buildings along the Luxembourg/French border. Chaumont Air Base was the home of the "Skyblazers," a jet acrobatic display team flying F86 Sabrejets. Our microwave radio site at Chaumont, which was close to the main runway, was continually being blasted by the roar of jets and their afterburners.

The very young lieutenant in charge of our radio site was a gung-ho officer with little military experience other than the Junior Reserve Officers' Training Corps (JROTC). The program started in high school with the promise of a scholarship to college in exchange for an extended period of active military service. After my discharge from the air force in 1958, my father showed me a letter that he had received from the lieutenant while I was stationed at Chaumont. In part, it read how interesting it was to work with me and how I performed my duties as a microwave technician with expertise and thoughtfulness (my father was pleased that I had gained some knowledge of the electronics field).

In the rest of the letter, the lieutenant tore me apart as a military man. Apparently I had little regard for military discipline, dress codes, haircuts, language, timetables, and a number of other military protocols. The lieutenant had observed me smoking, drinking beer, playing poker at the service club, and fraternizing with the local French population (with thousands of other GIs). The ultimate delinquency was spending my time reading *Downbeat* and listening to jazz. I didn't mind my military obligation, but I sure didn't plan on making the air force a career for the next thirty years like the lieutenant. I figured what I did on my off duty hours was my choice. My father thought the letter was very strange (so did I). The letter ended up saying the lieutenant thought I had the potential of being a first-class airman—and that he was going to do everything he could to make me one. It never happened.

Shortly after my arrival at Chaumont, I bought a 1952 Chevrolet convertible from an airman in my unit who was due to be deployed back to the States. He was anxious to sell the car before he left, and I was able to purchase it for a very low price. The Chevy was a classy red convertible with a white convertible top and whitewall tires. No wonder some Europeans were so envious of us Americans. Driving through the French countryside, I no doubt appeared to be a rich American tourist. Some Europeans despised us for being rich capitalists, but others loved us because of our effort in WWII and our economic aid after the war.

On my first trip to Basel, Switzerland, I went to see my grandmother's sister, Martha Vogelsanger. Jim, who was a drummer and a new friend of mine from the air base, went with me. Jim was fluent in French, and Martha spoke a little French, but mainly German. A lady who shared the apartment with Martha spoke German and French; between Martha's friend and my friend, they would translate English to French to German and German to French to English.

Martha was as delighted to meet her sister's grandson from America as I was to meet my grandmother's sister. Our delightful visit included many laughs as I tried to speak the few German and French words and phrases I knew, usually inappropriately. A large percentage of the Swiss people spoke German, French, Italian, English, and Spanish. I wrote a letter to my mother about my visit in Basel, and she was thrilled that I had met her aunt. Mom showed the letter to my grandfather, and he suggested a trip to the old country to visit relatives and see me. That idea developed into a trip they would make about six months later.

Basel is located on the Rhine River near where the Swiss, French, and German borders meet. The town dates back to the Roman times (third century BC). The town hall (*Basel Rathaus*) was built in the sixteenth century on the market square (*Marktplatz*). It is a spectacular building of arches, a tower, and a stunning courtyard decorated inside and out with beautiful murals.

In Basel, I usually stayed at the Touring Hotel near the *Mittlere Brucke* (the oldest bridge across the Rhine opened in the 1200s). I enjoyed the tasty food in the restaurant. I met a Swiss girl, and we dated for over a year. Kathy was fluent in English and spoke a number of other languages. She was in her midtwenties, was educated, had an adventurous spirit, and was a part owner of a hair salon in Basel. We enjoyed many trips around Switzerland, Italy, and France.

I had the option of working four or five days straight and then getting three or four days off, making possible a trip to Paris or Basel. Every time I would travel to Switzerland, I would stop at the border, check the exchange rate, and usually make a profit on the transaction.

Kathy was a great companion for an American's first visit to Europe. She introduced me to the history of Basel and taught me much about Swiss history and traditions. Although she didn't teach me to yodel, we made beautiful music together.

A friend once said, "Swiss lovemaking is probably the origin of Swiss yodeling." *Yodel-ay-ee-oooo.*

The music scene at Chaumont Air Base was encouraging. We had a number of good players, and I became involved with two bands. One band did commercial dance gigs at the service clubs, and the other was a jazz trio that played in Chaumont at the American Red Cross Center and at a little jazz cellar. Jonesy (bass) and Hite (drums) were two black musicians that I really enjoyed gigging with.

We played in Chaumont at a little bar in the basement of a hotel—after we brought in a piano that someone had donated to us to start a jazz club. We rolled the heavy acoustic piano down the stairs, around corners, and coaxed it into a small space in the bar. We'd pack the place with French nationals and American servicemen whenever we played.

In Chaumont, I met a French bass player. Gabriel and I formed a dance combo that we called the Continentals. He introduced me to French cuisine, French culture, and the French language. We spent many hours over bottles of Beaujolais, loaves of bread, and dishes of escargots.

I began to get interested in art, in particular the French Impressionist painters. As I made more and more trips to Paris, I experienced a greater appreciation for architecture, sculpture, painting, and drawing. I visited the museums and the jazz clubs in my favorite part of Paris, the Saint Germain-des-Pres district. The oldest district of Paris, on the Left Bank of the Seine River in the Latin Quarter, dates back to the third century.

Since the Middle Ages, the Latin Quarter has been the center of French intellectualism and culture, influenced by the Sorbonne University since 1231. This is the location of the Paris Bohemian café culture. San Germain-des-Pres was the haunt for many famous persons and writers throughout history, including Napoleon, Voltaire, Hugo, Sartre, Camus, Eliot, Fitzgerald, and Hemingway. Delacroix, Degas,

Monet, Renoir, Picasso, and other artists had a close association with the Left Bank. Ben Franklin and Thomas Jefferson were drawn to this section of Paris. I enjoyed the shops and cafés on the Boulevard Saint-Michel where I was within walking distance to Notre Dame Cathedral, a stroll along the illuminated Seine River, or a short ride on the Metro to the Moulin Rouge.

My favorite jazz club in San-Germain was the Mars Club. I caught many of the great American jazz musicians; most were playing in Europe because they were disillusioned with the music scene in the United States and with the New York City–imposed cabaret card license.

The NYC cabaret ID card was required for all workers in New York nightclubs, including performers. Many great musicians were denied cards at the discretion of the New York City Police Department on actual or trumped-up charges. The NYC cabaret card system was finally abolished in 1967.

Spending my off-duty hours in Paris became more and more frequent. The traffic around the *Arc de Triomphe*, at the western end of the *Avenue des Champs Elysees*, was always congested. Twelve avenues radiate from the hub of the *Arc de Triomphe* like spokes on a wheel. I fought my way though that traffic circle many times.

At the eastern end of the *Avenue des Champs Elysees* is one of the largest squares in Paris; the *Place de la Concorde* leads to the *Jardin des Tuileries* (botanical gardens) and the Louvre Museum. The square features two large fountains. In the center is a three-thousand-year-old, seventy-five-foot obelisk that originally stood at the entrance to the Luxor Temple in Egypt. The obelisk was put in place in the 1830s; a guillotine occupied the center of the square during the French Revolution. Three thousand people lost their heads there, including King Louis XVI and Marie Antoinette.

The *Place de la Concorde* has some of the most congested and confusing traffic in Paris. Automobiles, buses, motorcycles, motor scooters, bicycles, and vehicles of all sorts and sizes would seemingly be going in every direction around the square. On one of my visits to Paris, Jim and I were in a maddening race around the *Place de la Concorde* at rush hour. Just as I was about to turn my Chevy away from the square and head toward the Louvre, I collided with a Frenchman on a motor scooter.

Jim called out in French just as the motor scooter hit my car. I could tell that the Frenchman was injured. Someone called an ambulance, and the gendarmes arrived on the scene. Jim's knowledge of the French language was extremely helpful for dealing with the gendarmes and filling out an accident report. The man on the motor scooter suffered a broken leg, bloody cuts on his arm, and a demolished scooter. My Chevy had a dent in the fender, but Jim and I had no injuries. We were only slightly shaken up by the accident—and the sight of the bloodied Frenchman. A gendarme told me I would hear from the courts—and that I was not to leave the country until after the court appearance, to which he added something like "*ces fou* Americans" (crazy Americans).

A couple of weeks later, I received notice from my commanding officer about the accident, advising me of my rights under an American-French agreement regarding American military men in service in France. We were subject to French laws and had the right to a French lawyer. We could have a lawyer from the US Military Law Service only as an observer and an interrupter at the court proceedings. I was summoned to appear in civil court at a *tribunal d'instance* for small claims. I was being sued for damages by the scooter driver. On a date set by the court, I was to appear at the *Palais de Justice* in Paris. The *Palais de Justice* is a magnificent, enormous structure, and I thought it a shame to have to visit it on such a somber occasion.

I was in the courtroom early wearing my class "A" uniform—looking sharp. The trial was to decide who was to blame for the accident by degree of fault and to settle a claim for damages. The proceedings were officiated over by three judges, but they couldn't seem to get their acts together. The findings would be decided by a two-thirds majority.

Witnesses filed in, and then the scooter driver made his *grand entrée*, limping in on crutches with a large cast on his leg and bandages on one arm. He put on a great show for the judges. I became very nervous. *This looks bad for me. It looks like I really did a number on this guy.* I listened intently, trying to make sense of the gibberish in a language I knew very little of.

At a recess, I asked the interrupter about the hollering between the lawyers and judges. They were arguing over giving a figure to my guilt in the accident—whether it was 30 percent, 50 percent, 75 percent, or 100 percent. You were guilty or innocent by percentage. After the hearing, I asked my American lawyer what he thought the outcome would be.

He said, "I don't know. I don't speak French that well."

Jim was there as a witness, and I asked him about the bandying of words.

He told me it didn't look good for me. I might have to pay a huge fine plus serve time in the Bastille.

"Why? For what? I don't think I could do that, I would—"

Jim burst out laughing. "Just kidding," he said. "I don't know what the hell to think about all this."

That really didn't quiet my fears; he had really shaken me up with his little joke. I had heard and read horrible stories about French prisons. My imagination took me to the images of the Bastille in the books of Hugo (*Les Misérables*) and Dumas (*The Man in the Iron Mask*). Although the Bastille had been destroyed during the French Revolution, there were other French prisons—none in which I wished to spend any time.

A couple of weeks later, I received an official report on the trial. I was to pay a fine and damages that came to around three thousand dollars in US currency.

Having that ordeal behind me, I made numerous visits to Paris. I went sightseeing at historic places like the Cathedral of Notre Dame, the finest example of French Gothic architecture. I enjoyed the shops along the Champs, the museums, the sidewalk cafés and jazz clubs in Montmartre and Pigalle, the Moulin Rouge, and the Seine River. I tested my fear of heights again by going to the top of the Eiffel Tower to get a spectacular view of Paris.

In August 1955, my mother and grandfather flew to Zurich for a month's visit. I had accrued some leave time and took two weeks off to meet them in Switzerland. We stayed with relatives in Zurich for four days. Zurich was where my grandparents had built a house in the early 1920s after twenty years in America. The house was built in a municipality on the outskirts of Zurich. Schwamendingen later became a suburb of Zurich. My mom was about seventeen at the time, and her brother was twelve.

My grandfather and I strolled along the Limmat riverfront in Zurich on a beautiful late summer afternoon. We were looking at the shops along Lake Zurich. My mom and her relatives had gone on a shopping tour around Zurich, and we would meet for dinner at a café on the Lake Zurich waterfront. Grandpa suggested we head for the café, and he would buy me a stein of German beer. We made our way to the café and got a table on the shady patio. We ordered two steins of beer and told the waitress we would be expecting three more people for dinner. We had almost an hour before the dinner meal. Grandpa kept saying he wished he could remember more of his native language so he could communicate better with his relatives (even though most of the relatives spoke English). My grandfather was a very laid-back and somewhat stoic person. I noticed that the more beer we drank, the more he remembered his native language. He became more flamboyant—not in any obnoxious way, just more outgoing than usual.

Whenever the waitress came within earshot, he said, "*Fraeulein, vize biere, bitte.*" I had a great time with my grandfather. He did most of the talking, telling me about growing up in Switzerland.

Mom and the relatives arrived for dinner and Grandpa shouted, "Yah! Here are our dinner guests. *Willkommen, Herzlich Wilkommen meine Damen und Herren.*"

Mom gave Grandpa a stern look and said, "Dad, you're drunk."

Before he could answer, she started scolding him for being intoxicated. I jumped in and said it was my fault since I kept buying him steins of beer. "This was one of the best times I've ever spent with Grandpa."

Mom simmered down and said, "We'd all better get some food in us."

We had a delicious meal. As we were about to leave, my grandfather put his arm around me, gave me a hug, and said, "*Danke schoen, Enkel!*" (Thank you, Grandson). A loving moment I'll always remember.

The next day, we went to Schaffhausen, a short drive from Zurich. It is on the northern part of Switzerland, near the German border. Schaffhausen is a medieval town dating back to the eleventh century. It is built on the northern bank of the Rhine, near the Rhine Falls, the largest and most powerful waterfalls in Europe. Overlooking the city is a sixteenth-century fortress called the Munot and surrounding the old city the city walls. The Munot was built from a design by Albrecht Durer. It is an impressive structure with its citadel towering above the city.

The old city of Schaffhausen is a Swiss national heritage site. The baroque houses in the old city are exquisite and have ornately decorated windows; it was like being in a fantasy world. It was a warm summer, and there where displays of flowers everywhere. I wondered if this memory of Schaffhausen influenced my grandparents' decision to operate greenhouses in North Dakota. This is where my mom and uncle had spent part of their childhood, and this is where my grandparents and their families had been born and grown up. Looking at this Swiss gem of a city, I had an immense feeling of elation and wonder in knowing that this was part of my heritage.

After leaving Schaffhausen, we made a short journey to the little town of Beggingen. It is located almost on the German-Swiss border, about twenty miles from the Black Forest. Beggingen is where my grandparents spent their early childhood.

Driving into this little Swiss village in my red Chevy convertible caused many onlookers to stare in awe. They must have wondered who those rich American tourists were. We visited one of my grandfather's older brothers (he had four brothers). Grandpa's brother was in very poor health with emphysema, mainly due to the fact that he'd spent most of his life working and living in the forest in a damp cold environment. We stayed overnight in Beggingen and visited more relatives the next day.

One of my relatives spoke English and acted as the translator for us. He was very interested in my air force career; he was in the Swiss army and was getting ready to be deployed to his summer training camp. Swiss soldiers keep their uniforms, equipment, and weapons at home; if called to duty, they are immediately prepared to serve their country. Switzerland has an army—but a long history of neutrality—and does not fight in conflicts in other countries.

The next day, we headed back to Zurich for a day. We planned to go to Basel and then travel the autobahn to Mannheim. We would visit a friend of ours from Williston and head to Paris.

Our trip on the autobahn went smoothly—until we reached the outskirts of Mannheim. We had some serious car trouble and ended up having to stay in Mannheim for a few days while we had repairs done. We had a long visit with Mom's friend from Williston. Since I was running out of leave time, we decided to cancel the Paris visit and take Mom and Grandpa back to Zurich.

To and from Gigs

Back at Chaumont, I resumed my duties as microwave technician. The Cold War between Russia and the United States was escalating; in November 1956, the Suez Crisis put our air base and all American military bases in Europe on alert. The disagreement over the Suez Canal created tensions with an Egyptian-Israeli alliance between the United Kingdom and France. The Egyptian government wanted to nationalize the Suez Canal, and the disagreement developed into a conflict known as the Sinai War. The USSR threatened to intervene on behalf of Egypt and threatened to launch rocket attacks on Britain, France, and Israel. This threat by the Soviet Union put our Strategic Air Command (SAC) bombers on alert, armed with nuclear weapons.

There were heated debates in the United Nations over the Suez Crisis. Lester B. Pearson, Canada's secretary of state for external affairs at this time (also prime minister of Canada from 1963–68) proposed a plan to have United Nations forces act as a buffer zone between the opposing forces.

The Soviets withdrew the threat, and Pearson's plan gave birth to the UN peacekeeping operations. Pearson was awarded the Nobel Peace Prize in 1957 for his efforts in avoiding what could have been a global nuclear war.

In the beginning of 1957, I was reassigned to Chambley, France, a new air force base that had opened in the summer of 1956. Due to threats by the Soviet Union, this new base provided air support to NATO for military units and a communications link to all USAFE bases.

Chambley Air Base was ten miles west of Metz, France, a mile from the village of Chambley, and about thirty miles from the German and Luxembourg borders.

Shortly after arriving at Chambley, I was told that our radio unit was due for an inspection that spring. This was to be a class "A" inspection by a bigwig colonel from the Twelfth Air Force Headquarters. We scrubbed, polished, waxed, shined, shaved, and brushed up on our microwave maintenance and communications protocols.

The sergeant in charge of our unit had a very heavy Southern drawl. The morning of the inspection, he was fussing over us like a mother hen with her chicks. The sergeant would get very close to us and ask, "Do I smell? Y'all answer me truthfully now, ya hear!"

"No smell, sergeant, you're okay," we answered.

The sergeant had a stomach ulcer and had been told by a local farmer that the ulcer would go away if he drank goat's milk every day. For almost a year, he'd been drinking goat's milk every day, which he bought from the farmer. It seemed to keep his ulcer at bay, but he would smell like a goat, depending on how much milk he drank. One time I'd told him I had an over-acidic stomach, and he said I should try some goat's milk.

I took a sip and said, "No, thanks. I'll stay with my Tums."

In the radio site building, the sergeant had us line up in front of the wall-to-wall microwave equipment. Facing the door, we anticipated the arrival of the colonel.

Just before the door opened, the airman next to me said, "You forgot the US insignias for your lapels!" I'd removed the insignias to polish them and forgot to pin them back on.

The door opened, the sergeant hollered, "Attention!"

The colonel and his party stepped into the building. I froze at attention, and for just a moment, I closed my eyes and hoped I was dreaming. Opening my eyes, reality was at hand; if I was given a gig (a demerit) for an inspection infraction, the whole unit would be penalized.

The colonel began his inspection of the troops at my far right, starting with six airmen before me; there remained three after me. As the colonel and his party approached, I knew there was nothing I could do now. I took a deep breath and held it. The colonel stopped in front of me and looked me up and down. Just as he was about to say something, the airmen next to me started coughing.

The colonel looked at him and asked if he was okay.

"Yes, sir," the airman answered. "Just a tickle in my throat, sir."

"You'd better take care of that. We don't want anything contagious around here."

The colonel turned back to me and said, "What's your name, airman?"

Releasing my breath, I said, "Airman First Class, Herbert A. Hicks, Service Number AF17378507, sir!" I was amazed that I'd blurted out not only my name but my entire rank and service number. I think the colonel was just as taken back by this as I was.

"Very good, airman," he said and moved on to the next person. We passed the inspection with flying colors.

After the inspection, I thanked the airman next to me. I told him it was quick thinking to start coughing at that moment. He said he didn't plan to do it—he really did have a tickle in his throat.

Our sergeant came up to me and whispered, "By the way, Airman Hicks, don't ever let me or anyone see you without your insignias again."

I never did; to this day, I have those same silver insignias in a little box in my desk drawer, a souvenir of my air force inspections.

By the spring of 1957, I had met a number of musicians on the base, and we had put together a jazz sextet.

An airman in our squadron turned out to be an amazing alto sax player. John Duzzi was from Detroit and had been playing alto for only a few months. The tenor player in our group had been giving John saxophone lessons. Gigs were far fewer than they had been at Chaumont, but we would have great sessions at the service club, jamming and learning new tunes. We were able to play a few gigs in the town of Metz.

John and I were on leave and went to the French Riviera. The Mediterranean beaches in Nice were delightful; it was warm and sunny, and we saw a number of nude sunbathers. We enjoyed sunbathing on the beach, drinking wine, smoking Gauloises (a strong French cigarette), swimming, sunbathing, and meeting beautiful young ladies. We grew beards and were tanned by the Mediterranean sun; we looked more like GBs (Greek beachcombers) than GIs.

Traveling just a short distance east from Nice, we visited Monaco and Monte Carlo. Le Grand Casino de Monte Carlo was the first casino built in Monte Carlo in the 1860s. It is a spectacular plush building that invites you to explore the interior. Who could resist the temptation to gamble there? We couldn't. Although we didn't win big, we also didn't lose big; we were not high rollers.

Traveling west on the Riviera, we visited Cannes. The beautiful Mediterranean beaches had fine sand and were lined with palm trees. A number of expensive resorts lined the oceanfront; boats of all sizes—from small skiffs to large luxury yachts—gently bobbed in the harbor. The Cannes International Film Festival is held there every May.

On our way back to Nice, we had some minor car trouble. By the time we got to Nice, we had to find an auto shop for repairs. The parts needed had to be ordered, which would take about a week to receive. We had to get back to the air base in a few days and called the officer of the day to explain our situation.

A week later, we were on our way back to Chambley. We pulled up to the air base's main gate to report. Although we were about three days late, we didn't expect the hassle we were about to get.

The air police checked our identification and said, "Get out of the vehicle."

"Why?" Maybe they didn't believe we were airmen because of our scruffy beards and tans.

"Airmen, you are under arrest for being AWOL."

"Wait, we can explain."

"You can explain it to the provost marshal."

"Oh. Okay."

We knew the lieutenant who was the provost marshal; he was a sax player who played some commercial dance gigs with us. Two APs escorted us to the provost marshal's office. He was surprised to see us and asked us to explain the AWOL charges. We explained our situation and produced a bill of sale and date of the car repairs in Nice. After some checking, he found that we had called the base to inform the officer on duty of our anticipated late return from leave. It seems the OD never gave the message to the main gate; it was an air force SNAFU.

Having been cleared of the AWOL charges, we reported back to our unit and signed in from leave. The airman signing us in asked if we had seen the latest bulletin about early outs. We hadn't, and he showed us the bulletin. It stated that any airman due to be discharged from active duty in January or February 1958 could apply for an early out, starting in September 1957. That included me; my enlistment date was January 15, 1954, and my four years of active duty would be up in 1958. The increase in enlistments and the cutbacks in NATO bases in Europe made this possible. I immediately put in for the early out so I could be home for Thanksgiving and Christmas.

I received my orders to be shipped back to the States in September. I would take a train from Metz to Orly Field in Paris and then catch a flight to New York City. I was happy to be completing my tour of active duty early and getting back to the United States. After taking care of my affairs at Chambley Air Base, I took a bus to Metz. I stopped at a hotel sidewalk café across from the train depot to get some lunch and a glass of wine.

I had a couple of hours before catching the train to Paris. After lunch, I picked up my duffel bag and strolled down the avenue to do some window shopping. In a store window, I saw a beautiful metronome in a handsome polished wood case. I thought it would be a perfect souvenir of my tour of duty in France. I purchased the metronome and headed for the train station. I showed the ticket master my ticket to Paris. He looked at it and shook his head.

"*Mais monsieur, le train est parti.*"

"*Parti?*" I said. "Impossible!"

He pointed to the track and the closed gates, "*Parti.*" He then showed me a schedule of the next train to Paris.

"*Demain matin,*" he said, pointing to the schedule.

"Tomorrow morning?" I moaned.

"*Oui.* Tomorrow morning."

There was nothing I could do but wait for the morning train to Paris. I slung my duffel over my shoulder and crossed the street to get a room at the hotel.

The next morning, I was up early and on that train to Paris, the first leg of my journey back to the good old USA.

The metronome I bought in Metz sits in my bookcase today and is a reminder: *Keep time and don't miss the train. But if you do, don't sweat it, another one will be along.*

Chapter 7

Back in the Good Old USA

"*It's autumn in New York. Why does it seem so inviting?*"—asked the first lines of this beautiful jazz ballad.

In September 1957, I was thrilled to be back in New York. The foliage was beginning to tint the landscape with a warm palette. And even more thrilling—I was about to be mustered out of the air force.

I had made arrangements to hitch a ride to Minneapolis on an air force cargo plane. This ride would save me some bucks, and I had big plans for spending my mustering-out pay. After I had crossed all the Ts and dotted all the Is for my air force active duty discharge, I was on my way home to join the ranks of civilian life.

On the train from Minneapolis to Williston, I contemplated how fortunate I was to have been born in a country that allowed me freedom of thought, expression, movement, and choice. Over the last few years, I had learned an enormous amount about the human experience and had lost some of my naive outlook on life.

Traveling, meeting new people, experiencing different cultures and ideas, weighing the pros and cons of different lifestyles, and seeing discrimination of many kinds changed my view of the world. What impressed me the most was the juxtaposition of the attitudes that humans shared. Some people held hatred and intolerance, and other people embraced love and empathy. I realized that compassion is one of the single greatest attributes a human being can have. I had been taught by the greatest scholastic tutor ever: experience. I looked forward to continuing my studies and hoped I would be a worthy student in the "School of Trial and Error."

As soon as I arrived at the train station in Williston, I called my folks. Dad drove to the station to meet me.

"Where's Mom?" I asked.

"She's at home, warming up some supper for you." I knew that "warming up some supper" meant I would probably have the best and biggest meal I'd had in years.

My little brother wasn't home when I arrived and had no knowledge my homecoming. I was looking forward to seeing Bob again. We had exchanged many letters over the last few years and had a lot to talk about.

When I heard the door open and close and footsteps up the few stairs to the kitchen door, I expected to see my little brother. The door opened—and Bob was no longer my *little* brother. He was a seventeen-year-old young man. When I'd last seen him, he was barely a teenager.

"Surprise," I said, opening my arms.

We hugged, and I had the feeling that we were more than just brothers; we were to become the very best of friends.

Larry had married his high school sweetheart, Maryann, and they were busy raising a family and running a Texaco service station. Larry had a remarkable knowledge of automobiles and a good head on his shoulders for business. I knew very little about either subject. The one thing I knew about cars and business was that once you got them running, it was easy to crash them.

Larry asked if I wanted a job pumping gas. I took the offer and became a gas jockey with the Texaco motto: *Trust your car to the man who wears the star.*

Larry operated the service station with the emphasis on "service." In the fifties, a service station meant service, and Larry's was the epitome of "service." Today's service is based on quickness instead of quality.

On a snowy, bitter cold day, I was pumping gas for a customer. I clicked the nozzle to the on position so I could run back into the station to get warm. The nozzle was set to click off when the car's tank was full. The customer and I were talking, looking out the window at the blowing snow. All of a sudden, the gas tank began shooting a stream of gas into the air; the nozzle had malfunctioned and didn't turn off. I ran out to the pump island and slipped on the snow and ice, landing on my back and sliding under the spray of gasoline. The customer was right behind me. He grabbed the nozzle and clicked it off.

"Are you okay?" he asked.

"I'm okay. Just got some gas in my eyes," I said. "Don't light a cigarette."

Rich arrived in Williston about a month after I did. He had served most of his air force time in Alaska. He had married a girl who was originally from Williston. Zee was a feisty redhead who loved booze, conversation, books, and jazz (in that order). When she was young, her family resided not far from my house; she was a tomboy who would not take any crap from the other kids.

The first thing Rich and I did was work on putting a band together. Williston was in the middle of an oil boom, and a lot of people involved in the industry were moving to town. Among those newcomers was a young geologist who played bass.

We found a high school student who was a friend of my brother's to play drums. Doug Gordon had moved to Williston with his parents shortly before the oil boom. His dad was one of the first roughneck oilmen to come to western North Dakota and helped bring in the first oil well in the Williston basin.

We added a female vocalist to complete our little quintet: vibraphone, piano, bass, drums, and vocalist. Dee was a young jovial gal who added some class to us roughnecks.

The "Hole" is what everyone in town called the Athletic Club Bar. Located in a basement under a bowling alley, it had a quasi-setting of a New York jazz club—except for the audience. It didn't matter since no one really listened; they were there to drink and eat. Most of the patrons were heavy drinkers and took advantage of the low-priced drinks and free hors d'oeuvres at cocktail hour. We played what we wanted and didn't take requests—except for one time.

What we thought was going to be a complaint turned out to be a windfall for us. A large imposing figure of a man approached the bandstand and pointed his finger at us. He said, "I have a request."

He directed his request at Rich, who was standing in front of the group. Rich was always diplomatic and accommodating, but he felt a little intimated, even though he was shielded from the giant by his vibraphone. We expected a rude remark to be hurled at the band, but we were all surprised by the man's request.

"Do you guys know a George Shearing tune called 'Lullaby of Birdland'? I'll give you fifty bucks if you can play it."

"Yes, we can play it." We were as surprised by the request, and the requester was just as surprised that we knew the tune.

After the performance of Shearing's composition, this gentle giant motioned to the vocalist to hand him the microphone. "Attention everyone, let's give this band a round of applause. The best little band between Minneapolis and Seattle."

The patrons of the Hole gave us our one and only round of applause, and the gigantic man handed Rich a fifty-dollar bill. We later found out our number-one fan was the CEO of a company in Minneapolis, a jazz fan, and was traveling through on his way to Seattle. He showed up now and then at a number of gigs we played at the Hole, always ready with a jazz request and a tip for the band.

The band often talked about his generosity, and one day we had an opportunity to compare it to another tip we received. On one of our breaks, I found a wallet in the men's washroom; it contained over four hundred dollars in cash, a number of credit cards, and an ID. I showed the wallet and cash to the band, saying that's a *big* tip, but I took the wallet and cash to the bartender.

He looked at the ID and told me he knew the guy. "He's sitting at that table," he said, pointing.

I walked over to the guy and asked if he'd lost his billfold. He stared at me and mumbled, "I don't think so. I'll check." Not finding it, he said, "I must have lost the damn thing." I asked him his name, he told me, and it matched the name on the ID.

"This must be yours," I said, handing him the billfold full of cash.

"Yep, that's mine," he answered. He shouted to the bartender, "Give this guy a glass of beer and put it on my tab."

The bartender shrugged, gave me a bewildered look, and poured me a twenty-five-cent glass of beer.

I gave the man with the billfold a thumbs-up (which I really meant as a middle-finger salute) and sarcastically said, "Thank you."

The band was cracking up. As I approached the bandstand, they asked if I was going to share my reward with them for being honest.

"Nope. I alone earned it," I said proudly and drank my beer.

A number of local musicians would sit in on this gig. One particular drummer would perform with us when our regular drummer couldn't make the gig. He would hit the sauce hard and heavy; sometimes he would be totally smashed by the end of the gig. Drunk or sober, he was a good drummer. He had a drinking problem and a number of domestic problems, which at times made him very depressed. He eventually gave up his battle with depression and committed suicide. All of us wondered if there wasn't something we could have done to prevent this; it was a sad day for all Williston musicians.

Rich's family owned the three movie theaters in Williston. Rich and his wife worked for the family business. The oldest movie theater in town was the Grand Theater. Built around 1920, it was beautifully furnished with plush seats, a balcony, a stage, and orchestra pit.

Next door to the Grand Theater was a ladies' clothing store. One day when I met Rich for coffee, he said, "Come on, Herb, I've got something to show you in this shop."

"What is it?" I said. "Are you buying a skirt?"

"No," he said and laughed. "You are."

As we approached the large front window of the store, Rich pointed to a young lady inside, telling me she wanted to meet me. A fine-looking gal with long, dark hair and more curves than a Rococo painting was arranging some clothing on a display table.

Rich and his wife had met her and talked about me and our band. She said she had seen us play and would like to meet me. Rich said he would arrange a date.

Eldora was a French gal from a small hamlet north of Williston. Eldora and I became good friends, and we spent many dates together with Rich and Zee. The four of us took a trip to Minneapolis to see the Miles Davis Quintet featuring John Coltrane. Rich and I thoroughly enjoyed the concert, but Rich's wife and my girlfriend didn't appreciate Miles's eccentric behavior. Miles was in one of his mysterious mind spaces and had turned his back to the audience, playing the whole concert blowing into the stage curtains. We told Zee and Eldora that we didn't mind Miles doing that as we were there to "hear" his playing not to "see" his playing. The girls wanted to know why Miles thought he could get away with offending the audience by playing with his back to them.

I had no answer.

But Rich gave them the answer. He said, "Because he's Miles."

Rich and I decided to get a band together with a broader musical scope than our little combo. We formed an octet, which consisted of trumpet, trombone, tenor and alto sax, and a rhythm section of piano, bass, drums, and vibraphone. Our main reason for this group was to play jazz compositions, but we were also hoping to get a few commercial dance gigs so we included a number of standard dance tunes.

Our gigs with the octet were a musical joy for us musicians—but not all that successful with the audiences. The older people at the gigs liked to dance to the old standard tunes we'd play, but the younger crowd wanted the latest rock and roll. We could play tunes more like early rhythm and blues rather than rock and roll. This satisfied some, but others wanted a screaming vocalist with loud amplified guitars. Younger audiences were becoming attuned to the sounds of rock-and-roll stars like Bill Haley, Jerry Lee Lewis, and Elvis Presley. Groups with electric guitars, amplifiers, and lead vocalists were the fashion of the day. In our unamplified ensemble, we didn't have a lead vocalist, our lead was horns, our beat was the old "swing thing," and our library consisted mainly of jazz and American songbook standards.

We were a band that wasn't interested in the commercial pop scene of the day. Being a commercial success was not our main goal. We just wanted to play our music our way; if people didn't accept that, we could be satisfied with just being a rehearsal band. We had many discussions about being entertainers or artists. We were interested in the creative aspects of music and had strong feelings about prostituting our musical skills for money and the approved acceptance of an audience. These were a nice added bonus to our efforts, but they were not our main concern.

Were we elitists? Some thought so, but I don't believe we were. We were just trying to be honest with our values. We did have some people who thought highly of our music; on the other hand, there were a lot of people who absolutely detested it and would loudly let us know. It was as though we had committed one of the seven deadly sins by not aligning ourselves with the latest fads and fashions, and we had no right not to do so. It wasn't that we didn't recognize the talents of some of the pop stars; it was just that the pop style of music wasn't our interest.

The conflict between differences of tastes people have seems to be dependent on preconceived ideas about the most desirable aspects of something and the least desirable aspects of something. The problem with this is that all too often the preconditioning is based on misunderstandings and hyped media propaganda instead of knowledge. Constant exposure to an ideology breeds familiarity, which brings acceptance. If one is constantly led to believe that white is always good and black is always bad, that becomes the acceptance of the belief. You have to have knowledge, but it is more important to (paraphrasing the Zen way) "bring your bowl empty of preconceived experiences so you can fill it with the experience at hand."

In the late fall of 1958, I received a call from a lady wanting to know if our octet was available for a New Year's gig. I said we were available. I asked her if she had heard the band and if she knew what kind of music we played.

"Oh yes. We've heard you a couple of times around Williston," she said. "We really liked the band."

I asked where the gig would take place.

She told me the name of the town and that the dance would be at their community hall. To protect the innocent, civilized people at the dance from embarrassment, I will use the name "Row" for the small community where our New Year's gig would take place.

Row is a typical small North Dakota town in the middle of wheat and oil fields. I played at their high school graduation dance with my band in 1951. We also played some polkas and waltzes. I figured we could throw in a couple of old tunes and booked the gig.

The community hall was an old building in the middle of town and had many uses. There was a high stage for show productions and a hardwood floor that was used for basketball, but it was badly warped. The hall had a kitchen, which served food and booze. There were only a few folding tables near the kitchen/bar, and a row of uncomfortable wooden folding chairs lined the walls around the dance floor. The acoustics were horrible; sounds would reverberate off the far wall and return to the stage in delayed time.

There was a loading dock in the back with a door that opened onto the high stage, which made it easy to get our gear in and out of the performing area. But to get to the back door, we had to navigate around a large snowbank. The lady who had hired us was there to greet us with our pay in cash. She didn't want to carry the money around at the dance, and she paid us up front—lucky for us.

Setting up our equipment was easy because of the access to the stage. The thing that wasn't so easy was being bugged by some of the spectators who were already there. The bar wasn't open yet, but these people had their own bottles and were well on their way to toasting in the New Year. Four or five guys came on the stage and started rifling through our music, requesting tunes and asking if they could sing a song.

One guy said he played guitar and wanted to use our guitar player's instrument to sit in for a couple of tunes. We told him we didn't have a guitarist in the band.

He said, "What the fuck kind of band is this?"

I tried to maintain my cool and keep an optimistic outlook at this point, but that's sometimes very hard to do in the face of adversity. Trying to explain to him the nature of our music was futile, and he ranted and raved about the band before we had even started, exciting a couple of his drunken buddies to join in. Finally after completely intimidating the band, they left the stage in search of more drinks. The New Year's celebration was well on its way.

Before playing the first note of the evening, I had a feeling that the gig was going to be a struggle. It was more than a struggle—it became a war zone. We started our first set as the hall began to fill with noisy people. The place was packed, standing-room only, but very few people danced. The first couple of tunes bombed, and people began to shout requests—none of which we knew or had even heard of. The few waltzes, polkas, and schottisches we knew saved our asses—for a while.

We stretched out the time between tunes as long as we could and improvised some classic country tunes like Hank Williams's "Your Cheatin' Heart" and Eddy Arnold's "Any Time," and we played different versions a couple of times. For some of the intoxicated malcontents, even the classic country tunes were too classy for them.

In their drunken wisdom, they let us know loud and clear their disapproval of our band.

In gigs where you have written arrangements for the band, you play what you have and hope the audience goes for it. The drunkest members of this raucous crowd didn't go for it. But we did have one surprise in the form of a compliment. A couple came up to the stage and told us how much they liked our music. They said they always listened to a Canadian radio station that played our kind of music, and they were thrilled to see a band in person that performed that style. I believe this couple was from a galaxy far, far away.

Making it through our first set with misgivings about booking this gig, we cursed the lady who had hired us. I should have seen it coming. This wasn't a 1950s high school dance; this crowd was hardcore whiskey drinkers and brawling rednecks. This was the night for this group of people to howl, and howl they did! It was a good thing our second set was bringing us up to the midnight hour where we could play "Auld Lang Syne" over and over. Then a midnight lunch would be served, which we hoped would calm some of the belligerent troublemakers.

The lull in the battle was when everyone was stuffing themselves with mounds of cold cuts, processed cheese, and white bread. We started our third set with a nice slow waltz, which I thought would make things a little mellower. Wrong! It seemed the booze was working overtime, and a little food just added fuel to the fire. People began yelling, "Play some good old shit-kicking music, or we'll kick the shit out of you. Smash those fuckin' brass horns and get a gee-tar picker."

When we played a polka, everyone screamed and danced—and a fight broke out. Some people tried to stop it, but they only succeeded in moving it outside—and it continued in the snow. I announced an old time waltz for the last dance, and some drunk hollered, "You fuckin' a, this is the last dance—the last dance you'll ever play."

Most of the crowd had become extremely wild, intimidating the musicians, fighting, and shaking up the people who had come to celebrate New Year's in a civilized way. Just as soon as we hit the last note, we started packing our instruments. A group of drunks with hate in their eyes and shit for brains stormed the stage; this scared the hell out of us. They began yelling a string of obscenities and saying that they were going to help us pack up and get out of town.

Our adversaries opened the back door and began throwing our equipment out into the snow. The drums were some of the first to go; the horn players quickly packed and protected their instruments. Our music stands went flying out the door—and so did the bass. The one thing that saved us from having a lot of damage to ourselves and our equipment was the large snow drift by the back door; it cushioned our falls. It was a combat zone, but we were lucky and amazed there were no casualties. The woman who hired us was nowhere in sight; under my breath, I cursed her again for hiring us. I was thankful she had paid us in advance. We scrambled around in the snow, recovering our equipment while some guys standing in the doorway gave us the "Middle-Finger Row Town Hall Salute."

They cursed and hollered at us, telling us never to come back. I never did—and never wanted to.

Chapter 8

Into the Sunset to the American Riviera

*B*oarding the Great Northern Empire Builder, I started a long train ride from Williston to Los Angeles. I had prepared for the trip with plenty of reading material and a box Mom had packed with treats.

The train was late getting into Williston from Minneapolis. The afternoon sun was low, creating long purple patterns crawling across the snow. For a North Dakota January, the weather was quite nice, sunny with a thin ground cover of snow. The train gave a little lurch, and we slowly pulled away from the station into the sunset. I gave a last good-bye wave to my mom and dad on the platform. Mom was mouthing something, and Dad saluted with a gloved hand. I settled into a coach seat. I was on the road again, excited about traveling again. It didn't take long for the *clickety-clack* of the rails to provide the sedative needed for a good sleep.

I slept most of the way to Portland, where we headed south to LA. The train ride was hypnotic, and we sped through spectacular scenery filled with mountains, trees, and streams; night and day seemed to merge into one blur of time. Next thing I knew, the porter was shaking me and saying, "Union Station, Los Angeles, next stop."

Walking out of that famous railway station, which has been filmed as a backdrop for movies and replicated by movie companies on their movie lots, I realized I was really back in LA. I loaded my two bags onto a bus that said Hollywood and headed west, again into the sunset, to my old haunt. Seeing the familiar sights of Hollywood Boulevard, I got off the bus near Western Avenue, the street that led to my old address on Russell Avenue. I checked into a motel just up the block.

The setting sun cast an orange glow that filled my motel room as I began to unpack some of my stuff and take stock of my next move. *All right, so I'm out of the air force, away from North Dakota, and back in California, now what?* I had mixed feelings about going back to music school, at least right away. I had, since the air force, acquired some other interests, mainly art and electronics. I'd saved a little money from my mustering-out pay and gigs in Williston. Most of that money was in traveler's checks, which I thought would be the safest way to carry currency. Two things I knew for sure; I had to find a gig, whether it was a day gig or a music gig, and I had to find a place to live. After that, I would play it by ear.

First thing I did the next morning was scan the newspapers for jobs and a place to live. Nothing of interest in job offers. I did find a rental located near the Hollywood Farmers' Market.

A day later, I walked to the corner of Hollywood and Vine to check out Westlake College of Music. To my surprise, it wasn't there; in its place was a tower that looked like a giant stack of 45 rpm records. The Capitol Records Building had been constructed on that site in 1956. It is an awesome circular twelve-story building of offices and recording studios. I took a quick tour of the building and found out that the music college had moved to Laguna Beach. I had already decided to look for a job before going back to school, so I continued on that path.

A big city has a way of swallowing people as though they had never existed, and that's what seemed to have happened to people I knew from school. Somehow they disappeared into the maze of the megalopolis.

I went to the musicians' union, was reinstated, and put my name in for any available gigs. A few days later, I received a phone call.

"This is the musicians' union. Is this Herb Hicks?"

Ah, I thought, *a gig*. It was a freebie—and not even playing music. The union was looking for members to carry picket signs in front of the Pantages Theater because the theater was showing movies that used soundtracks with canned foreign music rather than live recorded American musicians. I accepted, hoping my name would get on a list for a real gig.

The Pantages Theater, on Hollywood Boulevard, was within walking distance of where I lived. The beautiful art deco old screen and stage theater was built in 1930. It is equaled only by Grauman's Chinese Theatre, located farther west on Hollywood Boulevard. Both theaters have hosted the Academy Awards.

A few days later, I met reps from the union in front of the Pantages. I was given a placard, and with a small gathering of musicians, I began to walk back and forth in front of the theater with my protest sign. This was my first protest march—but not my last. I joined the ranks of protesters on other occasions on a number of issues.

The art exhibits I saw in the LA galleries whetted my appetite even more to try my hand at painting. Two exhibits that had an enormous effect on me were the Van Gogh and the Monet retrospectives. Their use of color opened up a whole new visual world to me. Seeing the world in color, through the eyes of those painters, I discovered an exciting visual perspective about my surroundings that I had been blind to before. I began to spend more time painting and drawing. I landed a job at Decca Records in the shipping department, but that only lasted two weeks.

I came across an ad in the newspaper for workers for an electronic company in Burbank. I called the number, and they told me when they would be holding interviews. I decided to rent a car for the interview. The next day, I walked a couple of blocks to an auto rental and asked to rent a car.

"Okay," the rental agent said. "Fill out the information on the form—and let me see a driver's license and a credit card."

I put my driver's license on the counter and started filling out the form.

"A credit card, please."

"I'm paying by cash," I said.

"Cash?" he said as though he didn't understand the word. "We don't accept cash! You have to pay by credit card."

"All I have is cash or traveler's checks, no credit cards. I always pay in cash." I figured that would show what an honest person I was by letting him know I always paid my bills with cold, hard cash.

"You don't have a credit card? I can't rent you a car," he said in an arrogant and condescending manner.

"But I need a car. This is my chance for a job interview in Burbank." I showed him my billfold copy of my air force discharge, telling him to keep that until I came back with the car. I offered to pay an extra deposit fee for the rental.

"Damn it," he said. "No can do without a credit card."

"If I'm not back by this evening, call out the damn National Guard," I said sarcastically.

We argued for a minute, and he told me to get lost. I threw the forms across the counter and walked away. He swore at me as I walked down the street. I decided then and there I would get out of "Tinsel Town."

A week later, I headed north on a bus to Ventura, Santa Barbara, and San Francisco. I still had some cash and traveler's checks. I'd be okay for bread for a couple more months. I was still pissed that I couldn't negotiate a car rental when I was ready and able to pay with a billfold full of cash and a pocket of traveler's checks. My father never had a credit card; like him, I paid for everything with cash—or I didn't buy it. I was diametrically opposed to the American financial scheme of "if you can't afford it, charge it." The replacement of cash with a plastic credit card was turning some people's dreams for a better life into a debtor's nightmare for a bitter life. Little did I know that ten years later, after I was married, I'd succumb to the lure and join millions of other North Americans as a bona fide credit card holder. It seemed to be the right thing to do at that time; it was a necessary evil.

North Americans have the most affluent society on this planet, yet we are over our heads in debt, individually and nationally. I'm as guilty as anyone in charging beyond my limits, maybe even more so. Our governments are paying only the interest on their debts, and we have nothing new to show for the debt. We should have all those things everyone wishes for—lower taxes, better education, medical research, health care, lower gas and housing prices, and a clean environment—the list is endless. Every year, the debt figure escalates by billions as prices soar. There must be a saturation point; what happens when that is reached? Poof?

There is something horribly wrong when we look at the differences between *the want of a service* and *the need of a service*. North America is basically a hedonistic society where people are willing to pay extravagant amounts for a service they want, like an entertainment or sports event, but balk at paying the price for something that is of basic value, such as education. In our society, we have the freedom of choice, which we value, but don't have an understanding of what is valuable. It seems the American dream has become the American extreme.

As we pulled into Santa Barbara, my thoughts turned from dollars to sense—my senses were being overtaken by the beauty of this Spanish-style town by the sea. "The American Riviera" has a climate much like the French and the Italian Rivieras. I immediately fell in love with the beauty of the town; the more I explored the amazing community, the more infatuated I became.

Santa Barbara was founded by Spanish missionaries and soldiers in the early 1780s, and they constructed a mission on the town site. In 1812, an earthquake and tsunami destroyed the mission, but it was rebuilt and became known as the "Queen of California Missions." During the California Gold Rush in the 1850s, the town was a lawless place and became a haven for bandits. The 1860s and 1870s saw an influx of English-speaking people, and the Spanish language gave way to English as the official language.

Santa Barbara was advertised as a health resort, and rich tourists came from all parts of the United States. Oil was discovered in the early 1900s, adding to the influx of people. The world's largest movie studio (Flying A Studios) operated there from 1910 until it moved to Hollywood in 1922. In 1925, another earthquake destroyed a large portion of the town. The town was rebuilt with a Spanish Colonial theme and has continued that tradition throughout its history. The Santa Barbara County Courthouse is known as the most beautiful public building in the United States.

The city has the unfavorable honor of being the first area since the War of 1812 to experience a wartime attack by an enemy on the United States mainland. On February 23, 1942, a Japanese submarine surfaced offshore and fired shells at an oilfield about ten miles west of Santa Barbara.

Its pristine environment was amazing, and it felt great to be there. Santa Barbara inspires the creative mind, and I met some of the most stimulating, productive people in my life. But everything changes with time, good and bad, and it is too bad that Santa Barbara has lost some of its old charm. Human encroachment, economic inflation, offshore oil drilling leaks gumming up the sandy beaches, cutting down the orchard groves to make way for subdivisions, and the scramble of commercial enterprises to fleece the tourists have plagued the town. It is still, however, a beautiful place with a temperate climate and an abundance of floral scenery.

Walking a block from the bus stop to State Street, I found my way to the Santa Barbara Museum of Art. I was hooked; I had to stay here and check out this town. San Francisco could wait. That evening in my hotel room, I read an advertisement in the *Santa Barbara News Press* about a club called The Spigot (The House of Jazz) featuring live music Thursday, Friday, and Saturday nights and jam sessions on Sundays. I'd check out the Sunday show. That night I had only two thoughts—eat and sleep.

The next day, I took a taxi to 2611 De La Vina Street. As I walked through the door toward the bar, I could hear a sax player wailing away. The guy was good. The seating arrangement was like one I'd seen at a jazz club in San Francisco. As I became orientated to the club's dimly lit interior, I saw a small stage against the wall with the band. Facing the bandstand were rows of benches, like pews in a church, each with a small shelf for drinks. There were a few small tables to the right of the bandstand against the wall, but most patrons were seated at the benches and focused on the musicians. The band had just finished the set and was about to take a break. A long bar was on my right. I pulled up a stool and ordered a draft beer. The bartender (who I found out later was the owner) asked if I wanted a pitcher of beer.

"No, just a glass is fine." I said. "The sax man is good."

"You bet he is—the best. You sure you don't want a pitcher?"

"No, thanks, just a glass will do. What's the sax player's name?"

"Vince Wallace. He's from San Francisco, you know."

I didn't know and had never heard of him, but I was about to find out who the guy was who sounded like John Coltrane.

I took my glass of beer and headed for one of the small tables near the side of the bandstand. I had a feeling the bartender was watching me all the time. The gal who was waiting tables wanted to know if I needed another beer. Still nursing my first beer, I told her I was okay. She ambled off to hustle another customer. A group of musicians came on stage. It was an open jam session so you'd never know who would come to sit in.

As they prepared to play the first tune of the next set, I overheard the sax man say, "Let's play 'Jordu.'"

The lineup of musicians on the stand was: bass, drums, two conga players, and the sax man. What? No piano man?

At the side of the bandstand was this old, beat-up, upright piano (someone had painted it white with paint as thick as gesso). I went up to the bandstand and asked Vince if I could sit in on piano.

He said, "Yeah. We *need* a piano player." I sat down at the piano and did a couple of runs on the keyboard to get the feel for its action.

Vince asked what I wanted to play.

I said, "I heard you call 'Jordu.' That's a good tune—C minor?"

Vince took the pick-up notes to the tune and that, as they say, was the beginning of a beautiful friendship. Piano, bass, drummer, and two (too loud) congas joined in. Vince blew his ass off and must have taken at least a dozen choruses.

I sat in the rest of the night. I was introduced to the musicians with whom I soon became friends. I was also introduced to the bartender (the owner, George McClintock) and made another instant friend. He even bought me a drink, which was unusual for George.

Vince Wallace was from Oakland; he was twenty when I met him, but he played like a seasoned jazz musician. I was twenty-four and just learning. Vince, at his young age, had played with some name musicians, and he later played around LA and San Francisco with some of the top jazz players, including Hank Mobley, Dexter Gordon, Hampton Hawes, Eric Dolphy, and Jack Sheldon.

The drummer with this group was Chip Crosby. Chip was the brother of Dave Crosby of Crosby, Stills, and Nash. Chip also played bass and did a number of gigs in coffee houses with Dave and with folk and jazz groups in Santa Barbara. Chip had a big ego and could be standoffish, but he was always very friendly toward me. Years later, he moved to the mountains in Northern California and changed his name to Ethan. He became a recluse in the remote Trinity Alps Wilderness; disillusioned with life, he committed suicide in 1997.

Harry Vizzolini was the bass player. He was a Santa Barbara local who played with Chip frequently and with a local tenor man, Dave Sanchez. Dave would sit in with us quite often, and it was a treat to hear Vince and Dave exchange choruses and fours. Vince sounded like Coltrane and Dave played like Getz.

The conga players, Mitch and Holly, weren't part of the regular group, but they would sit in on Sunday jams. Mitch was a big guy, and Holly was a little guy. They were more or less living off the land in Santa Barbara and off of Mitch's girlfriend's generosity. They hung around Vince—not only because they dug his playing, but the three of them dug getting stoned together.

I don't remember the name of the piano player I replaced. I only know he became very ill and went home to San Francisco. Lennie Sequiera, also from San Francisco, was originally the bass player with the group; when he took the piano man back home, he decided to stay.

That night, toward the end of the gig, Vince asked if I would like to play with the group on a steady base. Of course I accepted without any hesitation. It was what I had been hoping for.

"We're going over to this cat's pad after the gig," said Vince. "Want to make it?"

"Sure. Can I hitch a ride?"

"We'll find one." I never did know of Vince owning a car, but he always seemed to find transportation. A group of us climbed into an old beater and took off thorough the sweet-smelling Santa Barbara fog.

When I commented on the nice smell, someone said, "That's night-blooming jasmine."

"Like us," someone else said. "Night-blooming jazzmen."

"Right on," someone said as we all cracked up.

People were drinking, eating, listening to music, and talking in a large Spanish-style house in a heavy wooded area. When we stepped inside, someone hollered, "Vince! Groovy set tonight."

Vince acknowledged the compliment, and the guy handed him a large rolled joint. "This is for you and the piano man."

Vince handed the joint to me and said, "Light up."

I said, "Okay. Got a match?" I lit it, took a big toke, and handed it back to Vince.

Someone said, "All right," and a few others applauded. Why the applause? I was a white, clean-cut, straight-looking guy who none of these people knew. I'd walked into a jazz club, sat in on piano, made friends with the musicians, and asked the owner the names of the players. Some people thought I was a narc. It was the paranoia of the times.

Vince said, "I knew he was cool."

After we'd established that I wasn't the law, we got stoned and enjoyed the party. We continued to joke about being "night-blooming jazzmen."

Early that morning, I bummed a ride back to my motel. Just before that moment when the real world around you dissolves and segues into the abyss of sleep and dreams, my mind became filled with thoughts of yesterday and plans for tomorrow.

I thought my first step would be to buy a used car so I'd have transportation to and from gigs. I checked the newspaper for used cars and found a dealer whose prices fit my budget. I ended up buying a 1947 Pontiac. Buying a car was different than renting a car; they accepted *cash*. The Pontiac was a gas-guzzler and an oil-burner, but the price was right—and it got me around town. The car was a viridian-green coupe with heavy, thick metal bumpers that someone had also painted green. My friends and I called it "The Green Hornet."

I looked for a place to rent and found a small apartment on State Street in an old house that was surrounded by a cluster of palm trees. It had a small balcony overlooking a yard of well-kept shrubs and flowers.

On that little balcony, I took in the sights and sounds of the beautiful surroundings. I felt pleased about my good fortune. In two days, I had acquired a gig, a car, and a place to live. I felt alive with a renewed sense of purpose, I looked forward to tomorrow. Santa Barbara was paradise; to hell with the big cities of Los Angeles and San Francisco.

I contemplated my next move. My choices seemed to be many, but one thought kept cropping up in my mind. I had to put my visual impressions of my world on paper. The next day, I bought a new supply of paints, canvases, drawing materials, and a sketchbook. I began my visual journey.

The gigs I played with Vince were a learning experience in improvising. He showed me new approaches to old standards, taught me new tunes, and opened my ears to new musical sounds. We cowrote a tune and called it "Sphinx Winks." It had a mysterious twist to the lead line, and we thought it held some kind of riddle, like the Sphinx, with a tongue-in-cheek wink. Vince would take long solos, sometimes taking the solo to a climax where he would end up playing choruses by himself, without the rhythm section, taking the listener to new highs in auditory emotions. The audience loved it; it was a very hip band and audience.

On one particular two-week gig I played in Santa Maria with Vince, we had a great bass man and a drummer from LA. I can't recall the bass player's name, but the drummer, George Valentine, had worked with Chet Baker. Sometimes the bass man and I would let Vince and George go "mano a mano," each trying to outdo the other—it was high-energy playing. The club owner was so impressed by Vince's playing that he bought him a new tenor sax. The tenor Vince had been playing had a lot of miles on it; tape, rubber bands, and glue held it together. Vince was elated with his new gift and would spend an hour or so before each gig bathing, so he would be shiny clean for his new shiny tenor.

After the Santa Maria gig, Vince moved on to LA. I went back to Santa Barbara and did some trio gigs at the Spigot with different drummers and bassists. I put a quartet together with Dave Sanchez on tenor. The Spigot was becoming a well-known jazz club between LA and San Francisco. George started to book name jazz musicians in the club for Sunday concerts. Jazz greats like Dizzy, Cannonball, Shelly Mann, Cal Tjader, Curtis Amy, Les McCann, and Billy Higgins all played there.

I began to feel the confines of my little apartment; I needed some studio space to do my painting. I found a nice little house to rent on Gillespie Street (no association with Diz).

Besides the Spigot gig, I played casual gigs around town with different groups. I'd transferred from the LA musicians' union to Santa Barbara. I played some casual gigs in Santa Barbara that left me wondering. I played a gig the first Monday of the month for a seniors' dance club in the gym of an old school. We were a trio with an unusual combination of drummer, trombone, and piano. The leader was the trombone player, and he instructed me to play a bass line with my left hand and chords with my right hand. Why did I take this gig? I kept reminding myself of the two reasons: I needed the bread (money) and I needed the bread (food). The gig paid well, and people brought fantastic potluck dinners. I'd wait all day before eating and then scarf down the food like a starving pig. I'd load my pockets and a satchel I carried my music in with plastic bags full of whatever foods I could salvage from the meal. Those leftovers became my midnight snacks—and sometimes the next day's dinner. Starving artist? Not really, but damn hungry.

The gigs at the Spigot were steady, and a number of good players would come by to sit in. Freddy Jackson (Junebug), an alto player, would sit in now and then. Junebug was a hot sax player who later ended up playing alto with Ray Charles.

A musician who played with us, that I was most impressed with, was a tenor sax player from Syracuse, New York. Sal Nistico had moved to California when his father had a change in job location. Sal walked into the Spigot one evening and asked if he could sit in. From the first note he played, he blew everyone away. Sal became a member of our group. Sal and I became good friends, and he moved in with me at the little house on Gillespie Street. We had some cool times together; no matter what we did, everything turned out to be a great adventure with Sal. He could play the hell out of that tenor sax and was as agile as a championship athlete when he blew that horn. In other areas, he could be a klutz, but then so could I. He and I double-klutzed around Santa Barbara.

Sal met a girl at the club and needed a car to take her out. He wondered if he could borrow the Green Hornet.

I said, "Sure you can. It's a gas- and oil-burner, but it'll get you around."

Sal took off that evening to pick up the girl. "I'll see you in the morning," he said.

I was up late painting and slept in the next morning. I was getting some breakfast and wondered where Sal was. No Green Hornet in front of the house—and no Sal in sight. I was beginning to worry about him. By noon, my concern for Sal heightened, and I pictured untold horrifying scenarios.

Then the front door opened, and Sal walked in.

"You okay, man," I asked.

"Yeah," he said, out of breath.

"Where's the car?"

"At the beach," he said. "Out of gas."

"No big deal, man. We'll get it later today. I'll get someone to give us a ride."

Sal's night with his date had ended up at a beach about five miles northwest of Santa Barbara. Sal was trying to make out with the girl, and she got pissed off. She wanted to go back to town. The old Pontiac made it about a block and stopped—out of gas. The girl was really pissed and started to walk. I guess she got a ride. Sal said he fell asleep in the car and woke with the sun shining on his face. Not having any money for gas, he left the car by the beach and hitched a ride to town.

With the help of some of my friends, we retrieved the car later that day.

It had been almost six months since I took up residence in Santa Barbara, and I had enjoyed every minute of my new home. Playing at the Spigot was such a great experience, and playing with Sal was probably my greatest experience in playing jazz.

Sal was moving to LA and would only be in Santa Barbara now and then. I had met a gal who was a regular customer at the Spigot. She and I had a relationship and decided to rent a house together. We found a large house with a studio where I could paint. Before moving in, I did some renovations to the house and the studio area. The house had an old refrigerator that we were replacing with a newer model we had purchased. I invited Sal to dinner since he happened to be in town that weekend. He said he would help me move the fridge.

The old fridge was heavy and awkward to move. Sal and I tipped the fridge on its side to manipulate it out the back door. I immediately got a whiff of ammonia. Sal thought the smell was coming from the top of the fridge where the coils were. He bent over the fridge, sucking in a big breath to smell the fumes. He let out a moan and stumbled down the half-dozen steps of the back entrance, overcome with the toxic ammonia gas.

There was a fire station next door to our house. I yelled for help, and two firemen responded. One climbed over the fence, and the other ran to get a respirator. Sal was on the ground, coughing and moaning, while the fireman leaned over him. The other fireman was over the fence with the respirator and applied it to Sal. Luckily, Sal was okay. I was shaken to think that Sal could have injured his lungs to the extent of not being able to blow his sax.

Sal stayed with us for a couple of days and went on to earn celebrity status as a jazz saxophonist in LA. He went with the Woody Herman

Band, the Count Basie Band, and the Buddy Rich Band. He played and did recordings with many, many great jazzmen. Playing together was exciting, but the time we spent talking and hanging out together was really special. We'd have Sal over for dinner often. He loved to eat and could he pack away the food. We shared a passion for ice cream; he could devour a quart in one sitting, and I could almost keep up with him.

Sal died in 1991 in Berne, Switzerland. He was only fifty-three. Sal's death was a great loss to the jazz community.

Harry, the bass man, worked for the Santa Barbara Sears, Roebuck & Company and asked whether I would be interested in getting a job with them. Sears was looking for a person to work in the shipping and receiving department. Sears was a good company to work for and had a profit-sharing plan for their employees. One day, while helping unload a shipment of tires, I twisted my lower back and injured a vertebral disc. I was taken to the hospital and spent a week in traction. This was the beginning of a long history of back problems that have plagued me the rest of my life.

I had a number of Latino friends in Santa Barbara. Every once in a while, we would take a trip to Tijuana to see a bullfight and do some shopping. On one trip, one of my friends bought some Dexedrine tablets, which you could buy over the counter in Tijuana. She asked if I wanted to try some, telling me the tablet would make me alert and give me a burst of energy. In other words, it was a speed drug. I popped a couple of tablets; by the time we were seated at the bullfights, I was flying high. I had enough energy to be in the ring fighting those bulls.

I saw the bullfight from the perspective of the bull and began cheering for the bull. I yelled "*Ole, toro.*" I booed the matador.

The Mexicans around me kept saying, "Loco gringo." We kept squirting streams of wine into our mouths (missing most of the time) from the wineskins we had. We must have looked like a scene from Hemingway's *The Sun Also Rises*. On the way back to Santa Barbara, I experienced a "speed crash" and sacked out till late the next day.

My brother and two of his friends drove to California from North Dakota. Bob stayed in Santa Barbara to visit me while the other two guys went to LA. Showing Bob the beautiful sights around the area, and he too fell in love with Santa Barbara. He had just graduated from high school and planned on going to radio broadcasting school at Brown Radio Institute in Minneapolis that fall.

Santa Barbara College offered adult education classes in art, and I enrolled in a painting class, sculpture class, and an art history course. I'd read a book on mono-printing techniques and entered some of my mono-prints in the First Press Art Gallery show. I sold two prints and was encouraged to do more. I began to paint more and do more drawings and prints.

My girlfriend and I were having problems and drifting apart. She was as headstrong as I was. She was seeing other guys; when she told me she was pregnant and I was the father, I doubted her word. She said she was going to have the baby and didn't care what the fuck I did. I felt it was my responsibility to act accordingly to any obligation I had. She told me she was leaving—and she didn't want anything to do with me. The conversation tore at my heart, and I felt like I'd been whacked in the gut with a crowbar. We got into a horrific quarrel, and rage overtook both of us. Flinging things around the house, she picked up a butcher knife and slashed one of my paintings. I grabbed a broom. We faced each other, knife and lance, like two gladiators ready to do battle. Shouting a barrage of insults and profanities at each other, our frenzied minds and bodies were reaching the boiling point. I experienced a beast of rage that wanted to release its fury. For some reason (I hope it was reason), we both realized how dangerous our argument had become. Not letting the quarrel escalate any further, we both held up our hands, palms out in surrender, and backed off.

It was over between us, and we made plans to separately move on. I was traumatized emotionally by the situation. I was in a quandary about what to think of her accusing me of getting her pregnant. It surely was possible, but it was hard to figure why she didn't want any commitment from me. If this was my child, what was my role? Not knowing the accuracy of this scenario has been the cross I've carried the rest of my life. I have no regrets for any of my actions in life—only questions. I thought I'd bury my past, start over again, and begin to live only for the immediacy of the moment. The moment was to move and start over in the picturesque little town of San Luis Obispo, where I'd had some of my artwork in exhibitions.

But instead I chose to go to Minnesota.

Through my correspondence with Bob, I learned that he was interested in sculpture and was taking courses at the Minneapolis School of Art on weekends. He sent me some information on the MSA, and I began the process of applying for admission. I was accepted as a student at the MSA for the fall of 1960.

In the beginning of that year and through the spring, I did a number of paintings and drawings. I crated some to be shipped back to my parents' house, and I left some others out by the back fence (they disappeared). One of my last acts before leaving Santa Barbara was to park my old Buick across the street from where I lived, sign the ownership registration card over to whoever found it, and leave the keys in the ignition. It disappeared too. The crate of paintings I had shipped by rail got sidetracked. I thought they disappeared too, but three months later the crate was found sitting in a boxcar on a rail siding in Oregon. It had finally been shipped to North Dakota.

Chapter 9

The Minneapolis School of Art

My first semester at the Minneapolis School of Art started in the fall of 1960. Bob and I rented an apartment on Twenty-Sixth Street and set up a studio there. The short walk to art school was beautiful. The fall air was crisp and invigorating as I hustled along the tree-lined streets with autumn leaves turning to yellow and orange. The sunlight filtering through the elms, cottonwoods, and oaks cast long, cool shadows across the avenue and complemented the warm hues of the leaves. I decided to do a painting of the lovely boulevard. A year later, I did the painting in an expressionist style and sold it with no record (unfortunately) of who owns it today.

I was eligible to go to school on the GI bill. I received eighty dollars a month from the government for my stint in the air force—the exact amount of our monthly rent. My brother was working at KSTP, the major radio-television station in the Minneapolis/St. Paul area, and we were able to cover our monthly living expenses.

MSA is a well-known art school with a prestigious reputation. The first two years of a four-year program consisted of foundation courses (design, drawing, and art history) and courses in other disciplines required for the BFA degree. I really appreciated those foundation courses. I've always believed that design and drawing courses were important essentials for being a visual artist; one could use those fundamentals as a springboard to further develop creative visual ideas.

It is also important for the audience to have this fundamental education to achieve a deeper understanding and a greater joy of a work of art. As an artist, I am appreciative of a knowledgeable, unbiased audience. The fundamentals are not meant as hard fast rules in order to be creative; some works purposely break the rules in order to create a new vision. But breaking the rules without understanding is purely being rebellious with no other purpose than to be a rebel; it is meaningless.

A disturbing fact is that too many school curriculums do not include creative problem-solving programs, such as art and music courses. The emphasis in education is too often placed on memorization of information through repetition. Straight-line thinking without any lateral investigation only leads you to the end of your nose. The future of the human race depends on innovative thinking to solve the complex problems our species are faced with today.

My education in art school changed my perception of the visual world. One noticeable change in my perception was the awareness of negative shapes in nature—as opposed to just seeing the positive shapes. I'd look at a tree and be aware of the shapes of the branches and leaves (positive shapes)—while being equally aware of the *spaces between* the branches and leaves (negative shapes). Paul Cezanne once said that he didn't paint objects; he painted the spaces between them.

Learning to see involves using both hemispheres of the brain, but with an emphasis on the right half of the brain. Most of my education, up to that point, had been focused on using the left side of the brain: verbal, logical, analytical, symbolic, temporal, and rational modes of consciousness. I realized that I needed to further educate myself by applying a greater use of my right-brain mode—nonverbal, spatial, nontemporal, nonrational, and intuitive modes.

The school had marvelous instructors and a number of exceptionally talented students. Carl Grupp was an amazing draftsman. He always had his sketchbook with him and was continuingly drawing wherever he went—either from nature or from his copious imagination. I marveled at the expressive drawings Carl would do—the human figure in action, animals, historic themes, biblical themes, caricatures, and cartoons. Wherever his imagination would take him, his talented drawing skills would bring the images to life on the page.

Carl, Bob, and I became very good friends—not only because of our similar interests in the visual arts, but also because we were jazz fans. Carl had an enormous jazz collection, which included every recording by Sonny Rollins. Bob and I were invited to dinner at Carl's parents' house many times, and we would spend hours listening to Carl's collection of jazz recordings. I'm privileged to have a number of works by Carl in my art collection.

When our landlord learned I was an art student, he asked if I could do a painting for him—and he'd make a deal for some free rent. I said I would. He wanted a painting of a clipper ship. I came up with a dynamic oil painting of a clipper under full sail smashing through the ocean waves. I sent a color slide of the painting to my dad since he was a fan of old ships (he and I had put together models of clippers when I was a kid). My dad loved the painting and said if the landlord didn't buy it, he would. With later regrets, I wished I would have given the painting to my dad as a gift. The landlord also loved the painting and gave us two months of rent ($160) in exchange for it. About a year later, a friend saw the painting for sale in an antique store. I went to see it; the price tag was $1,800 (worth over twenty-two months' rent). The frame looked expensive.

Bob had wanted to buy a sports car since he was in high school. All through school, he saved every penny from all the jobs he had. With a little help from our dad, he was able to purchase a new Austin-Healey. Bob ordered the car through an auto dealer in Williston. Up until this time, he was driving an old Ford. I had left my car on the streets of Santa Barbara, and although I was without wheels, I didn't really need a car to get back and forth to school. Bob offered his old Ford to me, but I told him to trade it to the dealer in Williston and get a few bucks out of it.

"Besides," I said, "That will give me an excuse to use your new Healey now and then."

When Dad called to tell Bob his Healey had arrived at the Williston Import Autos, we decided to drive to Williston that weekend, pick up the new car, and trade in the Ford. It was a beautiful fall ride back to Minneapolis in a new sports car—not like the freezing snowstorms Bob and I traveled in over that route in the winter months.

I had applied for student financial assistance at school and was awarded a position as a painting instructor for Saturday art classes. This was the beginning of my teaching experience, and I thoroughly enjoyed this new undertaking. The more I taught, the more I learned—and the more I learned, the better I taught. It was a revolving learning experience.

Bob's interest in music switched from playing alto sax to playing the bass violin. At this time, our drummer friend moved to Minneapolis. Doug Gordon had gone to high school with Bob, and the three of us formed a trio.

We opened our apartment to a number of weekend parties for musicians and artists. At one particular weekend party, I asked my brother if he'd seen Doug that day. Bob said Doug had called a while ago and would be here shortly.

When Doug arrived, he was accompanied by a black dude, and he said, "I'd like you to meet Les McCann."

Les McCann was a famous jazz pianist and vocalist. Doug had met Les at a club in downtown Minneapolis where Les was playing. After having a couple of drinks together, Doug invited Les to our party. Les was a great party guest, entertaining everyone by playing some numbers on our piano and telling stories of his travels with famous jazz musicians. Years later, I met Les again in Santa Barbara when we played at the same jazz club.

Bob, Doug, and I would have interesting—and sometimes heated—debates on politics, religion, art, world affairs, and philosophies from Aristotle the Greek to Zorba the Greek. One of our lengthy philosophical discussions centered on how reality can become distorted by the conditioning of one's senses. One's mind might conclude things actually exist as they may appear to be true to the senses, but it may be only delusional. We plunged into a heavy discussion of the distinction between empirical knowledge and theoretical knowledge. The nature of reality has been questioned since the time of Plato. We were always searching for answers to age-old questions.

I have often wondered why some people are so judgmental, me included. I've learned over the years to temper my judgments by remembering my dad's advice. "Don't pass judgment on something or someone by appearances alone; good judgment is dependent on good information."

On November 22, 1963, I came home from school for lunch. Doug was sitting on the couch with his attention glued to the TV. He motioned for me to be quiet and sit down. Blaring from the TV was the news report that President Kennedy had been shot. The report from Dallas was shocking, and my first reaction was that it had to do with communists and the Cold War. Many conspiracy theories grew out of Kennedy's assassination. The nation was in a state of paranoiac shock. Suspiciousness led to judgmental delusions.

Doug, Bob, and I sported beards in the early sixties. Walking in downtown Minneapolis, a couple of days after Kennedy's assassination, we were accosted by a car full of young guys. Pulling up alongside us, they began making obscene gestures and threats yelling, "Hey you commie hippies, go back to Cuba with Castro where you belong."

A police car in the next lane flashed its lights. The agitators took off into the flow of traffic. The police pulled up to the curb and asked us what was going on. We told them it was just some young guys mouthing off. The cops told us we'd better move along if we didn't want any trouble. My dad's words on being judgmental echoed in my mind.

One day, in his usual mysterious way, Doug took off, without a word, for parts unknown. Bob and I met a drummer, a student at art school, and we had a trio again. We began to play gigs with the trio and sometimes with a quartet and quintet. Making it to and from gigs in Bob's Austin-Healey was a feat in contortionism. We would load Bob's bass in the sports car with the neck stuck between the two front seats and the body of the bass sticking up into the backseat. Bob and I had just enough room in the front, and Bob had barely enough space to shift gears.

A fine trumpet player from St. Paul started playing gigs with us. Chris was a fun-loving guy with a peculiar sense of humor. Blowing that trumpet was Chris's main thing, but there was another thing that Chris enjoyed doing. He loved to shock people with his antics. You never knew when he would pull one of his crazy feats, like mooning or streaking.

On one occasion, we booked a dance gig for the truckers' union in Minneapolis. It was held in a large hall with a high stage where the band was set up. Chris was his usual jubilant, spirited self. I was soloing on piano, and my eyes were halfway closed. Opening my eyes as I went up the keyboard, I saw Chris mooning me and singing the tune we were playing. He crooned, "It's only a paper moon." It was a good thing we were above the audience where they couldn't see what he was up to; otherwise those truckers probably would have run us over. The guys in the band were cracking up, and I don't know if I was laughing so hard because I was embarrassed or if the situation had just hit me as being utterly out of sight and totally funny.

Chris's cousin, Dickey, played sax and did some gigs with us. Chris and Dickey were a comedy of errors, a theater of the absurd, and a vaudeville act all rolled into one.

After a gig, we would usually go out to eat and unwind. We had a favorite Italian restaurant that stayed open all night. After a gig, that's where we could be found. One night after a gig, Chris, Bob, and I were waiting for Dickey to join us at the restaurant. He had a gig with another band. After a long wait, Dickey and another musician arrived. Dickey was holding a handkerchief over his nose with blood down the front of his shirt. Having had a few drinks, Dickey was feeling no pain. Laughing, he said he'd stuck his nose in somebody's business. After his gig, he and some friends were looking for an after-hours jam session. They were given an address in the black part of town. They went to the address and knocked on the door.

A big black dude opened the door and asked, "What do you white honkies want?"

Dickey insisted that this was where the jam session was—and he was answered by a big black fist to the nose. We suspected that Dickey had knocked on a dope house or a house of prostitution. No matter what was going on in that house, the use of the word *honky* and a punch in the nose was proof that he was not welcome.

We took a look at Dickey's horribly bloodied and distorted nose and thought it must be broken. We decided to get him to a hospital. We looked in the phone book for the nearest hospital, ordered some pizza to go, and took off for the emergency ward. At four o'clock in the morning, we were eating pizza in the hospital emergency waiting room while a nurse was getting information from Dickey about his accident. The nurse said a doctor would be there shortly to take care of the nose.

Bob and I kept nodding off while Chris and Dickey laughed and played with a wheelchair. They were jokingly saying, "Where is Dr. Kildare when you need him?" in reference to a popular TV series in the sixties about hospitals and doctors.

Chris told Dickey to get in the wheelchair—and he'd push him down the hall to find the doctor. Bob and I watched Chris speed down the corridor with Dickey in the wheelchair. They disappeared around a corner. A few minutes later, the PA system crackled.

"Paging Dr. Kildare." It was unmistakably Chris's voice.

Chapter 10

Minneapolis to Mexico to Maine

I spent the first summer break from MSA back in Williston. I played a number of gigs and spent a lot of time painting and drawing in a studio I set up in my dad's workshop.

I was lucky to be in North Dakota that summer day; Bob was at work at KSTP when a tornado roared down Twenty-Sixth Street. Minneapolis is known for powerful thunderstorms in the summer, and this particular summer storm spawned a tornado that tore up buildings along our street. It blew in the large window in our apartment's living room and sent glass shards into the wall and couch where we watched TV. The bakery up the street lost its roof, and it was never found. A barbershop had its large glass window bowed outward, the curtains pulled onto the outside, and the glass snapped back in place with the curtains hanging from the inside of the glass to the outside. Luckily there were no fatalities.

That next summer, Bob and I planned a trip to California and Mexico. The Healey could pass anything on the road, and it did. Many times we would remind the driver, "Look at the speedometer. Jeez, do you realize you're going 120 miles an hour?"

We traveled day and night, taking shifts on our way to California. On one particular warm moonlit night, Bob was at the wheel as we sped down a straight-as-an-arrow highway across Nevada. We were traveling with the top down. The floor of the Healey against the firewall to the engine was so hot that it was roasting our feet. We wore sandals and wrapped our feet in T-shirts soaked in water. At three in the morning, the desert air cooled to a temperature where we felt comfortable. I was sacked out, slumped down in the passenger's seat. *Wham!* The impact woke me instantly. We swerved off the highway as Bob tried to control the car, skidding in the desert sand. Coming to a stop in a cloud of dust illuminated by a large desert moon, we both sighed deeply, coughing and spitting grit.

"Herb, are you okay?"

"I'm fine," I said. "What happened?"

"I fell asleep and hit a highway marker."

In the bright moonlight, we could see that the right door was dented with a long scrape along the side. We agreed that we had been pushing our traveling schedule and decided to "cool it."

When we arrived in Sacramento, we looked up a Healey dealer to see if Bob's insurance would cover the car's damage. The Healey dealer told us it would be covered—and the car could be repaired in just a day. We thought we'd just bum around town while waiting for the repairs. It was a very hot day, and we were tired and hungry. We had something to eat and shopped around town for a couple of hours. As evening approached, we bought some chips and cold drinks and decided to camp out in a little park just down the street from the auto shop.

We went to the auto shop early the next morning to check on the status of the repair job. The Healey would probably be ready by evening. After breakfast, we decided to go back to the park and hang out until evening. We took off our sandals and got comfortable on the lawn for a siesta. Waking from our midday nap, the sun was beating down on us. The people strolling through the park paid no attention to the two of us under a large tree—and the shade had completely missed us. Our feet were horribly sunburned. With much moaning and groaning, we strapped on our sandals and took off for a drug store to get some calamine lotion. After applying lavish gobs of lotion to our feet, we headed for the repair shop to pick up the Healey. We nursed our feet with wet towels and sunburn lotion—and our headaches with aspirin. We looked forward to getting to the cooler coast of California.

With the Healey looking new, our feet wrapped in wet cloths, and the anticipation of relaxing in Santa Barbara, we headed south.

In Santa Barbara, we checked into a motel by the harbor. We were relieved to be out of the heat of the desert and the California inland valley. The first day in Santa Barbara, we went to a Foster's Freeze. I was enjoying a cool banana split, and Bob was having a chocolate sundae. I would always try to get Bob to order a banana split. He'd tell me that he'd love to have one, but it had to be the right time—and he'd wait until that right time. In his lifetime, he never found the right time to enjoy a banana split.

All of a sudden, Bob started honking the horn, pointing over my right shoulder, waving his arms, and yelling, "Stop, stop."

I turned and saw a pickup truck slowly backing into the right side of the Healey. The Healey was below the line of sight of the truck driver. I joined in with Bob, yelling at the driver and moving over as far as I could. I felt the momentum of metal pushing metal and a loud crunch to the passenger's side door. The door—that just a day earlier had been restored to its original beauty—was creased again.

The driver of the truck stopped with a jerk and opened the door to see what he had backed into. Before he could get all the way out of the cab, Bob was running toward him with his fists clinched.

I jumped out over the back of the Healey and ran to stop my brother before he could punch the driver. Bob was furious. He was usually a very cool person, but this really upset him. The poor driver, a Latino, was really shaken. Bob was yelling at the Latino, who was shouting in English and Spanish. I was yelling at both of them, and a few people came over to see what had caused the commotion. After everyone cooled down and apologies had been exchanged, we began to sort out our concerns.

Bob said, "I just had that damn door repaired yesterday."

The pickup driver said he had insurance that would pay for repairs, but he had his insurance papers at home. We should follow him to his house to get them.

We followed the pickup driver to his house. On the porch, he opened the door and motioned for us to go inside. As we stepped inside, we were met by a lady who immediately started screaming at us in Spanish.

The truck driver said something to her in Spanish. Then she broke into English and said, "You know you can't bring them in here—get out of here!"

"*Ay ay*—I forgot about the quarantine," he said.

Backing out the door and onto the porch, we saw the sign from the California Health Department. *Quarantine—Measles.*

"Too late now," Bob said.

"Besides, we've already had the measles," I added.

After getting all the insurance information, we found an auto repair shop and left the car to be repaired (again). We had some nice days in Santa Barbara, spent a day in LA, and headed to Mexico. In Tijuana, you could get some of the finest handmade leather articles at very cheap prices. We couldn't find the seat covers we wanted for the Healey, and we settled for a couple of pairs of handmade sandals. The soles, made from old automobile tires, left tread marks wherever we'd walk on the beach.

One hot afternoon, we had a drink in a Tijuana cantina. We were approached by a Mexican bartender who told us he could get us anything we wanted. He mentioned Dexedrine, cocaine, and marijuana and also pointed to a beautiful dark-haired girl. He said he had two beautiful girls looking for a date tonight. Bob and I looked at one another and said we may be interested. The bartender said to meet him in ten minutes at the door next to the bar, and he'd introduce us to the girls.

We waited at the door for a few minutes, and the bartender came with a key to open it.

"*Entrar, amigos,*" he said.

In the room, two ugly old women were drinking at a table. They had more body hair than we did.

Bob and I said, "We're out of here."

When we turned to leave, the bartender reached out and grabbed Bob by the shirt. He said, "Gringo, you owe me dollars."

We pushed him aside, ran down the street to the Healey, and headed for the border. We drove to San Diego, got a cheap hotel room, and joked about "our beautiful Spanish senoritas." The bartender had to keep them behind a locked door—God knows what would happen if they had gotten out. The sandals were enough of a souvenir from Mexico without bringing back souvenirs from those mangy Mexican maidens.

Our trip back to Minneapolis was uneventful and quick. We were glad to get back to our little apartment. We were tanned, tired, and itching to get back to the art studio and to the bass and piano. We were looking forward to playing more gigs.

I was making abstract expressionistic paintings, using mainly earth colors. I was fortunate enough one year to sell two of my paintings to major collections. The Minneapolis Institute of Art bought a small painting, and a large painting sold to a major Minneapolis manufacturing company.

When I couldn't carry the large painting to the school sale, Bob and I tied it to the top of his car to deliver it. We arrived at school and removed the painting from the car top.

Bob said, "Put it down a minute—look at that mess on the painting."

There are lots of robins in Minneapolis in the spring, and one had made a large deposit in the middle of my painting.

Bob, looking at the painting with his critical eye, said, "I like the addition, it works with the earth colors. I think you should leave it in the work."

I thanked him for the critique but didn't think I could claim it as an original work of mine.

Bob held the painting on the steps of the school while I ran inside to get some wet paper towels to restore my painting to its original state.

During my third year at MSA, I was awarded a summer scholarship to the Skowhegan School of Art in Maine. The school was known for its staff of famous artists and alumni. Three months of studying with well-known artists and meeting art students from many parts of the country was a unique experience in my art education. I also welcomed the opportunity to explore New England. I visited the Farnsworth Art Museum in Rockland, Maine, which houses a large collection of works by Andrew Wyeth. A majority of his work had the same impact on me as his most famous tempera painting, *Christina's World*. Wyeth's ability to express a serene surrealistic mood in his images of troubled conditions fascinated me. *Christina's World* is a haunting image of Wyeth's neighbor, Christina Olson, crippled by polio, crawling across a field and looking toward her house on the horizon. It is one of the most recognized American paintings of the twentieth century. It hangs in the Museum of Modern Art in New York.

Eating fresh Maine lobster burgers was a delight, and they were as easy to buy as a hamburger in the Midwest. Glutton that I was, I could never get my fill of lobster.

Inspired by the school and its instructors, I acquired knowledge of painting and drawing skills that led me to be awarded first place in Skowhegan's painting category. Summer school ended in August. A girl I'd met at school invited me to her home in Boston. I spent two days in Boston and took a bus to New York to catch a plane home.

On the flight back to Minneapolis, it seemed as though I had just taken the flight *from* Minneapolis. Soaring thirty thousand feet above the earth at five hundred miles per hour, I watched the checkerboard landscape slowly unfold beneath me. I wondered about the significance of humans; we were so tiny compared to the earth below—and the earth was so miniscule compared to the universe. It was mind-boggling to think about the nature of the design of the universe and the meaning of our existence. What did it all mean? I kept searching, but I had no answer.

The concepts I'd been exposed to the past summer brought me to a new level of conscious reasoning about trying to find the significance of *self*. Although there was no clear answer, I felt closer to knowing myself than I had ever before. Every once in a while, I'd have a renewal in self-faith, and the questions and doubts about my existence seemed less important than the mere fact that I existed. I committed myself to study diligently and was absorbed with becoming successful.

My concept of success was changing. I was redefining what success was to me. I felt that success for me was not gaining fame and fortune—but attaining my better self. I had no definitive answer for how to obtain success, but I had numerous questions. Was success happiness? Was happiness success? As a youth, my mind had been filled with concepts of doing *hard work*, busy activities (to keep one from being idle), and fearing punishment for failure. I had believed these were the things that helped you to gain material success. I began to realize that the real joy of success is within. Enjoying the pleasure of the process, the journey of better self-becoming became the important part of success for me.

Successful creativeness seems to happen when there is knowledge mixed with an open mind that is not being obsessed by the formality of an agenda—not methodically analyzing every detail in a clinical manner so that it becomes unemotional. Keeping an open mind that floats with your thoughts and does not become obsessed by your thoughts releases one from prejudgments.

The mind must be clear of preconceived concepts and prejudgments that lead to prejudice. Meditating to keep an open mind and my thoughts free from my controlling selfish center became one of my goals after being introduced to books on Zen by Alan Watts and Eugen Herrigel. I'm reminded of my favorite Zen story:

A student, studying with a Zen master, expounded on his concepts of Zen and its meaning. The master, pouring the student a cup of tea, filling it to the brim, kept on pouring.

"Stop," The student exclaimed. "The cup won't hold any more. It's overflowing."

"You are like this cup," the master replied. "You are overflowing with ideas about the Zen way. You ask for teaching, but your cup is already full; I can't put anything in. Before I can teach you, you'll have to empty your cup."

I enjoy the Zen nature of haikus. A famous poem by Matsuo Basho, the seventeenth-century Japanese haiku poet, is one of my favorites:

The old pond:
A frog jumps in,
The sound of the water.

In haikus, it is said that some of the important things are left out of the poem so one must read between the lines for the experience of the meaning.

A critique on the haiku above by Eugen Herrigel in *The Method of Zen* states that while it is minimal poetry it contains the whole universe. "Suddenly, in the midst of motionless calm—movement, life, spreading rings of sound, then vanishing again. And what is all this commotion compared with the voice of silence, which is the beginning and the end?" One must link relationships of your experiences to find the meaning.

My last year at MSA was an end of a beginning and the beginning of a new happenchance. It was a fulfilling journey in art, music, creativeness, and discovery of *self*. I was on a path of awareness about how much I *actually* knew, how much I *thought* I knew, and how much I *didn't* know. I found new takes from which to view life after traveling numerous paths. It was comforting to know I had companions on these routes to new discoveries (albeit for a big part of my life, I've traveled the paths alone).

My brother and I always had a close bond and empathy for each other's sentiments. Early in 1964, I began to notice a change in Bob's behavior. He seemed depressed and wouldn't communicate with me. Much later, I found out that Bob's girlfriend had dumped him and gotten married. I don't know why Bob didn't confide in me, but keeping his frustration locked inside made his depression worse.

One day, he exploded over a little disagreement about the interpretation of a piece of music. He misinterpreted my advice as trying to be controlling, and I mistook his remarks as being demeaning. It was as though the ground was knocked out from under me, and I was dumbfounded by his action—and by my reaction. Our quarrel went from bad to worse, and we were the closest to exchanging blows we'd ever been. I freaked out over not being able help him.

Bob said he was leaving and packed his suitcase.

I told him to wait a day to think it over.

There was no way to change his mind. He said, "No. I've thought about doing this for some time. I'm going to California to look for a job."

I pleaded with him to reconsider, but he refused to talk. Putting the cover on his bass, he picked it up, carried it down the stairs, and loaded it in his car. He came back upstairs and got his luggage. As he went out the apartment door, I reached out to stop him. He slammed the door on my hand. He was gone—down the stairs, out the door, and out of our association.

I was consumed with feelings of remorse and tried to console myself by reminding myself that I was not my brother's keeper. But was that true? I always had an innate feeling of protection for my brother and felt a strong obligation to that mandate. For a couple of weeks, I was beside myself with worry. I figured he may have gone to Santa Barbara and called friends there to inquire about him.

About two weeks later, Bob called from Santa Barbara. We immediately began apologizing for our behavior. The time and space factor gave perspective to our confrontation—and awareness about our senseless disagreement. Why does rage deep inside us erupt like an ancient volcano? This is a mystery of human behavior. We acknowledged shame for our uncontrolled behavior and promised to control our actions better in the future. Having settled our differences, we pledged to continue our friendship forever—and we did.

On June 4, 1964, I received my bachelor of fine arts degree from the Minneapolis School of Art. Mom and Dad drove from North Dakota for the commencement ceremony and to help me pack up the apartment. We rented a trailer to haul all my books and art supplies back to Williston. On the way to North Dakota, we ran into a horrific rainstorm. The trailer had only a tarp covering, and everything in it couldn't have gotten more thoroughly soaked if we'd gone through a car wash.

In Williston, we unpacked the waterlogged contents of the trailer. More rain was predicted, and all the items were put out to dry in the basement. I opened all the books and spread them out like unfolded tents across the floor. The various colors of the covers glistening under the lights made them look like a field of drowned butterflies.

Chapter 11

Return to Paradise

I enjoyed spending the summer of 1964 in the company of old friends, going fishing with my folks, eating home-cooked meals, and playing gigs with Rich. I did a lot of landscape drawings, self-portraits, a portrait of my father, and a portrait of Ole Moe, the town's most colorful character. I had a bit part in an Old West play—not because I was any kind of an actor but mainly because I had long hair and a beard. It was a fun-filled summer.

Wanderlust urges began to stir in me; by fall, I was ready to move on. It is said that once you have experienced the beauty of Santa Barbara, you'll always want to return. I sure did. I had two other reasons for wanting to return. The University of California at Santa Barbara had a master's degree program in the visual arts that interested me—and my brother was still living there. Bob was playing bass with a Latin jazz trio in Santa Barbara.

Bob encouraged me to return to Santa Barbara and said we could easily get some gigs. He said he had a surprise for me; someone wanted to talk to me.

A low, gruff voice came over the phone and I wondered who was trying to disguise their voice. After kidding around for a minute, the voice sang out, "This is Doug." Doug Gordon had shown up in Santa Barbara. We could get the old trio back together. Bob and Doug had found a beautiful house to rent in the hills above Santa Barbara.

Bob picked me up at the LA airport, and we immediately took off up the coast on Highway 101. The ninety-mile drive to Santa Barbara gave us some time to catch up with each other's lives over the last nine months. When we reached Santa Barbara, we traveled up San Marcos Pass Road and followed Painted Cave Road to the top of the mountain. The road was dusty, steep, narrow, and winding. It was an edgy ride in the Healey, but it was beautiful. Near the top was a small community called Painted Cave. The place took its name from a cave formed into the side of a small cliff that contained intriguing pictograph images and colorful designs created by the Chumash natives from about a thousand years ago.

Near the top of the mountain range, we turned into a little driveway and parked beside a California-style bungalow. The breathtaking view from Bob and Doug's place reminded me of the French Riviera. The hilly landscape, Spanish-style roofs, the harbor, and the aqua-blue Pacific Ocean made me think I was in paradise.

Doug wasn't home, but a note said he'd gone to the Brooks Institute of Photography and would be back by evening.

The little house at Painted Cave was a two-bedroom rental, and Bob and Doug had fixed up the attached garage as an added bedroom for me. The garage was a comfortable, open-beamed space with enough room to set up a painting studio, which I did later.

My brother and I had just sat down to our evening meal when Doug walked in; the three of us continued our meal and talked like we were still at our apartment in Minneapolis. It was good to renew old friendships. We discussed our plans in terms of getting some gigs. Bob suggested I talk to George at the Spigot since he was still hiring jazz groups.

"Tomorrow I'll see him," I said.

The next day, George hired our trio to play Friday and Saturday nights. We also performed as the house band for an open jam session on Sunday evenings. Bob and I were making it to and from gigs in his Austin Healey; this time we went up and down a winding mountain road with the bass in my lap.

The Spigot had made a few changes in the four years I was gone. Two new additions delighted me. George had installed a new bandstand—and a six-foot grand piano.

We had a number of local musicians sit in on Sundays—some were really good, and some were not so good. At one of these Sunday sessions, I met a very good drummer who would become one of our permanent sidemen. Tony Cappiello had recently been discharged from the navy and had moved back to his hometown. He was playing with a group of jazz musicians who were stationed at Vandenberg Air Force Base.

Bob, Doug, and I did the trio gig for about three weeks. One morning, Doug was gone when we woke up. It was a familiar situation—just like in Minneapolis. There was no advance notice or even a hint of leaving. At least Doug left a note referring to his wanderlust as his "Gauguin complex." Doug's behavior didn't surprise us, and we accepted Doug for what he was—an enigma. As luck would have it, I had met a fine musician who was a vibraphone player, a trombonist, and a drummer who was looking for work. Harry Smallenberg was a student at UCSB. I contacted him about the gig, and we had a drummer for our trio.

In the sixties, rock-and-roll music was in, and the British rock bands were invading North America. California surfing music, psychedelic LSD-inspired music, and art were all part of the counterculture genre being dug by music fans.

The sixties were a time of revolution against established morals and attitudes of society. With the hippie movement, hip music fans had shifted from the "Jazz-Goes-to-College" concept to drop out, get high, and dig the message that rock-and-roll music had in its screaming lyrics and earsplitting distorted guitars. The hippie movement grew out of the bohemian counterculture of the forties and fifties Beat Generation hipster beatniks that described the jazz and swing musicians.

The hippies' counterculture lifestyle opposed the Vietnam War; they were for civil rights and the personal freedom to experiment with lifestyles—from sex to drugs. They were far left—but not a left-wing political party. They had no aspirations to replace a political party. The hippie movement was more social than it was political. In the sixties, I wasn't left or right; I was in the center. Although I was not a hippie, I did sympathize with some of their concepts that were in opposition to the "Establishment." In particular, I was for being eco-friendly and showing love and compassion for others—no matter their race, religion, gender, national origin, or ability. I was in favor of the opposition to war and nuclear weapons.

Some of the sixties' rock musicians were very talented and made significant contributions to the pop music scene in terms of message songs. Others offered nothing but gimmicks and mindless antics that were hyped by greedy promoters. The music we played was acoustic instrumental jazz—no words, just sounds. I'd heard many music fans admit they couldn't dig and wouldn't listen to instrumental music (jazz or classical) since it had no meaning without words.

Our trio played the Spigot gig until that fall. Harry had to take leave of the trio because of full-time commitments to his studies at the university. Tony became our drummer and played with different combinations of groups we had over the next three years. Bob, Tony, and I formed a very close friendship; Bob's bass and Tony's drums worked magic on our tunes, clicking into a solid groove that we called "the circle."

Early in 1965, Harry returned to gig with us on vibes and trombone. Our quartet was quite popular with local jazz fans (and even with people who weren't necessarily jazz buffs).

George was usually a tough and fickle boss, but he really liked our group. He was a nice enough guy, but there were some things he'd do that would irk the band. For instance, he'd send notes up to the bandstand for us to play a crowd-pleaser. Sometimes we'd be obligated to play the Ramsey Lewis pop-jazz hit "The In Crowd" two or three times a night. George's little notes would sometimes crack us up (take a request for a round of drinks, smile when you play, etc.). We would purposely make grimacing faces.

The band's schedule was changed to play Wednesday through Saturday and cut out the Sunday gig. George thought musicians were a strange bunch, but he said he dug us and knew that we were probably the most trustworthy of all the musicians he'd met. He asked if I'd like to work the bar on Sunday afternoons; even though I was a musician, he thought I could be trusted to run the bar. I accepted his backhanded compliment.

I needed all the work I could get while waiting a year to get my resident requirement before going to graduate school. I told him we would clean the place if he'd let us rehearse in the club on Sundays before it opened. It was okay with him, and he gave me the keys to the bar. We'd come in early to vacuum the floors, clean the tables, and look for any change the patrons had dropped that the barmaids had missed (it was amazing the amount of money we would sometimes find).

The order of the day at rehearsals was for the musicians to have pickled eggs, pepperoncini peppers, pickled polish sausages, and glasses of beer. For some of us financially strapped students, the bohemian cuisine of fart food was our main meal of the day.

Even though George knew we were into the food and beer at rehearsals, he told me to go easy and not eat or drink him out of house and home. He knew he was getting a deal with the band. One time he took Bob and me to dinner in LA and a night at Shelly's Manne Hole Jazz Club—all expenses paid. Old George was really a softy underneath his tough exterior, but I wouldn't want to tangle with him and the baseball bat he kept under the bar.

We'd get all types of patrons in this funky little jazz bar—white-collar and blue-collar workers, professional people, and college students. There was also a mix of rough customers, including oil rig workers and Hells Angels bikers who would sometimes clash.

By March 1965, the quartet had expanded to a quintet. A very talented tenor sax player joined the group. Charlie Orena was a music student at UCSB and played alto and tenor. Charlie's forte was his imaginative tenor solos. Today Charlie is a well-respected saxophone player working gigs with top musicians in LA.

That summer, Harry graduated from the UCSB and planned on doing graduate studies at Berkeley. We had met a valve trombone player who would fill his spot. Clark Meyer had done some gigs in Las Vegas with Sam Butera (saxophonist for Louis Prima's band, the Witnesses). Clark was a great improviser, creating some lush solos on his valve trombone. He lived a very bohemian lifestyle and was a positive guy with a subtle sense of humor. These qualities were reflected in his 'bone solos.

When we weren't gigging at the Spigot, Tony, Charley, Bob and I played a number of casual gigs. One interesting gig on the second Thursday of every month was at a Devereux School. Devereux Schools, located throughout the United States, offer programs for intellectually and developmentally disabled young adults. The monthly dances at the Santa Barbara campus were an anticipated event for the students.

Among the students, there were some who were family members of a number of well-known celebrities. We had a great rapport with the students. They loved the band, always listening and dancing with great appreciation for the music and asking us to sign autographs. It was the best kind of therapy for the students—and for the musicians. I felt a deep appreciation for the fact that being born without a disablement was a blessing—and in some small way, I could aid those who were not so fortunate.

Every monthly dance had a memorable event. On one occasion, a staff member asked if he could sing a song with the band. The handsome, well-dressed young man said he'd like to sing "I Left My Heart in San Francisco" in the key of B flat.

I agreed. Usually people who want to sing a tune with the band have no idea what key they sang in. I did a four-bar intro for him, but he missed coming in. I played the intro again and gave him a cue when to start. This time, he was right on time and right on key. I stared at him in disbelief as he sang the first four bars; instead of going to the next phrase, he started singing the first four bars again. At first I thought he was just nervous and wanted to start over again. He kept repeating those four bars: "I left my heart in San Francisco . . . I left my heart in San Francisco . . . I left my heart in San Francisco."

I realized I'd been had; the young man was a student. The band went along with his vocal rendition and played the phrase over and over with him. When he decided to stop, he just put down the mic, took a bow, and thanked the audience. The place went wild with applause.

A staff member came up to the band and thanked him for singing.

He thanked me, grabbed me, shook my hand enthusiastically, and planted a big kiss on my cheek. I felt honored that we had given this young man his proud five minutes of fame. He went into the dance crowd singing, "I left my heart in San Francisco." Eat your heart out Tony Bennett.

That spring and summer, I was busy playing gigs and doing my Sunday bartending gig. I submitted a portfolio of artwork to apply for graduate school and was accepted to start in the fall. The drive from Painted Cave was becoming a drag, but there had also been a big brush fire in the hills. The ash falling all around our place and the smoke turning the sun into a red-orange ball in the sky made it look like the last days of Pompeii.

Bob and I moved into Santa Barbara and found a little house to rent just a couple of houses down from where Sal and I had rented the place on Gillespie Street. We found an old piano for sale and hauled it out of a basement and into our new home.

We had a following of fans that would show up regularly at the Spigot. We became friends with some interesting characters, including two brothers who were talented artists and did design work for movie studios in Hollywood. They did the initial designs for the Batman vehicles—and an interesting caricature of the band.

We met a lawyer who gave up his successful practice in New York and moved to Santa Barbara to live an alternative lifestyle in a remote area of the Santa Barbara hills. There were some *real* jazz fans who listened attentively to our music. There were also the usual barflies, alcoholics, used-to-be's, going-to-be's, and all assortments of "shuckers and jivers." Some patrons were high rollers, and some were down on their luck. One young dude was an heir to the Kellogg's family fortune. He had a party after a gig, and some of the band members attended. As dawn approached with a beautiful sunrise, he invited some of his party guests to hop on board his private jet and fly to Acapulco for breakfast. None of the band members joined the flight to Mexico; instead we spent our breakfast at one of our favorite Mexican restaurants in Santa Barbara, eating *huevos rancheros* that were as good, if not better, than Acapulco ones.

My brother and I always had a great appetite for good old Dakota/Montana beef steaks. Tucked away in a suburban neighborhood in an old remodeled house we found a mom-and-pop restaurant that served large portions of tender beef steaks. Their T-bones were close to what we'd get back at the State Line Nightclub in North Dakota.

We ate at this little restaurant often. One time while waiting to dine, I happened to look out the window at the street below us. Two young men were walking along the street, one on the sidewalk and one in the street, looking in the cars and trying the doors to see if any were unlocked. They tried the doors on Bob's Healey, which was parked right below us, but it was locked. Moving on to the next car the guy opened the door and grabbed a purse from the front seat. He stuck the purse under his jacket, and the two strolled casually down the street.

I jumped out of my seat and hollered at Bob. "He stole a purse!" I ran down the short flight of stairs and out into the street.

The two hoods were still walking slowly down the street, but they took off as soon as they saw me running toward them. One ran across the road and down a side street. The one holding the purse took off down the street and into a park just ahead of us. Even though he'd had a head start, I poured on the steam and started to gain on him. He kept looking back at me, and seeing that he wasn't outrunning me, he flung the purse into some bushes.

I gave up the chase and retrieved the purse.

Bob was standing in front of the restaurant when I returned. "What was that all about?" he asked.

Holding up the purse and catching my breath, I said, "Some guy stole this purse from a car."

I asked if the purse belonged to anyone; an elderly gentleman said, "That looks like my wife's."

A gray-haired lady replied, "Yes, indeed. That looks like mine."

After I explained the purse-snatching incident the elderly couple thanked me and said they would buy us dinner—and we could order anything we wanted. I told them we had already ordered T-bone steaks.

"Good choice," said the old gentlemen. "The steaks and a bottle of wine are on us."

Looking forward to the master's art program at the university, I began spending more time painting and drawing. I was accepted as a member of the Santa Barbara Art Association, and my work was represented by the First Press Art Gallery. I was beginning to make a few sales; with the Spigot gigs, I saved enough dough to buy an old Ford station wagon.

My brother met his future wife in Santa Barbara in 1965. Ev Scoville was a nurse at Cottage Hospital in Santa Barbara. She and her friend, Joyce Nieboer (also a nurse at Cottage) and a group of their friends used to come to the Spigot often to listen to us. Ev and Joyce were from Alberta, Canada; as fate would have it, Bob, Ev, and I would end up residing in Alberta within twenty years.

Among the nurses' friends who were patrons at the Spigot was a technologist who worked at the blood bank. Jerry Roberts was a demonstrative guy and skippered a huge beautiful sailboat, *La Volpe*, which was owned by a Santa Barbara doctor. On a number of occasions,

Bob and Ev would be among the crew as *La Volpe* sailed out of the harbor.

One of the few times I was on board was when we did a Columbus Day pageant. We sailed into the harbor, and everyone on board was dressed in the attire of 1492. We enacted Columbus's important historical event as we docked in front of a group of Indians dressed in period costumes. A large crowd gathered.

One of onlookers shouted, "Look, the first pirate to land in America!"

When I viewed a photograph of our landing in the *News Press,* I saw the pirate. I was standing on the deck of the ship, waiting for Columbus to disembark. I had a bandana on my head and a patch over one eye. I did look more like a Caribbean pirate than a fifteenth-century Spanish sailor discovering the New World. One of my childhood visions of becoming a pirate had come true.

Bob and Ev got married that September. Ev decided to visit her parents in Canada before the wedding. She would fly to Calgary the second week in August. Bob was busy working the day of her flight, and I borrowed Bob's Healey to drive Ev to LA.

In August 1965, all hell broke loose in Los Angeles in an African American neighborhood. The Watts Riots were the most violent disturbance LA had ever seen. Racial tension had been building due to a number of issues, including miserable living conditions, poor education, unemployment, and discrimination and police mistreatment of Black Muslims. Fifteen thousand troops of the California National Guard had been deployed to help the police end the rioting.

The LA airport was near Watts, and we had heard reports of rioters cruising near the end of the runways and firing handguns and rifles at planes as they took off. I don't know if they expected to bring down a jumbo jet with a .22-caliber bullet, but it was a violent act of defiance. We were a little concerned about driving through that part of LA. As we neared the airport, we could see smoke rising from burning buildings in Watts, but we were lucky and had no problems arriving or departing.

Arriving safely back in Santa Barbara a few hours later, I was thankful that I had made the decision to move out of LA. Even Santa Barbara was beginning to take on the hustle and bustle of LA. By the nineties, Santa Barbara was like an extension of the megalopolis to the south. There are things I like about the big cities—the immediate availability of the diversity of everything I enjoy. There are cities I love to visit, but the idea of living there as a permanent resident no longer appealed to me. Maybe it's my roots that go back to the open spaces on the prairies: "Don't fence me in."

The sixties in the United States were plagued with a number of contentious issues. Among them were the civil rights movement, Vietnam antiwar demonstrations, the Cuban missile crisis, and nuclear threats. It was a time of great unrest for Americans, but the time for change was long overdue for some issues. Although I empathized with the issues at hand, I was neither socially nor politically activated by the conflicts of the times. I didn't embrace the lifestyles or the pop music of the time. In a negative sense, I was wearing blinders in relation to the problems of the day. I had my own agenda, was quite self-centered, and was more wrapped up in my own quandaries. In a positive sense, I was trying to be true to myself, to know myself, and be independent of outside influences, fads, and fashions. I had been treading water for a while, but I was beginning to swim against the current to the goals I had in my sights.

Trying to find myself, to be true to myself, and know myself was (is) a frustrating undertaking. I was frightened of knowing myself. I had already discovered that I was not a demon or a saint—I contained parts of both. I wanted to know myself deep down, to find my self-worth, and figure out if I liked me being me. Much later in life, I found the answer; sometimes I liked myself, and sometimes I didn't. And much, much later in life, I liked myself most of the time. Is that progress? I guess it depends on what there is to like.

My metaphysical search had taken me on countless twists and turns to find myself. I found some aspects of self that were intrinsic to my principles. I liked the arts; more than that, I had a great *passion* for the arts. I attentively read books, listened to recordings, went to concerts, looked at paintings, and watched plays and films for countless hours. I marveled at the men and women whose creativeness had fashioned great achievements over the course of history.

I knew I wanted to be an artist. The major obstacle I had to overcome was my lack of self-confidence; the more I knew, the less confident I became. Was I competing with the titans in art—Michelangelo, Da Vinci, and Picasso? I searched my soul to change my attitude and realized that the only one I was competing with was myself. The uniqueness of me being the only one that is me was my prominence. Be true to myself. Being oneself is a hard gig.

I had an innate sense of my abilities and my limitations. I came to realize that doing my best would be my unique creativeness for my own aspirations. Setting my sights on my first goal, going to graduate school at UCSB, was coming into focus. I begin drawing and painting more and submitting my work to various art exhibits. I was still doing the weekend music gigs, which I enjoyed immensely, and Sunday bartending gig, which I was finding more and more tedious. I sustained myself with a little income and had the good fortune to find time for my artwork.

I don't remember why I walked into the little Santa Barbara bar in the middle of the week, sat at a table, ordered a drink, and started eating peanuts from the bowl in front of me. It may have been because I was interested in hearing the trio that was playing—or maybe I just wanted a cold beer. Whatever brought me to that bar was one of the strange, almost surreal moments I've encountered now and again.

Swept away by the music of the trio, the dim lights of the club, and a refreshing beer, I was drifting, totally relaxed.

A voice brought me back to earth. "You're Herb Hicks, aren't you?" Before I could answer, a hand was thrust in my direction. "Hi. I'm Jean." A beautiful, sexy gal was standing at my table with her hand out waiting for mine.

"Yeah, I'm Herb." I sounded self-conscious—as though I wasn't sure what my name was. I grasped her hand and said, "Pull up a chair and have a peanut." I was flabbergasted by her stunning beauty.

She sat down beside me. Before I could ask how she knew me, she said she had seen me playing piano at the Spigot last weekend. She told me she was a jazz fan and had enjoyed seeing various jazz greats back East.

I was in awe.

This was her first time in California, and she had been in Los Angeles for the last couple of weeks. "Tell me about you," she said.

"Well . . . originally, I'm from North Dakota—"

"Oh my god. I know nothing about what goes on in the Dakotas."

"Me neither," I said, laughing with embarrassment.

Her laughter was the icebreaker since I had felt a little intimated by her forward behavior. Before I knew it, I was spilling out my life's story to her.

She listened attentively, and we ordered a couple more drinks. I asked her about her life. "My name is Jean." She turned on the charm and flashed a lovely smile. "That is all I can tell you. No more questions."

I've never considered myself a ladies' man; although I have known a number of women of various types, I had never met a gal as enigmatic as Jean. Over the next two months, we became good friends, but I still didn't know anything about her background—or even her last name. I knew she liked jazz and art, was without inhibitions, and was completely self-reliant—my kind of woman. Our relationship became more intimate as time went by, and Jean began modeling for some of my drawings. This helped me put together a portfolio of drawings of the nude figure for my master's art program.

One Sunday afternoon, Jean met me at the Spigot while I was bartending. The bar was full of the usual regulars, soaking up beer on a warm Sunday afternoon. As she walked through the door and up to the bar, everyone's eyes turned in her direction. There were a few catcalls and whistles. Most of the people in the bar knew that Jean and I were an item. She sat at the bar, having a glass of beer and looking very sexy. We were having a conversation about a trip we were planning to LA.

A big hand and arm slapped the bar beside Jean and a loud drunken voice said, "Bartender, get this gorgeous thing a beer."

I hadn't seen this burly, ugly guy before; he was not one of our regular customers. I knew all our regulars and I trusted them—drunk or sober—but I didn't like this guy's rudeness or looks. I told him to back off. I had my eye on him—and on George's baseball bat behind the bar. I looked down the bar at some of my regulars—in case I needed their help.

Jean told me to never mind; this guy couldn't bug her. The drunk became more obnoxious, moving closer to Jean and putting his arm around her. She slid off the barstool, did a quick turn, and landed a swift kick to his crotch.

He went down on his knees like a sack of potatoes. Swearing and snorting like a bull, he started to get up and yelled, "You bitch—"

Someone grabbed him, spun him around, and landed a punch square to his nose. A couple more guys joined in the "fun." Adrenalin was racing through my body; I had one hand on George's baseball bat and the other on the phone.

The police showed up in a matter of minutes. I remembered George's advice about any trouble at the bar—always phone the cops.

Early one morning, as the cool Pacific fog was drifting over Santa Barbara, I was awakened by someone shaking me. Opening my sleepy eyes, I saw Jean standing over my bed. I made a move to get up, but she pushed me back down.

"Don't get up. I can only stay a minute," she said. "I just wanted to see you to say good-bye."

"Good-bye? Why? What's wrong?"

"Nothing's wrong. I just have to go."

"Go where? Why?"

Putting her finger to my lips she said, "No questions, remember? All I can tell you is that I have to go to Florida. I like you very much, and we had a great time. Didn't we?"

I agreed.

Jean left my life just as she had arrived; one minute she was there, the next she wasn't. Other than her name, I never knew who she really was. A few people told me they knew something about her. Bizarre stories surfaced from some about who she was. Whether these strange stories were fictitious or real, I'll never know. I only know she captivated me. The most mysterious woman I'd known came and went like the morning Santa Barbara fog.

Chapter 12

Ice Cream Delight

Located by the Pacific Ocean, the University of California at Santa Barbara is one of the most beautiful academic campuses in the United States—and one of the most distinguished in the Association of American Universities. I was honored to be accepted to a master of fine arts program and looked forward with great anticipation to my first semester there.

I started UCSB in the fall of 1965 and continued to play weekends at the Spigot and bartend on Sundays. We were still having rehearsals on Sundays, using a quintet, and were doing charts arranged by our new trumpet player, Tony Birabent.

We usually had good crowds at the gig, and George was so pleased he threw a beach barbecue and beer bust for the band and regular customers of the club. George supplied hamburgers and kegs and kegs of beer from the Spigot. People brought all kinds of salads and desserts, and the band brought a special "whipped cream pie."

I always enjoyed Soupy Sales's pie-in-the-face slapstick comedy routine. The band planned on getting George with the pie routine. On the pretense of honoring George for hiring us for so long, we had one of the club's most frequent customers and I pose for a photograph with him. As the three of us posed on the beach, my brother handed me a whipped cream pie.

On cue from the photographer, I said, "This is from the band." I delivered the pie to George's face with such force that whipped cream covered his nose, mouth, ears, and hair. Everyone was laughing as George choked and gasped for breath.

Tony gave a pie to Bob, and Bob planted it on my kisser. He said, "This is from the band."

George recovered from his choking and remarked that he was glad to see my brother had pied me so he didn't have to.

Continuing to do my thing in music and art, I questioned if I had the stamina to really serve two mistresses. As hard as it might be to juggle a number of vocations, when you love something, you can find the time and energy. There were times when I found it difficult to distinguish love from short-term fascination, which sometimes existed in my capricious mind. Having a full agenda had always been my modus operandi, and I served both love and fascination.

Shortly after Bob and Ev were married, they acquired two new additions. They bought a Volkswagen mini-van. They enjoyed camping and didn't need a hot little sports car to zip around in. Bob could haul his bass in the van with their other new addition—a dog. Their little puppy grew to be a large, beautiful German shepherd; it was one of the smartest animals I ever knew.

At Skowhegan Art School, I had an inspiring Italian art instructor who owned a beautiful German shepherd named Tiber. I was so taken by that intelligent animal that I thought Bob and Ev's German shepherd should have that namesake. I suggested the name to Bob and Ev for their new puppy. They agreed—and Tiber it was.

Tiber was a fitting name for Bob and Ev's dog. In the seventh century BC, King Thebris drowned in the Albula River, which was renamed the Tiber River in his honor. According to legend, Jupiter made him a god and guardian spirit of the river. The Romans depicted Tiber as a powerful river god with water flowing from his hair and beard. The legend says that Rome's founders, the twin brothers Romulus and Remus, were thrown into the Tiber River—and they were rescued, nurtured, and raised by a she-wolf. Rome was founded on the shores of the Tiber River.

The Fine Arts Department at UCSB had professors and students of notable fame. One of the most well-known drama students was Michael Douglas. Michael's path and mine crossed a couple of times; although he hadn't established himself as a celebrity actor in 1965, he was known as the son of the famous actor Kirk Douglas.

I was an admirer of the Italian artist Rico Lebrun and would have liked to study with him. He was an art professor at UCSB from 1960 until his death in 1964. A student and colleague of Lebrun's, Howard Warshaw, was my drawing instructor. He appointed me as an academic assistant to teach an undergrad drawing class, and I acquired a tremendous amount of skill and information about drawing.

The graduate program critiques on our works-in-progress took place bimonthly. The critique sessions analyzed our technical abilities, but the focus was on the art student's expressive content—a subjective understanding of the work's emotional message. These sessions were captivating for me since I could make a correlation between my aural and visual art.

The sessions were a great place to observe human interactions, in particular the clash of enormous egos that artists are legendary for having. Some people's self-esteem was easily punctured, and their egos were deflated; others were easily enraged and inflated.

Pauline McGeorge was a graduate student a year ahead of me. She had a great facility for drawing and would go tit-for-tat in debates with Warshaw in the critiques. Pauline was a free soul with tremendous perception; she was well-read and a true humanitarian. A few years later, she would be responsible for employing me as an art professor at a Canadian university.

The Jolly Tiger Restaurant in Santa Barbara was one of the "open-all-night" joints in town where after the gig the band would go to have our morning dose of cholesterol. It doesn't take two brain cells to figure out why, some thirty years later, I had blocked arteries and was a type 2 diabetic. When I was young, I gave little thought to the concept of my mortality and would try most anything—screw the consequences and forge ahead to the future.

We were pigging out at the Jolly Tiger early one Sunday morning when I heard a familiar voice call out my name. Mort Weiss walked into the restaurant. I hadn't seen him since we'd met in New York ten years before. He was in town with a band. It would be thirty-eight years before I heard about Mort again. In 2003, I bought a CD of his quartet. It included Mort on clarinet, a guitar man, and a drummer and the swinging Hammond B3 Organ player, Joey DeFrancesco.

In late 1965, Doug returned to Santa Barbara. He was no longer playing drums; he'd become a full-time cinema photographer, doing documentaries for Rex Fleming Films. Doug had been back to Minneapolis and had married. His wife, Carol, had sat in front of me in a design class at the Minneapolis School of Art. So many people reappear at different times and places in my life. These occasions are like marks on concentric circles that line up without appearing at the same point in the time-space continuum. Is the miraculous journey of life predestined by some unseen mystical force or is it the result of unintentional circumstances?

Doug seemed to have his act together; he was totally committed to his photography and his new married life. Somewhere from my subconscious mind, thoughts began to clamber around about my lifestyle—and my old haunt of finding success and self-worth was again questioned. I was almost thirty and had set a course for my upcoming journey. I had found a measure of fulfillment in the music and art I was experiencing, but something was missing in my life.

I was soon to find out what it was.

I love ice cream. I've always loved ice cream. As I write this, I dream of ice cream. I dare not have any since I'm a diabetic. Years ago, I made a promise to myself. Each day, I remind myself of that promise—no more of that sugar cholesterol delight!

Before I imposed my abstinence from ice cream, McConnell's Ice Cream Parlor in Santa Barbara was my Shangri-La. When I discovered chocolate pistachio nut, it was love at first bite. I was hooked. I would make frequent trips to buy chocolate pistachio nut ice cream by the gallon. And I ate it by the gallon too.

On a beautiful fall afternoon, I stopped at the ice cream shop to get my usual crème glacée. I was met at the counter by the most gorgeous brown eyes, long, shining dark chocolate-brown hair, and a delightfully lovely smile.

The young lady said, "Can I help you?"

It was love at first sight. I was hooked. Trying to control my rapture, I said, "I'll have one of each." One of my clever corny attempts at being amusing came out of my mouth before I could think of anything intelligent to say. I composed myself long enough to order a gallon of ice cream and a double cone so I could hang around a little longer and enjoy the beautiful view.

In that moment, I knew what I was missing in life—love. Love, that potent sensation, is more mind-altering than any drug. Love, the top of the human emotional scale, is rivaled only by hate and pain. Love, in its copious configurations, had smitten me. I was flabbergasted, tongue-tied, and enamored. I did not have the courage to do anything but leave—and that's what I did.

I spent a week pondering how I could introduce myself and ask her for a date without being intrusive. I had no one to introduce us; it was all up to me. Doug and Carol had asked me if I wanted to see a movie that was playing in town. It was a solution to asking my ice cream dream girl for a date. It would be the perfect ploy. She would probably feel more comfortable going on a first date with another couple.

I hatched my plan. As I approached the ice cream parlor, I felt self-assured, knowing that my rehearsed plan would go well without the use of corny clichés.

"I'll have a double chocolate pistachio nut cone."

"You want just a double cone? No gallon?"

"Just a cone. I've a gallon at home." It was encouraging that she remembered what I had ordered before. I extended my hand and said, "I'm Herb."

"Hi," she said in a low soft voice, putting her hand in mine. "I'm Claudia."

We were people of few words—but great passion.

I'm usually poor at remembering names, but I paid particular attention to her name and never forgot it.

Her name was Miss Claudia Otto, but it would change in six months to Mrs. Claudia Hicks. We were engaged on Valentine's Day in 1966 and married in a Unitarian Church in Santa Barbara on April 2.

Claudia had an unusual pet—a four-and-a-half-foot iguana that she had raised since it was a hatchling. It was a magnificent creature with a name that matched. Claudia had spent over six years taming Lord Gabriel Stewart Michael. I was amazed by the iguana's responses to Claudia's commands. The lizard couldn't be called intelligent, but it was conditioned to certain commands. I once had a pet bull snake, but it was as dumb as mud; reptiles really were not my choice of pets.

Claudia could put it over her shoulder and walk around with it sitting there seemingly contented until it signaled it had enough handling. That signal was displayed by extending its dewlap (a fan-shaped flap of skin under its jaw), doing head bobs, or twitching its tail; these signs of aggression meant the iguana was ready to defend itself. Michael would display these features whenever I would try to pick it up; I left the handling to Claudia.

The reptile was the perfect art model; it would freeze in a pose for hours. It was a stunning creature with exotic colors of bright green, yellow, blue, and brown and an elongated reptilian prehistoric-like form that conjured up images of dinosaurs. The reptile was intimidating and had a remarkable arsenal of weapons. Its mouth had sharp teeth, a row of sharp dorsal spines that ran from head to tail, long, sharp claws, and a powerful whip-like tail used for defense that could become detached if grabbed by a predator (which it could regenerate).

It was an herbivore; one of its favorite foods was nasturtium flowers, which Claudia grew in our garden. The iguana is referred to as "the chicken of the trees" in Latin America; in some places, it is cooked and eaten. If you order a chicken taco in South America, ask if it is chicken or iguana.

On our honeymoon, we headed up the California coast to San Francisco in Claudia's little Austin-Healey 100. That Healey 100 was no comparison to the 3000 model Bob had owned, but it could get up and go. We thought it would be easier to get around San Francisco in it than my old Ford station wagon.

We got as far as San Jose before we had major car trouble (a repeat of my love-hate relationship with autos). It would take mega bucks and almost a week for repairs. I phoned Bob in Santa Barbara and told him of our dilemma, asking if he could wire some money to us at our motel (I still didn't use credit cards). Bob said he would wire money right away—and suggested that I call an acquaintance of ours from North Dakota who lived near San Jose. I didn't know the person that well, but I thought I'd give him a call anyway just to say hello from Bob. I was surprised when he sounded glad to hear from me. When he asked what we were doing in San Jose, I told him of our predicament. He insisted that we come to dinner at his house. He was a deputy sheriff for a county near San Jose.

He picked us up at the motel in his squad car and drove us to his home to meet his wife and have dinner. The minute we walked in the door, I had an uneasy feeling. This was nothing new for me; I've always felt uncomfortable when meeting someone new or being in an unfamiliar situation. Maybe being in the presence of a law officer made me feel uneasy.

I soon remembered who the deputy was. He was the younger brother of a boyhood acquaintance of mine who I'd gotten into a fight with and somehow managed to break his little finger. I wondered if the deputy remembered this. Throughout dinner, this thought gnawed at my conscience. I guess I still felt some guilt about the kid running home in tears with his broken finger. Maybe it was time for a reprisal by the law, but the younger brother made no mention of it. I didn't relax until we were back to our motel.

San Jose is home to the Rosicrucian Egyptian Museum. When I was an undergrad at the Minneapolis School of Art, I became interested in Etruscan and Egyptian art and culture. When we found out about the museum, we were thrilled to be able to visit its spectacular displays. The Rosicrucian Order is a system of metaphysical studies; it has roots in mystery traditions, philosophy, and myths of ancient Egypt that date back to 1500 BC. The Ancient Mystical Order *Rosae Crucis* (AMORC)) is not a religion but a study of self-improvement. The name Rosicrucian first appeared in 1598 in Germany; the name derived from *rosa* (a rose) and *crux* (a cross). One of my favorite jazz musicians, Sonny Rollins, is a Rosicrucian; if AMORC is a system of self-improvement, Rollins is a prime example of its realization.

Claudia and I spent several days at the museum, impressed by the marvelous Egyptian artifacts, the mummified bodies, and tableaus of ancient Egypt. I scrutinized every display like a crime-scene investigator, and my reaction to the museum display was exhilarating and hard to explain. I don't know if one could call it spiritual, metaphysical, otherworldly—or if my overactive imagination tripped me off to some cerebral fantasy. It wasn't the first time I'd had that perception—and it would not be the last. I also had that sensation when I viewed the King Tut exhibit and when I was excavating fossils. The bizarre feeling occurred when I was in a serious car accident, had a heart attack, and during other stressful or transcendent experiences. It has happened to me since I was about ten—and I've never gotten a handle on it.

Albert Einstein once wrote, "The most beautiful and most profound experience is the sensation of the mystical. It is the sower of all true science. He to whom this emotion is a stranger, who can no longer wonder and stand rapt in awe, is as good as dead."

Back in Santa Barbara, I continued my studies at the university and played gigs on weekends. Claudia took a job as a bookkeeper for Firestone Company. She was good with figures and financial matters—the opposite of me. We put a lot of time into our little house on Gillespie Street, renovating, doing repairs, and grooming our little yard, which had some very productive orange and avocado trees.

We both loved nature and traveling and decided to take a trip to North Dakota. Claudia and my parents had not met, and this was a chance for them to get acquainted. When the spring semester ended in June, we planned to take our trip—traveling routes I had been over a number of times before.

With our station wagon packed with gear, we headed for Las Vegas. After a couple of nights in Vegas, we traveled to Salt Lake and headed west for Yellowstone Park. At the Little Big Horn battle site in Montana, we spent the day exploring the famous battlefield where the Seventh Cavalry and General George Custer made their last stand in the Great Sioux War of 1876. The only survivor of Custer's regiment was a mixed breed Morgan-Mustang horse called Comanche.

Claudia had never traveled outside of California. Since I was familiar with the country and history of the northwestern part of the United States, I acted as tour guide. As a boy, I was interested in the history of the northwestern plains and had spent many hours roaming the Dakota/Montana prairies looking for Native American archaeological items. I found a number of artifacts and built an interesting collection—only to have it taken by a thief.

After wandering around the Little Bighorn site in Montana, we took off for South Dakota.

I remember my first visit to South Dakota in 1939. I was six; my mom, dad, and I went on a camping/fishing trip to the Black Hills. We had a huge heavy green cotton duck canvas tent that looked like an army tent with its sloping, peaked roof and enough room for a dozen troopers to stand up in. Dad had a mixture of oils and turpentine that he used to soak the canvas with to make it waterproof. I loved its pungent odor, which I can recall at any time and experience some of the most memorable camping outings of my childhood. On this camping trip, my dad and I were introduced to fly fishing.

We chose a campsite where we could view Mount Rushmore. In 1939, the sculpting of Mount Rushmore's sixty-foot granite portraits of four presidents was not yet finished. I was privileged to see this amazing historic event taking shape before my eyes. I watched with binoculars as the workmen, hanging from sling chairs on the face of the mountain, chiseled and blasted out the features of the four presidents' heads. It was almost as though the portraits were just below the surface—and all the workmen had to do was remove the unwanted rock to expose the features.

When I was a student at the Minneapolis Art School, I tried my hand at stone carving. I soon found out that sculpting using the subtractive carving method was not for me. If I chiseled off part of a nose, I couldn't add it back on; instead, I had to carve every part of the stone down to have enough material to shape the nose again. I enjoyed the additive/subtractive method of modeling with clay and was more successful with that. I have a deep admiration for stone sculptors and stand in awe of a work like Michelangelo's masterpiece, *David*. If Michelangelo's deft chisel would have slipped—*David* might have been circumcised.

When we arrived at Mount Rushmore June 1966, viewing the finished sculpture from what I had seen twenty-seven years earlier was beyond belief. On the face of Mount Rushmore the giant portraits of George Washington, Thomas Jefferson, Theodore Roosevelt, and Abraham Lincoln, facing toward the southeast, were suffused by the afternoon summer sun; the emotional impact was incredible. It was hard to comprehend the massiveness of scale of this monument.

The information center supplied us with answers to our many questions about the sculpture. Mount Rushmore is a 5,725-foot-high mountain with a granite cliff near the top where the six-story-high heads are carved. The sculptor with this grand vision was Gutzon Borglum; he employed four hundred workmen to sculpt this enormous sculpture. The carving began in 1927 and was finished in 1941.

We stayed for two days in historic Deadwood, South Dakota. We visited the barroom where Wild Bill Hickok was gunned down while holding aces and eights, known thereafter as the dead man's hand. After visiting the Badlands of North Dakota, Claudia and I arrived in Williston to the delight of my parents. We spent a busy month in North Dakota, visited friends and relatives, and then headed back to California.

In the fall of 1966, I taught a drawing class and a basic design class to undergrad art students. Along with painting classes, I was studying printmaking and loved the intaglio process. I made numerous etchings and would spend late nights, sometimes all night, at the university printmaking studios drawing, inking, and printing plates. The medium lent itself to discover a wide range of shades from the depths of penetrating blacks to opulent grays.

My interest in my work, at this time, was the human figure. I was inspired by themes from classics in literature, works that had a disconsolate side resembling Dante's *Inferno*, Homer's *The Iliad*, and the ferocious images by contemporary artists, such as Picasso and de Kooning. I was also interested in Egyptian and Greek mythology and did a series of prints based on those themes. Anthropomorphic images showed up in my drawings, paintings, and prints at the time.

During the winter of 1966, I did a suite of small prints. *Series from a Generation of Vipers* was influenced by Philip Wylie's book *Generation of Vipers*, which was an attack on the complacencies of the American way of life. Written in 1943, it is equally relevant today. The book's title is from the Bible; in Matthew 23:33, Jesus talks about a generation of vipers, referring to teachers who give false information. After an exhibit of these works at the Faulkner Art Gallery in Santa Barbara, I received a review from an art critic who said they were beautifully morbid; the paradox in that critic's response was very perceptive.

Humanity and the forces of nature have been the two main themes in my art. My work has been critiqued as being understood, not understood, and misunderstood. For a spectator to admit to understanding a work is admirable; to admit to not understanding a work is also admirable. But to misunderstand and misinterpret a work is a misfortune.

In June 1967, I received my master of fine arts degree from the University of California, Santa Barbara. I immediately began searching for employment. I was excited to know that Claudia was pregnant; we were expecting our first child in September. I was overjoyed in anticipation of our new beginnings as a family.

On September 1, 1967, a beautiful baby girl came into our lives. She was the first of my three wonderful children. Tucked away in my memories is every sound, sight, and impression of that gorgeous fall day as I made my way to Cottage Hospital. Our doctor told me we had a beautiful baby girl with all the necessary parts in all the right places. I thought this was a peculiar observation; why wouldn't she have all the parts?

I looked through the nursery window at this tiny person wrapped in a blanket in a tiny bed with a sign above it that read "Hicks" and some other information I couldn't focus on. She was fast asleep and looked so peaceful and content that my urge to tap on the window was suppressed; I just stood and looked at her in wonder.

We chose the name Joanne Marie for our beautiful daughter. The name had a beautiful rhythmical sound to it; it was like music to me.

Without a doubt, our purpose in life focused on our little daughter. Joanne seemed to be allergic to every formula of milk we tried. Our nights were filled with woe as we tried to soothe our little girl's colic affliction. We sang to her, rubbed her tiny aching tummy, and walked the floor with her over a shoulder, gently urging up a burp. We drove around Santa Barbara at night with Joanne cradled in Claudia's arms, rocking to the rhythm of the moving vehicle. We dedicated ourselves to comforting our baby daughter. When we found a formula of milk that agreed with Joanne, everyone began to get some sleep at night.

Every day, our little girl became more aware of her surroundings, and she impressed us with her pointing and reaching for things as her eyes focused on us and everything around her. Her smiles, gurgles, and bubbles were charming antics, and her waving of arms and kicking of legs were delightful gymnastics. She would attentively listen to my voice as I told her fantastic tales and read stories to her.

I sent out hundreds of applications after graduation, but I only heard from a couple of junior colleges. The positions were mainly in English or history—with a possibility of teaching an art class. There were countless applicants in the teaching job market in the late sixties, and funding cuts to universities were prevalent. Getting hired was a ride on a merry-go-round; you can't find a job if you have no experience, and you can't get experience if you haven't had a job.

In November, I received a phone call from Pauline McGeorge. She said, "Hi, Herb, remember me? I was in the master's painting class at UCSB."

"Indeed I do remember you, Pauline."

"I'm calling you from Canada. I'm the chairperson of the Art Department of a new university in Alberta. I was in touch with UCSB and saw you had graduated with your master of fine arts degree this summer. I was wondering if you were looking for a teaching job."

"Yes, I am," I said enthusiastically.

The University of Lethbridge, Canada's newest Centennial University, was hiring professors—and had an opening for an art professor. They needed someone to teach a basic design course, a painting course, and a drawing course to help develop the department's art curriculum. She knew I had taught these courses at UCSB. Canada had a lack of MFA graduates, and the few who had applied were not interested after looking at the university's lack of facilities. American candidates were next on the list for finding new professors.

"If you're interested in the position, we could fly you up here so we can take a look at one another."

Interested? Of course I was interested. Finally, a possibility for a university art teaching position. She told me that time was of the essence; they wanted to make a decision by December 1 at the latest. The appointment would start in January.

Claudia and I talked about the possibility of moving to Canada, and I returned Pauline's call with an affirmative answer. Within the next couple of days, the University of Lethbridge made arrangements for me to fly to Calgary and then to Lethbridge.

Stepping off the plane at the Lethbridge airport, I was met with a ferocious wind. Surprisingly the temperature was not that cold—colder than Santa Barbara, but somewhat warmer than November in North Dakota. It was my first encounter with a weather phenomenon known as the Chinook wind.

I was welcomed by the newest member of the art department; Mac Gimse was a sculptor. The department consisted of Pauline and Mac. I was surprised to learn that Mac was born and raised in Minot, North Dakota. We hit it off from the very beginning, and I was amazed to learn that Mac had gone to Minot High School with a musician friend of mine. Another fortuitous event played a part in my life's drama.

The university was temporarily located on the Lethbridge College Campus and used some of the science building classrooms for art studios. They were small and had poor lighting, far from an ideal situation for art studios. Mac and Pauline had the arduous job of handling a curriculum for a department that consisted of two professors and inadequate classroom space. They were in dire need of studio space and a couple more faculty members.

At first, I was not too impressed with what this new university and art department had to offer, but I was impressed with the tenacity that Pauline and Mac displayed in getting an art curriculum up and running. They explained their ideas for building a reputable university art department. It sounded great, but how was it going to happen? They said the government of Alberta had funds to support a new university—in capital and operating funding.

I asked, "What about studios? Won't it take a few years before studios can be built?"

Mac invited me to come on a little tour of a structure known locally as the Old Fort Whoop-up Building, the Fort, and the Barn.

On the edge of the junior college campus, next to fenced pastures that held grazing horses and cattle, was a magnificent huge building that had been used as a roller skating rink, a farm show exhibition arena, and a dance hall. Mac turned the key, unlocked the Fort, and invited me in. I looked at the floor to see where I was stepping and saw a thick carpet of dead flies. The building hadn't been used for a number of years, and a zillion flies from the neighboring pastures had found their final resting places on this vast floor. I dubbed the building, "The Floor of Flies."

Getting past the initial shock of the floor covering, I was taken aback by the enormous open space. Like an airport hangar, the interior was open. There were no floor-to-ceiling posts; instead, huge beamed trusses crossed the width of the building about thirty feet up, along the ceiling. It was a delightful space. I scanned the far end of the building, which seemed miles away, and turned my eyes toward the enormous ceiling.

Mac said, "We are negotiating with the university to rent this building for art department studios."

I said, "That would be fantastic."

A little over a week later, back in Santa Barbara, I received a phone call from Pauline. If I wanted the position, it was mine. I would start as an assistant professor in January 1968. She also said the university had approved the use of the Fort to house the Art Department.

"That's fantastic," I replied.

It was a thankful 1967 Thanksgiving for our family.

Chapter 13

LA North

We had a month to settle our affairs in California. We packed our possessions (house and studio), made a trip to the Canadian Consulate in Los Angeles for an interview, and obtained the required documents for immigrant status in Canada.

Pauline informed us that finding houses for rent in Lethbridge was impossible, but there were some older homes on the market at reasonable prices. With some help from my parents and Claudia's father, we made a down payment on a house—sight unseen.

I planned to drive our Chevy station wagon to Canada, transporting Michael (our iguana) and Bruce (Pauline's teenage son), who I would pick up in Sacramento where he was living with his dad. Pauline asked if I would give him a ride to Canada since he was going to live with her.

Claudia and Joanne would stay in Santa Barbara with Claudia's mom until December, and I would meet them at my parents' place for Christmas. At the beginning of the New Year we'd head for Lethbridge, Alberta—or as some local residents refer to it as "L. A."

Having grown up in North Dakota, I knew the dangers of winter travel. I prepared myself and the station wagon with whatever emergency items I thought I'd need. I anticipated there would be some rough winter roads, and I purchased tire chains.

I had built a large glass-sided cage that fit in the back of the station wagon to carry our huge iguana. Hooking up a hose from the Chevy's heater vent, I ran it to the back of Michael's cage to provide him with heat. At overnight motel stops, we'd have to unload the iguana—and his cage—and bring him inside to keep him warm.

After picking up Bruce in Sacramento, we headed for Nevada. A massive storm closed Donner Pass in the Sierra Nevada Mountains to travelers without tire chains. While putting on the chains, memories of winters past came flooding back to me. This familiar scene of freezing feet, fingers, ears, and nose was reminiscent of my winter days as a youth in North Dakota. Two more times on our trip, we had to go through the freezing task of putting on tire chains.

At the border crossing of Sweetgrass, Montana, and Coutts, Alberta, Bruce and I provided the customs officers with all the necessary documents for immigration to Canada. A customs officer asked about the pet I was bringing into the country—and if I had a health certificate for it. I said it was in the car.

The officer wanted to see the document and the animal. I told him if he wanted to see the iguana, he could follow me to the car. I'd left it running to keep the animal warm in its cage. I don't think the officer knew what an iguana was, but he was about to find out.

I took the health certificate out of the glove compartment and handed it to him. I opened the back door and lifted the top of Michael's cage.

"Oh, wow! What a beast!" the officer exclaimed. "Okay, come back into the office with me." He still had the health certificate in his hand. As we entered the customs office, he handed the paper to a colleague and said he wanted him to check out the health of an iguana.

The colleague asked, "An iguana? Isn't that some kind of tropical bird?"

The three of us trudged back through the snow to the station wagon. I opened the door, and Bruce asked what the holdup was. I told him another officer had to check out Michael.

"Michael? That's the name of your pet?" asked the officer.

I lifted the top of the cage again; Michael was in his four-foot regal glory. Agitated by the movement of his cage being opened again, he began head bobbing with his dewlap fully extended, his spines bristling. He was raised up on all fours with a claw extended over his water bowl; he looked like a ferocious mythological dragon.

"Michael looks damn healthy to me," said the examining officer.

To and from Gigs

The other officer burst out laughing—and we were on our way to Lethbridge.

I delivered Bruce and Michael to Pauline's house in Lethbridge. Pauline and her son were happy to be reunited, and we got Michael and his cage situated on a table in the front room. Pauline, her two daughters, two sons, and a large German shepherd all pressed their noses against the glass cage, observing the large iguana as it bobbed its head as if to say, "Hola."

Driving to North Dakota the next morning, I was faced with more snow and icy roads. Twelve hours later, I arrived safely in Williston. My folks and I spent the next couple of days getting ready for Christmas and waiting for Claudia and Joanne to fly in from California.

There was a lot of snow on the day the plane was due from Great Falls, the last leg of the journey from California. As I waited at the airport with my parents, I was somewhat worried. The flight was late due to weather conditions, but when it finally arrived, the weather was looking good. The sun was peeking out from the steel-gray clouds. My anxieties left me as I watched the aircraft taxi up to the deplaning area. It slowly came to a stop, and a crewman pushed and positioned a moveable metal staircase up to the aircraft's passenger door. My folks and I were excited to see Joanne and Claudia; it would be the grandparents' first meeting with their granddaughter.

The door opened, and Claudia was the first passenger to disembark. She was cradling our three-and-a-half-month-old daughter. Claudia took a step onto the ice-covered metal stairway. In disbelief, I watched as she—with Joanne in her arms—slipped and fell from the top step, tumbling down the stairway and onto the frozen tarmac.

I shoved people out of my way and pushed open the door to the runway. I faintly heard someone hollering that I couldn't go out there.

I yelled back, "The hell I can't. That's my wife and child that just fell out of that plane." I reached out to Claudia and Joanne as they moaned and cried on the cold pavement.

Claudia's knees and elbows were scraped and bleeding from trying to protect Joanne from the fall. Joanne had a large bump on her forehead.

My mom and dad were right behind me, and the three of us helped Joanne and Claudia up off the pavement. Dad scooped up a handful of snow to put on Joanne's bump and said he'd bring the car around and we'd get to the hospital.

On the way to the hospital, Mom said, "Where in God's name was the airline stewardess?"

Everything checked out okay at the hospital; there was no trauma to Joanne's head injury, and Claudia's lacerations were treated and dressed. After getting everyone settled at home, I returned to the airport to pick up my wife's luggage. The Williston airport, in the sixties, was relatively small with limited hours of operation. By the time I arrived at the terminal, it was closed. I would have to pick up the baggage the next day. It was probably for the best since I was filled with anger. I wanted to talk with someone in charge at the airport and confront the negligent stewardess.

In January, Claudia, Joanne, and I headed to our new home in Canada. We were admitted at the Canadian border with landed immigrant status. As we crossed the border, it began to snow, the wind picked up, and the temperature dropped rapidly. Within a few minutes, we were engulfed in a full-blown blizzard. Visibility was zero; it was a complete whiteout. The snow was blowing horizontally as we inched our way along the highway. Claudia, with her head pressed against the window, was trying to give me instructions about how close I was to the edge of the road and the ditch. After an agonizing half hour of struggling at a snail's pace along the snow-blown highway, we saw a sign announcing a town ahead of us. We could just make out the dim lights of the village through the swirling snow. I drove into the town's center.

We were relieved to see an old hotel and bar sign glowing in the snowstorm. There were a few pickup trucks parked in front of the hotel. I pulled the station wagon into a parking space as close as I could to the front door and ran inside to book a room.

Behind the counter with a bell and a shelf of mailboxes, a door led to the bar. I could hear loud voices. Nobody was present, and I rang the bell again and again. No answer. I pushed open the door to the bar, and the familiar odor of stale beer and smoke hit me. I asked the bartender if someone could book me a room. He said he would find someone. I ran back out to the station wagon to let Claudia know what was happening. Joanne was fast asleep, and Claudia said they would wait in the warm car until I had booked the room.

When somebody took care of the registration for the room, I went to get my wife and daughter. The storm was still raging when I opened the back of the station wagon to get our luggage. We climbed the stairs to the second floor and found our sparsely furnished room. The room was lit by a single bulb hanging from the ceiling, but it was warm—with a bed. We were thankful to find shelter from our first Canadian snowstorm.

I returned to the station wagon to retrieve another piece of luggage. When I went around to the back of the car, I saw that someone had collided with the back of the station wagon, crumpling the tailgate. It couldn't be opened. Cursing the hit-and-run accident, I got our luggage out the side door and stomped up to our room. I told Claudia what had happened and went to the lobby to call the police.

I told the hotel clerk what had happened and asked if he would call the cops. Within a short time, an RCMP patrol car pulled up in front of the hotel. I told the officer what had happened and showed him my smashed tailgate. He looked at the damage and began writing a report while we sat in his patrol car.

"California license plates, eh? You're a long ways from home. What are you doing in this part of the world?"

I told him how we were on our way to Lethbridge where I would be teaching at the university. I had given him my California driver's license and car registration, which he was inspecting.

He asked if we had any other identification.

I said I had all our immigration papers in the glove compartment. He said he wanted to see them.

I began to feel intimated by his questions and wondered why I was being treated with such suspicion. I guess it's the nature of law enforcement officers to be suspicious; it keeps them on their toes.

I asked him about finding the hit-and-run vehicle and driver. He said it would be next to impossible, but if something came up, I'd be contacted (I never was). I exited the patrol car.

The officer did a quick U-turn, and sped down the snow-covered street, his taillights disappearing with each swirl of snow.

I stood in the street for a moment. The wind had subsided, and the snow was falling in a gentle pattern. I was blanketed in a grayish-white world. I noticed the beauty mixed with the harshness of winter. Memories of my winters as a youth came rushing back to me.

Welcome back to the Great White North.

We arrived in Lethbridge the next afternoon and found the house we had bought. It was in an older neighborhood, and there were only about ten feet between the houses. The old two-story house had a fireplace and was cozy and warm.

After unpacking the station wagon, we made a bed out of our sleeping bags on the front room's hardwood floor with a place for Joanne beside us. The house had a stove and refrigerator. We had no furniture; the moving company that was supposed to have arrived ahead of us from Santa Barbara would be about a week late. We had a large cooler with food for our journey from North Dakota, which my folks had packed. True to their fashion, it was filled with enough food and drink to take us through a winter in Alaska.

Joanne, Claudia, and I huddled around our little campsite in our living room and devoured some of the delicious food from our cooler. The low January sun was already disappearing in the west; for the first time in days, I gave a sigh of relief to have finally arrived at our Canadian home. My belly full of good food—and my wife and child beside me—I huddled down for a long winter night's sleep.

The next morning, we were up early, eager to begin our new life in Canada. Full of vigor for the day's activities, I began by making a list, which was my habitual routine. My list was long; I had to purchase groceries, a few cooking utensils, some picnic paper plates, and silverware. We could camp out—or camp in, as the case was—until our furnishings arrived from California. We planned to go to Pauline's house to pick up the iguana. We'd bring Pauline a bottle of wine and get one for ourselves to celebrate our new home.

We bundled up against the January weather and headed for the downtown district to look for a grocery store. Only a few cars were on the streets that Sunday morning. We pulled into a grocery store's parking lot, and it was empty except for large shoveled snow piles. Walking up to the door of the grocery store I saw the sign: *Closed Sundays.* Alberta had similar Sunday laws as North Dakota. Claudia, living in California all her life, where so many businesses are open twenty-four-seven thought it was very strange. As we continued our search for open stores, I reminded myself I should have expected as much since we were back in an ultra-conservative Bible Belt community.

Not able to find anything open, we decided to pick up Michael at Pauline's and ask her if she knew of anything that was open.

Pauline was delighted to see that we had made the trip safely. We asked her about open stores.

She laughed and said, "Well, you won't find any stores open on Sunday. You're not in California anymore."

I told her I was familiar with this situation; the puritan blue laws in North Dakota prohibited anyone from working on Sundays.

The Sunday closing law in Alberta, known as the Lord's Day Act, was implemented in 1906. In 1985, the Supreme Court of Canada declared the law unconstitutional as it violated the Canadian Charter of Rights and Freedoms. Today, a dozen or so years into the twenty-first century, we still have those who would infringe their beliefs unto everyone by bringing the Lord's Day Act back into law.

On Monday morning, we went to a grocery store, purchased our supply of food—but we couldn't find any wine. When I asked the clerk where the wine section was, she looked at us like we were from another planet.

"Grocery stores don't sell liquor. You'll have to go to an Alberta Liquor Control Board (ALCB) outlet." Since 1924, the Alberta government has run the liquor stores.

The ALCB had complete control over liquor sales and the conditions under which they were sold. They firmly controlled the beer parlors, which were divided into sections—one side for men and one side for ladies with escorts. It wasn't until 1967 that the bars could be used together by men and women without escorts. In 1993, the first private liquor retailers opened. The law went so far as to state that airplanes flying over the province of Alberta on Sunday could not serve any alcoholic beverages in that airspace. I wonder how the authorities policed that policy.

We felt like we'd journeyed back in time, landing in some puritan state where people were suspicious of pleasure. We questioned our decision in making this move north. Considering the severity of the weather, the antiquated laws, the remoteness from contemporary culture, and my old paranoia, fear of the unfamiliar crept into our assessment. We seriously questioned this major transition we were experiencing.

I would be remiss not to mention a number of the positive aspects about our move, such as the low-key hustle and bustle of a smaller community, the relatively clean environment (water, air, and streets), the beauty of the wilderness of the nearby Rockies, the amity of some people we'd met, and the opportunity to be a founding member of a new art department in a new university with a full-time teaching position.

Since the spring semester would begin in February, we had about a month to remodel the skating rink building, which was called the Fort in reference to nearby Fort Hamilton. Established in 1869, it later became known as Fort Whoop-Up. It was a trading post known for its illegal whisky sales.

Fort Whoop-Up was located at the junction of the Oldman River and the St. Mary's River on a bull train trail leading from Montana to Alberta. It is speculation that the trail became known as the Whoop-up Trail because a bull whacker driving the bull train would walk alongside the wagons, cracking his whip to get the team moving was called "whooping them up." It is also suspected that the name had an association with the whisky trade at the fort.

In the seventies, I visited the commemorative plaque on the top of a coulee that marked and pointed to the original site of Fort Whoop-Up in the river valley below. As I stood there envisioning the Fort of the late 1800s, a car of tourists pulled into the parking area and began questioning me about the Fort. They were interested in Indian arrowheads and asked me if there were any artifacts to be found in this area. I told them I didn't know—but it was a possibility.

After they drove away, I started walking along the top of the hill. Looking to where I was stepping, I saw a large stone hammer head, half buried in the prairie soil. I couldn't believe my eyes and my luck in the discovery of this unique artifact. I dug it the rest of the way out of the ground and retrieved a beautiful large stone mallet with a neatly chiseled groove around its circumference where there had probably once been a handle attached. Finding an Indian artifact was a *possibility*.

The remodeling of the roller rink building was left to the three members of the art staff and one student assistant. Mac, Pauline, Garry, and I had our work cut out for us. Garry had moved from northern Alberta to southern Alberta to obtain an art education degree. He was an energetic, creative person with a great sense of humor and the same pioneering spirit as us three faculty members.

Coming from parallel backgrounds of growing up with the outdoors, hunting, fishing, cold winters, and hot summers in the northland where hard work just to survive was no stranger, Garry and I found a common bond. I have been good friends with Garry and his wife for forty years.

I've had many delightful meals with the Shillidays. In the early 2000s, my son, Allan, was visiting me from Seattle. Garry and Arlene invited us over for dinner. We were served an appetizing pot roast.

Carving off juicy slabs of meat, Garry served us generous portions. "Taste this roast and tell me what kind of meat this is."

It was the sweetest, most succulent meat I'd ever tasted. We guessed every wild and domestic meat source we could think of—from caribou to Japanese "tenderized-on-the-hoof" Kobe beef. After much tasting and guessing, Garry told us the meat was muskox.

Muskox, the Arctic Bovidae, is about four feet tall with thick, long shaggy hair that almost reaches the ground. The large, ugly head and horns—and its musky odor—makes it a peculiar animal indeed. Its ancestors were contemporaries of the woolly mammoth. Muskox survived the last ice age (Wisconsin glaciation, 26,000 to 13,300 years ago) and the hunting efforts of prehistoric people.

Garry had been on a fishing trip to the Arctic region of Canada and met hunters who had bagged a muskox. They wanted to make a trade for some fish Garry's party had caught. The trade of fish for some muskox meat was made, and we were the beneficiaries of the exchange. It's a good thing there are stringent hunting regulations concerning the muskox—and that not many people have tasted the meat—otherwise the muskox would probably go the way of the woolly mammoth.

Cleaning the Fort to ready it for renovations was a huge task since; for a number of years, it had collected dirt, flies, mice, and cobwebs. We came up with the idea of making large panels of stretched burlap—much like one would make for a large painting—and then used the panels to create temporary dividers between the studios. This gave the Fort the appearance of an open studio workshop.

We obtained large burlap bags from the local Sheep Growers Association. Cutting the sacks into huge strips, we stretched the burlap on three-by-seven-foot frames. Fire regulations demanded that the burlap be fireproofed, and Garry spent many hours soaking the burlap with a fire retardant. The panels worked great by hooking them together in a zigzag design for the construction of the walls. The dividers gave the studios some privacy and could easily be moved to change the studio's size and location.

Garry and I were resolute in our undertaking to transform the Fort into art studios. We were at best "jackknife carpenters," but managed to get the renovations done through on-the-job training. We measured once and cut twice, which happened now and then, giving us a good laugh. When one has a goal in mind, without the knowledge of how to obtain it, the best way to proceed is to experiment without any fear of failure. We had no fear of trying our hands at any renovations.

Many visitors checked out the art studios. On one occasion, the president of the university visited. Showing him around the Fort, we entered a studio where Pauline was teaching a nude figure drawing class.

The president froze in his tracks as we entered the studio. A nude female model was motionless in a pose for the drawing class.

Pauline looked at the president and said, "Are you here to model or to draw?"

"Neither," he answered. "Just looking."

Pauline laughed and said, "You'll have to do one or the other to be here in this classroom." She didn't miss a beat as she instructed the drawing class, and she put out one cigarette and lit up another one. She was a chain smoker who never really put her cigarette out; she smoked it down near the filter tip, stood it on its tip, and lit another. You could always tell where Pauline had been by the trail of cigarette filters standing on end. This, of course, was in the days when there were few restrictions on smoking.

The students taking art courses were a mixture of those with a little background in art to those with no exposure to art whatsoever. Lethbridge had no major galleries and only a few art programs.

The Canadian artist Dennis Burton stated, "Lethbridge was a cultural desert, with the only culture being agricultural."

It was a little exaggerated—but not far from the truth.

The Art Department had its work cut out for it. We offered studio art courses and began art history courses. We started an art gallery and a visiting artist program to expose students—and the general public—to professional artwork done by national and international artists. By the turn of the century, those offerings had grown into significant components of the university's art program.

Our early art students were thirsty for knowledge and soaked up the information like dry sponges. A large percentage of our students were brilliant and worked hard. A few were *non compos mentis*. A number of "without-the-use-of-common-sense" incidents agitated the staff.

While trying to light the gas kilns in the ceramics studio, a student turned on the burners but she didn't have a match. She looked around the department for a light, leaving the gas running. Luckily a faculty member smelled the gas and turned the jets off before we became "Fort Blew-Up."

While I was critiquing three-dimensional works with modeling clay, a student showed me a little sculpture she had made with chocolate fudge. Not only hadn't she used the material assigned to do the project, but the piece was more two dimensional then three. The fudge had been stamped out with a cookie cutter.

I told her that it was categorically kitsch.

"Oh no," she replied. "It's chocolate and quite tasty."

Is this person for real?

She reached over to get me a piece of chocolate from the sculpture and knocked a brick off the table. It landed squarely on my big toe, smashing it with a force that felt like a ton of bricks. As I hopped around in pain, the student handed me a piece of fudge and said, "Have a piece of chocolate; it'll calm you."

Another student wrote a letter to the dean complaining that the Art Department was conducting drawing classes with unclothed models. She wanted to obtain credit for figure-drawing courses by only doing still-life drawings because looking at naked people was a sin. Apparently she had never appreciated the countless nude paintings and sculptures created over the centuries by great masters of the art world.

I suggested she read Sir Kenneth Clark's *The Nude: A Study in Ideal Form* to gain some insight into the study of the human figure in art. Clark said, "The nude does not simply represent the body, but relates it, by analogy, to all structures that have become part of our imaginative experience."

Our figure-drawing courses were part of our foundation courses, training the mind to think in visual terms. Drawing from life frees the mind from self as students apply full concentration to the difficult task of finding the relationship of anatomical forms.

Our first open house and art exhibition attracted a crowd of people from the surrounding community. Mac, the department chair, made a sculpture that was based on a well-known feature of Lethbridge, the Irrigation Capital of Canada. He put together (like a giant erector set) irrigation pipes that ran the length and height of the Fort, starting at the front entrance and ending in the gallery at the far end. The pipes transformed the high, open ceiling space into a semblance of a Gothic cathedral. He piped classical music through the tubes that resounded from one end to the other in a subtle reverberation.

Mac attended the opening in tux, tails, and top hat. He promenaded through the department, asking people's opinions about the sculpture artwork.

Some replied, "What sculpture?"

Others said, "That's not art."

They could only see irrigation pipes. Mac had two pockets of candy—one held sweet candies and the other held sour grapes. If people gave him a response that was positive in any way, he'd say, "Have a sweet."

If the response was negative, he'd say, "Have a sour grape."

A whole new world of art was opened to the community.

Within a year, I was appointed art gallery director. Within two years, I was appointed chairman of the Art Department. The department was growing, and we added two new faculty members. Charlie Crane became our art historian, and Larry Weaver filled a position as ceramics/sculpture professor. The department—with five full-time faculty members and one assistant—could now offer a program that became our core for a bachelor of fine arts degree.

All the art faculty members became good friends. Besides teaching, we shared a lot of activities together. Our support for one another in our teaching and university duties was unrivaled, and our dedication to our students led to the making of some very fine alumni. The harmony we experienced facilitated the growth and success of our program in those formative years. There was no clashing of egos or professional jealousies that so often happen in career occupations. Larger corporations (and larger educational institutions) seem to breed this type of competition; they create competitive rivalries that can sometimes be disruptive to the overall operation. When treated with respect, they can help promote healthy growth. Years later, our department would experience this phenomenon.

My teaching gigs opened another approach to understanding the world. Teaching was not just the dissemination of information—as had been most of my experience as a student. I found teaching to be a great learning process for understanding the depth of a subject. To communicate the significant concepts of the subjects I taught (drawing, design, and painting), it was necessary to reexamine my knowledge of the topic and clarify that knowledge in detail. If I were to be a successful teacher, passing knowledge on to a student who was willing and able to assimilate the information, I could teach the techniques of my discipline successfully, in a methodical process, *if* I had experience with the techniques myself. I could not teach creativity in any methodical way because there is no formulation. I could motivate students toward creativeness by having them explore all possible solutions to a problem—even the most bizarre—in a search for personal expression.

All human beings—in all vocations—have an innate hunger for creativeness. For whatever reason, the need for expression can be found in naive children and sophisticated adults—from the artists that created the images in the caves of Lascaux to the artists of computer-generated images of the twenty-first century. For some, this need may be buried deep in the subconscious; for others, it may be a dominant feature of rational conscious being. We all have *it*. It's a matter of finding and recognizing the hunger—and then nourishing it. The path to becoming creative is more of an intuitive experience than a structured, logical technique.

Our development of the art gallery program was motivated by the fact that the more genuine the exposure was, the more enlightening the involvement was. If students could see art in its original form—not just secondhand through reproductions in books—or hear and see actual music performances instead of listening to a recording, their familiarity would become tangible in a way that would lead to an experience of greater appreciation, pleasure, and knowledge.

That spring and summer, we explored southern Alberta. We discovered the abrupt grandeur of the Canadian Rockies; they rose from the prairies less than a hundred miles to the west of us. Waterton Lakes National Park, a sister park to Glacier National Park in Montana, was a gorgeous place to visit with its historical Prince of Wales Hotel. The hotel was built in 1927 by the Great Northern Railway and sits high on a bluff with a spectacular view of Waterton Lake and the town of Waterton. In 1932, Waterton Lakes National Park and Glacier National Park united to form the first International Peace Park. The park symbolizes the peace and friendship between the United States and Canada. I've played many gigs in the Prince of Wales Hotel. Every time I've driven up that hill to the stately alpine-styled hotel, I'm reminded of chalets in the Swiss Alps.

On the way to Waterton, we found a lake tucked away in the foothills. For years, our visits would usually get us a nice catch of rainbow trout. Fishing that lake was a year-round adventure—from winter ice fishing to summer fly fishing. I also discovered an abundance of pheasants, grouse, and partridge around southern Alberta. Hunting and fishing, which I had missed since leaving Minnesota and North Dakota, became an option for me again.

In September, I saw, for the first time, the house that would be my home for the greater part of my life. The real estate lady took us for a short ride to a little acreage about a mile outside the city limits. Turning down a tree-lined gravel road, I couldn't help but notice a large Southern plantation-style mansion complete with manicured lawns. We turned into the next driveway and parked in a semicircle driveway that supported a covered carport.

The house was a California-style bungalow surrounded by large cottonwoods and a feature that grabbed my attention. We opened a door just off of the main entrance, and I walked into a bright art studio with north-facing windows that ran from counter height to the top of a twelve-foot ceiling. We toured the rest of the house and learned that the house had been built by a local artist who had attended Chouinard Art School in Los Angeles (a school I had once thought about attending).

Thanks to the credibility I had as a university professor, we obtained a mortgage and joined the growing ranks of mortgagors. I'm thankful we made the decision to buy this house since it has been my comfortable home for more than forty years. A man's home is his castle. I have the freedom to enjoy my diverse interests and the privilege of individual privacy. I have the good fortune to live in a country where autonomy is assured and the necessities of life are readily attainable. At the top of my wish list is for every living creature on this planet to be ensured such good fortune.

Human beings, with our superior intelligence, wealth, and technological advances have the ability to create a more humane world where all creatures are permitted their basic needs for a comfortable way of life. Of all the variables around the globe that create the differences in the distribution of wealth, greed is at the top, and it is perpetuated by white-collar criminals. The difference between the salaries of a corporate CEO and the average taxpayer is outrageous—and it is growing by leaps and bounds. The capitalist system, originally implemented to help the ordinary person work to get a reasonable share, seems to have reversed to the feudal system it was meant to replace. The riches and the power are in the hands of morally irresponsible companies and oppressive dictators. These bullies have cheated, deceived, swindled, and betrayed average citizens of their quotidian existence.

The noble thing about most nations is that people will not stand for such bullying; sooner or later (sadly usually later), they will rebel against such behavior. I'm always amazed that the human race has continued through the centuries, considering all the cruel acts we have committed against one another. The hands on the doomsday clock keep fluctuating forward and backward, putting our species in a vagarious position to that cataclysmic midnight hour. We seem to be encoded to repeat the same old crap; do we have to step in it over and over, making the same mistakes history has shown us to be detrimental? Is this a case of not using our common sense?

"A handful of common sense is worth a bushel of learning."
—Unknown

Chapter 14

Sixties' Shrapnel, Seventies' Splendor

In January 1969, Claudia, Joanne, and I took a train with friends to Shelby, Montana. We disembarked from the train in the middle of the night; the temperatures were near twenty below freezing. The Great Northern Empire Builder's coaches, lounge car, and dome car were overcrowded with disgruntled passengers—who were more than twelve hours late—arriving from the East. The passengers' cars were covered with frost and snow, and the engine, spewing out great billows of smoke and steam, was completely encased in ice. The train had the appearance of a winter scene from Boris Pasternak's *Dr. Zhivago*.

Larry Weaver, his wife, Nina, and their son Mathew (a few months older than Joanne) were on the train when we boarded at Williston. They had been traveling for a couple days as the train plowed its way from Minneapolis, delayed by one of the coldest, most brutal winter storms in decades. We had all spent the holidays at our respective parents' homes and had planned on friends meeting us at Shelby for the two-hour drive back to Lethbridge. We anticipated that our ride would not be waiting for us, considering the late hour and weather conditions.

While waiting for our baggage in the depot, we talked about trying to find overnight lodging in Shelby. A taxi driver approached us and asked where we were going. We told him we needed to get to Lethbridge, and he offered to drive us there. It had been a tiresome ride, and we were anxious to get home. We decided to take the expensive taxi trip home.

We crammed into the taxicab—four adults, two small children, and our luggage—and head for Canada. When we arrived at the border crossing, the guard couldn't believe we were taking a taxi from Montana to Alberta. After he asked us where we lived, we were waved on through the border.

Not having the experience (or the fortitude) to deal with the harshness of Canadian winters can bend one's psychological outlook to the point of depression. I saw that strain in Claudia around the end of January. It was more than just the winter blues. I had the feeling we were drifting apart; we had different views on what paths our lives should take. She had been invited to spend some time with her older sister in Palo Alto, California, and she and Joanne could get away from the winter for a while.

I saw the handwriting on the wall; when I took them to the Calgary airport, I sensed this was the beginning of the end. I played the hand I was dealt and threw myself into my work. I made two big mistakes: working too hard at making a living without working hard enough at living, and letting my wife become influenced by her sister's viewpoints. By spring, we had drifted apart. We separated and divorced. Claudia and Joanne moved back to the States, became involved with other people, and ended up in Baltimore. Even though we remained friends, we were worlds apart.

Although I wasn't living in the States in 1969, I was well aware of the problems that plagued America: the Vietnam War, the assassination of Reverend Martin Luther King (April 4, 1968), and the assassinations of Senator Robert Kennedy (June 5, 1968) and President John F. Kennedy (November 22, 1963). The civil unrest and riots that were happening in my homeland disturbed and shamed me as an American.

One of my friends said, "Thank God that violent civil disobedience doesn't happen in Canada."

Civil disobedience, like the wind, can blow across borders. During the 1970 October Crisis the *Front de liberation du Quebec* (FLQ) caused bombings and riots in the Montreal area, and kidnapped

Quebec's minister of labour. They killed Pierre Laporte on October 17, 1970. No nation is immune to the rebellion of civilians. Their guilt or innocence is weighed by classification—revolutionist or terrorist.

In August 1969, Bob, Ev, and Tiber, visited me from Oakland. Bob was working on his BFA degree at the California College of Arts and Crafts, and Ev was doing her nursing gig at the Oakland Kaiser Medical Center. My mom and dad came for a visit, and we all went to Westcastle to fish, camp, and enjoy the mountain wilderness.

Enjoying the grandeur of the wilderness areas of Westcastle with my family was part of a remedy I needed for the despairs I had accumulated during the sixties. Those swinging, groovy sixties brought some heavy issues—from changes of residence, employment, and lifestyle to change of marital status and a number of smaller issues. The other part of my prescription for relaxing was a return to doing music gigs; at times, they were more like digressions than therapy.

At the end of their August visit, Bob and Ev took Tiber to the vet to get him a tranquilizer shot for the plane trip. I drove them to Great Falls so they could catch an early flight to San Francisco. Great Falls was having a large convention, and no motel rooms were available. We were desperate to find accommodations, and the dog was getting dizzy from the tranquilizer. One motel owner suggested we try a certain hotel. He called the hotel for us, and they had a vacancy.

It was getting late when we arrived at the hotel. I went in to register. The hotel clerk asked how many guests, I said, "Three—plus a large dog."

He paused, shook his head, and said, "Sorry. No pets allowed."

"No pets?"

"No pets!"

"This dog is not a pet. It's a seeing-eye dog," I quickly replied.

"Oh," he said. "That's different; we can make an exception for a seeing-eye dog."

To confirm my fib and ease the clerk's suspicions I added, "My blind brother has a seeing-eye shepherd."

I signed the hotel register, went back to the car, and explained the situation to Bob and Ev. I told Bob, "Put on some dark sunglasses."

We were not sure if Tiber could walk under the influence of the tranquilizer. We'd just have to force him to walk. Ev and I grabbed a couple of suitcases while Bob led Tiber around the car a couple of times, trying to get him to walk straight.

We approached the lobby door. I held the door open as Ev went in with Tiber and Bob following. The hotel clerk looked up from what he was doing, and I gave him a thumbs-up.

He waved and returned to his task. We slowly crossed the lobby and headed for the elevators. Bob was more or less pulling Tiber when the dog, on his wobbly legs, collided with a pillar in the lobby.

We froze in our tracks for a moment while Bob bent down, petting Tiber and whispering soothing words to him. When we got to the elevator doors, we were giggling like mischievous children. We didn't dare look at the hotel clerk for fear he was looking at us.

The elevator doors opened, and we hustled in the dog and our suitcases. By the time we got to our room, we were howling with laughter.

I said, "Man, that was the blind leading the blind."

In the morning, we repeated the scenario in reverse. Tiber was really sedated by then, and we more or less carried him to the car. No one seemed to pay much attention, and we were off to the airport.

That fall, I received a call from a Lethbridge tenor sax player asking if I would play in his quartet, which played for local dances. I was required to play a bass line with my left hand and chord with my right (much as I had done with a band in Santa Barbara). I didn't know what I was getting into, but at the first gig, I realized there were only two *musicians* in the group—the sax man and me. He could play any tune he had heard one time and commit it to memory forever.

The drummer was a young kid who knew only one drum technique—extremely loud rock. The trumpet player was really a maraca player, but he didn't play them as they were meant to be played. He just shook them on every downbeat, which he played on every song—whether it was a Latin tune or not. He had a lung condition that inhibited him from blowing his horn for any length of time. It was a strange group. Why did I play gigs with them? I had child maintenance and mortgage payments to make.

I told the sax man I would only play a couple more gigs and then he'd have to find a different piano man. At our next gig, the drummer couldn't make the date—and the sax player had his daughter play drums. His daughter had been playing with another group, but she was free to do gigs with her dad. I didn't even know he had a daughter—let alone one who played drums. At the first gig she played with us, I was pleasantly surprised by her drumming. She kept excellent time—nothing flashy technique-wise but good solid rudiments—and she was a real cutie.

For the first time, I really enjoyed playing with the group. I told the sax man I would stay with the group as long as his daughter played drums with us. And so it was. The drummer and I became good friends and started dating. Playing with this drummer gal, our tempos were right on—and we had a solid beat.

In the 1970 spring semester, we initiated a number of new courses. Our enrollment was increasing by leaps and bounds, our gallery exhibits were expanding, and we started a visiting artist program. We hired Jeff Olson as a department technician and John Nava (a fine draftsman who had been an art student of mine in California) as an assistant art professor to teach printmaking. I was preparing for a painting exhibition in the spring and tackling the duties of department chairman.

That summer, I went to an art conference in Seattle. Jeff Olson and I drove from Lethbridge to Shelby to catch the train to Seattle. Jeff and I were American citizens with landed immigrant status in Canada. Crossing the border many times, we both made sure we had all our necessary papers.

The American government, in their infinite wisdom, had seen fit to implement the military draft to place young American men between eighteen and twenty-five in harm's way in a civil war in Vietnam. Many American boys of draft age protested this action, dodging the draft by moving to Canada. These "draft dodgers" were thought of by some as the scourge of America's youth and cowards because they didn't believe in going to fight someone's civil war in a remote foreign country and end up getting killed for it.

When Jeff and I arrived at the border crossing at Montana, the border guard asked us where we were headed, what our citizenship was, and for some identification. We gave him our landed immigrant IDs and driver's licenses.

He looked at them and said, "American citizens, both of you, huh? Let's see your draft cards."

I didn't have a draft card because I had already done my military service. I carried a reduced photocopy of my honorable discharge from the air force. I handed it to the officer.

He glanced at it and said, "You were a fly boy, huh?"

He asked for Jeff's draft card.

Jeff handed his card to him.

The officer said, "You're classified as 1-A. If your draft number was called, would you come back to the States to serve?"

Jeff bent forward in the front seat of the car, looked the officer in the eyes, and said, "I don't know. Would you?"

The officer stepped back from the car, clutching our cards, and said, "Park your car over there and come inside."

The border guard asked me for my car keys and told us to sit down and wait. He and another officer went to my station wagon and tore it apart, looking for anything illegal. When he came back into the station, he took us into a small room and told us to wait while he made some phone calls.

I tried to explain that we would miss our train connection if we didn't leave soon. The bureaucratic SOB said we could go when he said we could go. He left, and another officer came into the room and asked how we were doing. He seemed like an agreeable person, but at that point, I didn't trust anyone. The guards had taken on the appearance of the Gestapo.

I asked the officer why we were being held, and he told us they were checking on our identification, military records, and criminal records. The other officer was waiting for a reply from the Pentagon to verify my air force service. "Then we'll know what the score is. So just wait."

We waited. Other officers looked in the room now and then. With our long hair and large mustaches, we felt like (and probably looked like) desperados in detention. After over an hour of waiting and asking why we were being held, a female officer came into the room. She said, "You guys still here?"

We explained our situation one more time, and she said she'd check to see why we were still being detained. When she returned, she said we were free to go. We told her that the officer who put us in there still had our papers and car keys. She found our belongings, returned them, and told us to have a safe trip. Jeff and I thought about making a comment, but we decided to keep our mouths shut.

As we pulled away from the border to catch a later train to Seattle, I told Jeff to say yes the next time he was asked about the draft.

"I don't think I could do that," Jeff said.

"Neither could I," I replied.

At Thanksgiving, I received a phone call that renewed my life. Bill Otto, my ex-father-in-law, and I had been good friends ever since I met his daughter. Bill called from his home in Fresno and said that Claudia and Joanne were there and wanted to talk to me. Claudia, to my surprise, said she wanted to get back together; she had discovered I was the only one she really loved. Truth be told, she was the only one I really loved.

After a long conversation, we agreed to try to work things out. I really wanted Claudia, Joanne, and I to be a family again—and I knew it would be the best thing we could do for our lovely daughter.

Old Blue Eyes sang, "Love is lovelier—the second time around." On December 11, 1970, Claudia and I were married for the second time. We had a lovely wedding at our home in Lethbridge. Joanne and a number of our friends were in attendance. The ceremony was performed by a Buddhist priest we were friends with; his wife was an outstanding art student of mine.

That Christmas, we traveled to Seattle to join my mom and dad and Bob and Ev for the holidays. Bob and Ev had moved to Seattle, and Bob was working on his MFA at the University of Washington. Ev had a nursing gig at the Swedish Hospital and Medical Center. The get-together was a reunification of family traditions that my soul knew were of great significance—and life was a beautiful gig again.

The next few years were some of the happiest times of my life. Claudia and I were enthusiastic about making our little house on the outskirts of town into a home. We began to do some remodeling and yard work. With the help of friends, I constructed a building north of my studio that became a chicken coop and a greenhouse. Years later, it was converted into a jewelry studio that my brother occupied. We had lovely vegetables in winter—along with fresh eggs and fried chicken. Joanne loved playing in the yard—summer and winter—and the greenhouse was her favorite place to hang out.

One day we decided to cook a chicken for dinner, and I told Claudia I'd pick one out. She told me to take Joanne, but I thought it wouldn't be a good idea since she might not like the idea of butchering an animal for food. Claudia said it would be good for her to know some truths about life. I disagreed and said I thought it was a good idea that kids had some buffers from some of life's realities until they were more mature. While they were young, believing in fairy tales, Santa Claus, and the Tooth Fairy should be a pleasurable part of their world. Claudia disagreed, and I gave in to her line of thinking.

Walking with my four-year-old daughter out to the chicken coop, I had mixed feelings about what was going to take place. I explained what farmers have to do to eat fried chicken. For a young child, she seemed to understand the meaning of it all, but I didn't believe for one minute that she understood what this fact of life was all about. Nevertheless, I continued on with my task.

With an ax in hand, I picked out a plump chicken and proceeded with my little ritual. The first step was to hypnotize the chicken. To do this, I held the chicken's head to the ground and repeatedly drew a line straight out from its beak to about six or seven inches. When the chicken was mesmerized, I put it on the chopping block and whacked off its head. I told Joanne that the chicken wouldn't feel a thing—how was I to know that?

As the chicken flopped around with blood spurting from its headless neck, I looked at Joanne. I expected her to cry or scream or at least show some sign of disgust. Instead, she looked at me and said, "We're real farmers now, huh, Dad?"

At dinner, Joanne said how much she liked the delicious chicken. I thought about how my child was teaching me what life is all about as I was trying to teach her all about life. We still have that father-daughter relationship today.

In the spring of 1971, we bought a pickup truck and a camper and enjoyed numerous camping and fishing trips. Our favorite fishing lake was located in the foothills of the Canadian Rockies where there was a stunning view of the mountains. One spring, while fishing from the shores of that lake, we huddled comfortably in our camper as the wind howled outside and our fishing rods, stuck in pole holders on the shore, were pumping up and down as choppy waves on the lake tossed our lines about. We had observed on previous fishing trips that the rougher the waves, the better the chance of the fish taking the bait. We were relaxing with a hot meal and a cup of coffee, keeping an eye on our rods for a strike. Claudia was pregnant with our second child.

Claudia yelled, "I've got a strike!" She jumped up and started for the camper door.

I was right behind her, shouting, "Take it easy."

Before the words were out of my mouth, she opened the door, jumped to the ground, stumbled, and ran down to her fishing rod. Her pole was jerking violently up and down as a fish trying to shake the hook pulled the line farther into the lake.

I yelled, "Take it easy."

Joanne was yelling right along with me.

The wind was blowing off the lake as Claudia reeled in the line. She said, "Okay, I've got him hooked."

I wasn't worried about catching the fish. I was worried about Claudia jumping around when she was pregnant. I shook my head in awe at the scene.

Joanne was jumping up and down, excited about catching a fish.

Claudia was leaning backward to keep her balance as her swollen belly protruded in front of her. She was reeling and pumping the rod, but the fish was putting up the fight of its life.

At that moment, my fishing rod started bobbing up and down, and all three of us started laughing. Claudia and I reeled in two beautiful rainbow trout, each weighing about four pounds. Not to be left out of the fishing activity, Joanne picked up the fishing net and was trying to recatch the trout as they flopped around on the shore.

Years later, I told my son—an avid fisherman with a degree in fishery sciences—that one of the reasons he became so interested in fisheries research was due to his mother's tenacity as a fisherwomen while he was still in the womb.

Allan Charles Hicks was born September 25, 1971, in Lethbridge. After getting Claudia checked into the hospital, I went to the waiting room to settle in and watch a football game. I had no sooner tuned the TV to the sports channel when the doctor came into the room.

He said, "Congratulations—you have a baby boy."

I was elated and said, "Already?"

The doctor told me the delivery had been quick and easy. Allan had my middle name, and his middle name was in honor of the great jazz musician Charlie Parker.

Allan was the second incredible human being who had come into my life and given me a sense of purpose. Allan took after his father; he would sometimes throw caution to the wind as he investigated everything in his surroundings. He would push, pull, turn, twist, chew, grasp, and examine the whole shebang; nothing escaped his scrutiny. He never sat still for a moment, and he is still like that today in his forties.

Joanne took it on herself to ride herd on Allan when both were young, and her affection and regard for her younger brother (and later for her younger sister) was a delight for me to observe. Joanne's innate sense to safeguard her siblings was akin to my sentiments toward my brother. I was pleased to know that this attribute had been passed on through our genes.

In the spring of 1972, Claudia and I decided we would buy a couple of horses since we enjoyed riding. Claudia liked Arabians, but I thought they were hot-blooded horses. I was not in favor of buying horses with such high-spirited dispositions. The two Arabians we looked at proved my point. We didn't even get a chance to ride the first one we saw, and after what happened when we first met the horse, we didn't even want to.

The horse was in a corral next to the Fort. The lady who was showing us the horse had it tied by its halter to a fence. When she swung the saddle up to the horse's back, the Arabian bucked and reared back, pulling the board from the fence. The horse swung around with part of the fence at the end of its halter. It was like flinging a medieval flail as the board whacked me across my midsection. The horse galloped off to the far end of the corral, dragging the fence plank with it as I doubled over with the wind knocked out of me.

Another Arabian horse we looked at seemed to have a much better disposition. I rode this horse around a field and felt the intelligence and power of the animal. Claudia wanted to ride the horse, but I told her maybe she'd better not since it was a little spirited. The real reason I hesitated for her to ride was that I was worried because she was pregnant with our third child.

She insisted and rode off on the back of the Arabian.

Yeah! That is a beautiful animal and rider!

In an instant, the horse started bucking—and off went Claudia into the plowed field. Luckily, she landed on her feet in the soft field. She fell to her knees, and I ran to her.

As she was dusting herself off, she said, "No more Arabians."

When our third child was born, I believe it was an early, quick, easy birth because Janine wanted to get into this world fast. She wanted to be on her own rather than be confined to traumas in a small space.

We finally found a horse that suited us. It was a mixed breed of quarter horse and thoroughbred with white and chestnut pinto spotting. The breed was called Paint. When the owner told me the horse's name was Painter, I knew it would be a cool horse for us.

The owner was up-front with us and told us that the horse was very good with female and children riders, but it didn't take to unfamiliar male riders. He said I could see how the horse acted if I wanted to ride him. I agreed, and he suggested that I try to saddle and bridle the horse to see what kind of reaction I got.

I said hello to Painter and talked to him for a moment before I put the blanket on him and swung the saddle onto his back.

He turned his head and looked at me while I tightened the cinch. I put the bit in his mouth, and he objected a little, but I bridled him, took the reins, and stepped into the stirrup. I swung myself into the saddle while the owner stood beside us.

The owner said, "Well, I'll be damned."

I spurred the horse gently, and we took off around the pasture. Painter obeyed every command I gave him; it was as though we'd been horse and rider all our lives.

Claudia rode him with no trouble, and we decided to buy the horse, the saddle, and the bridle. The horse owner's spiel about the horse not taking kindly to unfamiliar male riders was a good sales pitch, but isn't that what horse traders do?

The place where we bought Painter was five or six miles from our house. I rode the horse while Claudia drove home. Riding along a gravel road, I came to a railroad crossing about a mile from our house. Painter halted when he saw the tracks—and he wasn't about to trot over them. To Painter, the crossing must have appeared like a "Texas Gate," as we called them in North Dakota. The Texas Gate was usually just a grid of piping or other linear material placed across a road that prevented livestock from going over to the other side of the fence, but it would allow a vehicle to drive through without having to open or close a fence gate.

I wondered if Painter would just gallop over the crossing if I took him at a faster pace. I rode the horse back down the road, turned around, and spurred him toward the crossing.

At the crossing, he stopped abruptly, almost throwing me over his head. We farted around in front of the crossing. When Painter had enough of this contest, he started bucking—and I decided it was time to dismount. If I couldn't ride him over the crossing, maybe I could lead him.

I was ready for a fight, knowing there wouldn't be much a 170-pound man could do against more than a thousand pounds of horse flesh. I was supposed to be smarter than this horse, right? I decided to bribe him.

The ditches beside the road were thick with vegetation. I led him over to get a taste of those sweet-smelling grasses. As Painter chomped, I pulled up a large handful of grass and led him back onto the road.

I gave him a few pats on the neck and said, "All right, you *dumb* animal. Let's get going home." I took his reins and started to lead him to the railroad crossing. I went very slowly, taking deliberate steps and holding the grass out to him, as he began to follow me across the tracks.

No problem! He wasn't even interested in the grass I offered him. Painter wouldn't let me ride him over the tracks; he just wanted me to show him that the way was safe and lead him over. I apologized for calling him a dumb animal; I found out what an intelligent dumb animal he really was.

On December 16, 1972, our third child was born—my third sense of purpose. Janine Lorraine was named after two jazz standard compositions—Duke Pearson's *Jeannine* and Nat King Cole's rendition of *Sweet Lorraine*. The song's opening phrase—"I just found joy"—expresses my delight at having Janine come into our lives. J9—as she is known to a lot of her friends and family—is a compassionate daughter who chose nursing as her profession, which is so characteristic of her demeanor. As a child, she was very shy around strangers (like her father), but she was full of curiosity and liveliness. I don't know where she got her energy from since she didn't like most foods—unless they were sweet. She would hide her food rather than eating it. When she was a young tot, she would sit at the dinner table on a keg that had been a soy sauce container. This little barrel had a bunghole in it, and Janine would drop food in it that she didn't like to eat. Eventually the broccoli, carrots, mushrooms, and other vegetables became rancid, and J9's stash was discovered by her mom.

My kids enjoyed staying at my house since there were trees to climb, large lawns, and nearby pastures with horses, donkeys, dogs, and kittens. A loving aunt and uncle lived next door. Along the south side of my property, a long row of stacked logs had been cut from huge cottonwood trees years before I moved there. The kids found these logs irresistible to climb upon.

While sitting on my deck one hot summer day, I heard Janine scream. I looked up and saw her flailing about on top of the stacked logs. I ran across the lawn to find that she had disturbed a nest of wasps and was covered with them. Grabbing her in my arms, I ran into the house and turned on the shower to flush the wasps away. We received multiple stings. I was worried about an allergic reaction, which has killed people. We were lucky not to have been allergic to the poison. Janine asked why God had made wasps that could sting and harm us, but I had no answer.

Going to and from gigs, I have found myriad variables that make up human behavior—ranging in degrees from love and compassion to anger and hate. The more experiences I have in life, the more I realize that my ignorance about reality is my greatest hindrance to being content. How I appear to be, how I am, and how the world appears to be are impressions that I attempt to explain, but the truth to the questions are distorted by my opinions and senses. Any insight into how things actually exist is hard to comprehend. To know myself, without any fabrication, is foremost to developing my comprehension.

Know thyself—a carved inscription on the sixth-century BC Temple of Apollo at Delphi shows us that humans have always been concerned with this quest.

Chapter 15

Transitions

The seventies were full of more changes in my life. For the second time, Claudia and I separated, and we were divorced in 1974. This separation hit me hard, and I sought a number of ways to fight my depression. I had a number of self-prescriptions. I occupied my mind, body, and time with drawing, painting, music, art research, teaching, reading, and transcendental meditation, seeking to come to grips with the despair that had taken over me. A combination of these remedies helped me maintain a somewhat normal balance in my daily operation.

At times, I felt like a duck—cool, calm, and collected above the water, but paddling frantically underneath to keep moving. My most effective therapy was when I would get a chance to visit with my children; they were my bright hope for the future and eased my angst. My love *for* my children and the love *from* my children has always been a stabilizing component of my life.

In 1971, the university moved from its location on the college campus in Lethbridge, on the east side of the Oldman River, to the newly developed part of the city on the west side. The renowned architect Arthur Erickson designed the new campus. The university received international acclaim for its architectural originality and functional design—and was a cover story featured in *Time Magazine Canada*. Our enrollment was climbing; we hired Carl Granzow to teach sculpture and searched for other new faculty. The Art Department was now offering a BFA degree in studio art.

We had a number of opening celebrations and appearances of celebrities at the new university campus, including various artists and scientists from David Suzuki to Peter Ustinov.

Pete Barbutti, a comedian and musician who had made many appearances on the *Tonight Show* with Johnny Carson, performed too. I had a trio that was playing in the atrium, and Barbutti stopped where we were performing. He sat down beside me on the piano bench and asked if I knew "Moonlight in Vermont." I told him I did, and he said if I would play the chords on the lower half of the keyboard, he would play the melody on the upper half—with his nose. We did—and the audience loved it.

He said, "Oh yeah, I'm an old nose-picker from way back, and I get a lot of help from my friend Herb."

The Jazz Scene Quartet featured Dale Ketcheson on guitar, Bill McCarroll on bass, Ron Yoshida on drums, and me on piano. We soon grew into a quintet, adding a tenor sax player. Vern Dorge, a talented sax player, was still in high school at this time. Vern went to Toronto to study music and has performed with a number of famous musicians. He is now a familiar name on the Canadian music scene.

I purchased a vibraphone and began to double on piano and vibes. I was fed up with playing on out-of-tune and beyond-repair pianos that most clubs had. I decided to get a Fender Rhodes electric piano that I could haul around. I looked in music stores in Lethbridge and Calgary, but they were more than double the price of the ones I'd seen in the States. A friend in Santa Barbara told me about a sale they were having—and offered me a cheap piano. He shipped the keyboard to my friend in Montana, and I drove my camper to pick it up.

At the border, the officer asked where I lived. I told him, and he waved me through. I had every intention of declaring the keyboard and paying whatever taxes were due, which would still be cheaper than buying a piano in Canada. Without volunteering to declare it, I took my good intentions and the Fender Rhodes and drove home.

A month later, two policemen came to my house and inquired about the purchase of my Fender Rhodes. Someone had informed the Rhodes keyboard dealer in town about my deal on the piano, and I was busted. I had to pay a heavy fine for smuggling—plus the taxes that were due on the piano. I could have purchased three pianos if it were not for my stupid mistake. The road to debt and hell is undeniably paved with good intentions.

In the late seventies, Ernie Block and I formed a dance band called Chameleon. Ernie has played more gigs around Lethbridge and played in more different music groups than any other musician from the area. Ernie does things his own way. Anyone who knows this congenial man knows his one-liners by heart and knows of his compassion and sincerity. He is a self-made musician—proficient on *every* musical instrument. He is also a fine music arranger; the calligraphy of his handwritten manuscripts is impeccable. Chameleon changed its personnel and configuration many times over the years; Ernie switched to every instrument needed, and I stayed on piano or doubled on piano and vibes.

We chose the name because we could change our music to suit all the ballroom dancing styles. But we didn't change the category of music from ballroom dancing to rock. Our hardest gigs were usually weddings where we would perform to a wide range of ages and musical tastes. We didn't have a front line of guitars, screaming vocals, and towers of amplifiers; we were not a heavy metal rock band or even a "light metal band."

In the 1970s, music audiences were saturated, mesmerized, and swayed by the media and the persistence of DJs (on radio and in clubs) who endorsed the music industry's hype of rock music. More and more, the standard tunes for dance gigs moved to the rock genre music that everyone had heard via the media (over and over and over). During this time, there was overwhelming attention placed on the exaggerated theatrical "super rock star" image.

A dance band like ours had changed from being a chameleon to being a dinosaur. We were faced with adversity on a number of jobs solely because we would play our arrangements that formed the band rather than playing some other style. Eventually, I stopped booking gigs—and Chameleon became extinct.

Whenever your gig puts you in the public eye, no matter what your vocation, you become vulnerable. You're bound to meet some opposition. It is a person's right to have opinions and beliefs. But differences clash when one becomes opinionated to the point of making the assertion that one's beliefs are absolutely right—and others' opinions are absolutely wrong. This behavior is frightening. Wrath is elevated beyond understanding to prove a point. Add conceit and greed to wrath—and, as history shows us, the results can be catastrophic, culminating in prejudice, violence, and war. The only (hypothetical) justification is that one side is right and deserves reward—and the other is wrong and deserves punishment.

The human race has made so many advances in technology, science, medicine, communication, the arts, and other endeavors, but very few in civilized behaviors. The only human instruction and maintenance manual we are given when we're born is our history, which has shown we have not made many advances for the full control of ourselves.

Rage, part of the human temperament, takes us to impulses that are repeatedly our darkest ignoble characteristics. Even though we make brilliant improvements in many of our accomplishments, our inhumane behaviors keep us, as a species, from being thoroughly compassionate beings. If we could absorb important lessons from history, maybe we could learn how to behave in a civilized manner. I'm constantly astounded at the atrocities that exist within the human community and amazed that the human race keeps persevering without annihilating itself.

I've tried to be optimistic about the caring nature of human beings, but our humanitarian track record is not that great. Consider the continual news reports of terrorism, genocide, homicide, suicide, rape, and other cruel deeds. It's getting damn hard to ignore the evidence. Maybe it's just that we're getting better at reporting bad news—or as some would believe—it's false information like the holocaust *never happened* or global warming is *not damaging* our planet or clear-cutting the rainforests does *no harm* to the environment. Although humans sometimes sink to the bottom of the abyss, we somehow manage to swim to the top and keep afloat. Survival is our tenacity in action, and our actions define our disposition as our species continues going to and from our gigs.

Jack DeJohnette, the renowned jazz drummer who had made a name playing with Miles Davis, brought a trio on a Canadian tour. When they did a gig in Lethbridge in 1975, Jack DeJohnette stayed a couple of days at my house—and we had an all-night bash after the gig. Jack loved my new Yamaha grand piano and ended up playing it into the early-morning hours—to the delight of everyone at the party.

At breakfast, Jack thanked me for my hospitality and gave me a record of his most recent recording, *Sorcery*. DeJohnette's trio had a gig the next evening in Calgary, and we loaded my camper with his equipment and hit the road. His two sidemen went on before us in another car.

On the way to Calgary, Jack played a tape he had made of the guitarist John Abercrombie. He liked Abercrombie's playing and said the guitarist was destined to make it big (which he did). As we listened to the recording on my truck's tape deck, the music suddenly became distorted. My grip tightened on the steering wheel, and my jaw fell open. Ribbons of tape spewed from the tape deck and unraveled on the truck's floor. I was upset that I had destroyed DeJohnette's tape and started apologizing.ABergracrombie's playing and said me not to sweat it because he had copies of the tape. He laughed and told me I could keep the recording as he scooped up the ribbons of tape from the floor.

That evening in Calgary, DeJohnette's trio played an incredible gig. Sadly, only a handful of jazz fans were at the gig. Whenever I hear a recording of him, I think of our brief encounter. I still marvel at his creative drumming, especially in the famous jazz trio with Keith Jarrett on piano and Gary Peacock on bass.

Through the Alberta Art Foundation—and by entering various art exhibitions in the seventies—my paintings and drawings were included in exhibits and collections in major cities in Alberta, Vancouver, Toronto, Montreal, New York City, Los Angeles, Seattle, London, Brussels, and Paris. Teaching was a focus of my career at this time, and I earned a promotion to associate professor of art.

I attended a number of art conferences. On one flight out of LA, I had a chance encounter with a well-known Hollywood celebrity. As I waited to board a flight to Great Falls, I noticed that the passenger ahead of me was Charles Bronson.

When we boarded, Bronson was beside me in the coach section. My first thought was this couldn't be *the* Charles Bronson; he'd be flying in the first-class section. When I sat beside the very bored passenger, I realized it was Charles Bronson.

As I was thinking of what to say to him, he said hello in his unmistakably low, gravelly voice.

I said, "Hello, Mr. Bronson."

He nodded as if he had expected me to recognize him.

I introduced myself, and he asked if I was from Great Falls. I explained that I was going to pick up my car at the airport and then drive to Canada where I taught art at a university in Alberta.

He was very sociable, and we had a great conversation. I asked if he was working on a film in Montana. He was doing some location shots in Great Falls and around the Canadian border. One of the scenes they were doing in Great Falls involved blowing up a building. There was an old school in the city that was set to be demolished, and they had permission to film the dynamiting of the building. A couple of years later, I saw the scene he had told me about. The 1977 movie was called *Telefon*—and they blew the hell out of that school!

He asked if I was Canadian. I told him I was an American immigrant teaching in Canada and had completed my master's studies at UCSB. He told me he really liked Santa Barbara; he had friends there and found the art galleries most interesting. He'd always had an interest in art but never did anything other than maintaining an interest.

At the airport, we walked toward the exit from the air terminal.

I asked him if I could give him a ride.

He said, "Thanks, but I should have a limo waiting for me."

At the front curb, a huge black limo was waiting with a swarm of autograph seekers crowded around it. We paused for a moment and shook hands. I told him how nice it was to meet him, and he said, "Likewise." He gave a little smile, and with his typical squint, he waved good-bye and disappeared into the throng. I walked slowly across the parking lot to my vehicle, thinking I should have asked him about *The Magnificent Seven* and *The Dirty Dozen* or—something that really piqued my curiosity—why he was flying in economy class!

I sat in my car for a few minutes and watched the throng of fans. Some had placards that read "Charlie Bronson, Great Falls Loves You." I pulled out of the parking lot and headed north toward Canada. Charles Bronson had confirmed my belief in the adage that *the bigger the star, the nicer they are.*

In 1976, my brother and sister-in-law moved to Alberta. Bob established a custom jewelry and gemstone-cutting business and taught art classes at the Lethbridge College and University. Ev was employed as a nurse at the hospital in town. Bob hadn't played much bass since he left Santa Barbara ten years earlier. He and I would get together once in a while, but his business and teaching didn't leave him much time for music.

I would take my children to see their grandparents in North Dakota every holiday I could. Bob and Ev would usually go with us. We'd load up the camper and take off across Montana on Highway 2, known as the High Line. It was flat, straight, hot, and dusty in the summer—and cold, snowy, icy, and treacherous in the winter. It was a ten-hour trip to Williston, but we would usually stop at Wolf Point, Montana, after eight hours to spend the night with Rich Snyder, his second wife, Donna, and their four children.

Rich had moved his family from Williston to Wolf Point to run the two movie theaters when the Snyder family expanded their theater business. The "Snyder Oasis" always included a number of our favorite activities. They also had a beautiful swimming pool. My kids and the Snyder kids would swim all afternoon and evening, and the adults would enjoy a midnight swim. I would get a chance to practice my backflip off the board, which sometimes would be a back-flop. After our midnight swim, we'd have a jam session till sunrise. We'd catch an hour or two of sleep and let the kids take an early swim.

After a huge breakfast, we would take off down Highway 2 toward North Dakota. When I think back on those times, it is amazing the vitality I had. More energy and requiring less sleep are two physical attributes I wish I could reclaim from my younger days.

Two days before Easter in 1979, as I was getting to leave for Williston, my phone rang.

Bob said, "Dad had a heart attack."

Bob, Ev, and I hastily took off for North Dakota and arrived late that evening.

In the hospital room, I watched my father, deep in a coma, hooked up to a life-support device. Sobbing, I called to him in a low, soft voice. My mind replayed the countless times we had spent together. For more than forty years, he had been my mentor. He was always there when I needed comfort and advice. He was always there as the perfect father. I didn't know what to do. Could I do anything?

I cried and said, "Dad, Dad, I'm here." I prayed and hoped he would wake up, open his eyes, and tell me not to worry—and that everything would be okay.

Dad was in a coma for three weeks, and all the tests showed he was brain dead. As the oldest living blood relative, I signed the form to take him off life support. The man I admired—the one who had taught me so many life skills and given me the gift of life—passed away on May 5, 1979, two days before my forty-fifth birthday.

Although I had a busy schedule with art and music, I found time for romance. Carol Johnston was studying for a degree in art education. She was smart, vivacious, and headstrong. We were good for each other at this period; both of us were going through trying times and recent divorces. We were perfect sounding boards for one another. We enjoyed traveling, the outdoors, horses, the theater, art, fine wine, and good books.

In 1978, we went to Seattle to take in the King Tut exhibit at the Seattle Center—and to view a print exhibit at the Seattle Art Museum that included one my prints. The Egyptian exhibit of artifacts from the tomb of the nineteen-year-old pharaoh Tutankhamen was absolutely amazing. There are some experiences in life that are flagged as extraordinary; viewing this exhibit was one of them.

The tomb of King Tut was discovered in 1922 in the Valley of the Kings at Thebes. All the seals were unbroken—and more than three thousand articles were found in the tomb, most of them gold. His 3,300-year-old mummy was found in a sarcophagus with a solid gold funeral mask. The funeral mask displayed an extraordinary sense of magic. I was captivated by its presence and I felt the same transcendental experience I'd had at the Rosicrucian Museum in San Jose.

A road trip took us to Las Vegas, Santa Barbara, Los Angeles, and Mexico. Visiting Santa Barbara one warm summer night, we decided to take in a double movie feature at an outdoor drive-in movie theater. It had been years since either of us had been to a drive-in theater. We planned on making our movie outing a "picnic at the theater." We bought fried chicken, potato salad, and a couple bottles of local California wine. We drove our camper into the parking area, hooked up the speaker to our window, and settled down for a night of food, wine, and movie entertainment.

While waiting for the last showing that night, we noticed that a nearby car was having trouble starting. Without enough juice in its battery to turn the engine over, the starter just whined and died.

Two guys stumbled out and opened and closed the hood. They were laughing and jumping around like hyper children.

One of the guys approached Carol's window. Carol opened her window just a crack.

Our visitor stuck his fingers in the opening and put his face against the glass. In a heavy Spanish accent, he whispered, "Man, can you give me a push?"

Wow, was he stoned!

I told him I couldn't push him through the drive-in parking places, but I had some jumper cables we could hook up.

He said, "Gracias, amigo."

I pulled my truck over to his old jalopy and hooked up the cables. After a couple of tries, the engine turned over, backfired, and spewed black exhaust.

As I wound up my jumper cables, the driver said they wanted to pay me for "humping" their car. We all laughed.

I said, "No. That's okay. The hump was free."

He thrust his hand out the window, grabbed my arm, and put a humongous rolled joint in my hand. "The best Acapulco Gold. Dig it, man."

Dig it, we did. Carol and I giggled as we ate our way through a bucket of fried chicken and a bushel basket of popcorn during the two showings of the movies. One was Cheech and Chong's *Up in Smoke*.

For a birthday present, Carol had given me a purebred Brittany spaniel puppy. Willie became my faithful furry friend for fourteen years of companionship and hunting. He had an inordinate instinct for pointing and retrieving. I wish I'd had more time to train the dog, but he did fine with just his on-the-job training. When my son was old enough to go hunting with us, it was amusing to watch Allan and Willie pursuing pheasants in the field. Both were enthusiastic hunters, and I'm not sure who was faster.

On one hunt, Bob took a long shot at a pheasant. It seemed to take forever as he tracked, led, and fired, bringing down the bird. I congratulated him on his skillful marksmanship. Allan and Willie took off to retrieve the bird. Allan's long legs propelled him through the knee-high brush, and Willie bobbed up and down as they raced. As Allan loped through the thicket—with his shotgun at his side—he flushed a pheasant. Without missing a step, he fired the shotgun from his hip and downed the bird.

Willie retrieved the first pheasant, and Allan picked up the second bird. Bob and I were amazed at Allan's shot, and we told him what a lucky shot he'd made. Allan insisted that his shot was just like his uncle's—skill, not luck. We gave him credit for his skillful marksmanship.

Hunting the deep, thick brush of the coulees can be exhausting work. The wild rosebush thorns, thistles, and cockleburs stuck to our clothes and coated the dog's fur. A person could walk right by a pheasant hunkered down in the thicket, and the bird wouldn't flush unless he almost stepped on it or had a good hunting dog.

Bob and I were hunting a large deep coulee when Willie froze in a pointing position. As we approached the dog, we were poised with our shotguns ready for pheasants to come flying out of the thicket like launched missiles. Within a couple of yards of the dog, we began to make loud noises to flush the birds. Nothing happened.

Willie jumped forward, and we thought he had found a porcupine or a skunk. I ran to Willie; if it was a porcupine, I wanted to get him out of there before he got a snout full of quills (as had happened in the past). The dog had his paw on two large garbage bags. The bags were filled with more than two dozen recently shot rooster and hen pheasants.

We'd run across this type of senseless act of wildlife killing before and were appalled by the fact that some idiots would kill just for the entertainment of shooting something. Hen pheasants were off limits since they produced next year's generation of birds; there was also a limit of three cock pheasants per hunter. Disgusted by our find, we returned to our truck and headed up a narrow dirt road toward a ridge. When we went up and over the ridge onto a flat plateau, we couldn't believe our eyes.

"Man, did we take a wrong turn."

"Wow—we must have gone through a time warp."

Ahead of us—as far as the eye could see—was a vast wheat field. About fifty yards into that yellow field was a spectacular three-story Victorian mansion, complete with turrets and dormers, flying a Texas flag. Around the mansion were some vintage automobiles from the 1920s, and an old threshing machine was in the wheat field. We had either driven into a time warp or a movie set. It turns out that it was a movie set.

Alberta had been chosen as a location for a number of Hollywood movies because of its diversity of landscape—and it was cheaper to film in Canada because of taxes. The movie crews were not filming at the time, but I'm sure they would have been as surprised as we were to find us driving out of the coulee.

The movie that was being filmed was *Days of Heaven* starring Richard Gere and Brooke Adams. It won an Academy Award in 1978 for best cinematography and has been described by film critic Roger Ebert as "one of the most beautiful films ever made." The scene we had happened upon was beautiful. The sun, low in the west, illuminated the tops of the yellow (ready to be harvested) wheat and made the shining field glow. The sides of the Victorian manor were like a sun-drenched alpine mountaintop, casting long purple shadows across the gold landscape. The urge to explore the mansion was strong, but we didn't want to disturb the movie site and continued to an old dirt road that took us down a hill to a highway—and back to the reality of our time.

East Kootenay in British Columbia is a beautiful part of the Canadian Rockies. The Elk River and the Fernie Alpine Resort are two big attractions for fishing and skiing. We went on a magnificent sunny day, and there was lots of powder on the slopes. Carol, Joanne and I were skiing at the Fernie Alpine Resort.

When we decided we'd had enough skiing and it was time to head back home, I said I was going to make one last run, and the girls could wait for me by the lodge at the bottom of the hill. I took the chairlift to the highest point of the mountain. I had a spectacular view of the snowcapped peaks and the valley below.

As the winter sun began to dip behind the mountaintops, I pushed off downhill. I skied into some moguls and flipped into the air. I did a half somersault and landed hard and flat on my back. The wind was knocked out of me, and it took a minute to catch my breath. I had hurt my back, adding to my chronic back problems.

I skied carefully down to the lodge. When Joanne and Carol saw me, they said I was as white as the snow. It was a miserable ride back to Lethbridge; by the time I arrived home, I could hardly walk. A few days later, I saw my doctor—and began the long, difficult journey of treating my back problems.

Chiropractors, physiotherapists, acupuncturists, and hypnotherapists all had a crack at treating my back ailment—with very little success. My doctor suggested I see an orthopedic doctor. I was given a myelogram test by a not-so-competent orthopedic doctor to determine what was going on with the nerves in my spinal cord. The procedure started with the injection of a liquid, impervious to x-rays, into the sheath surrounding the spinal cord. I was given too much of the liquid; in the morning, it felt as if the top of my head had been blown off.

The orthopedic doctor had me scheduled for a back operation that afternoon. In the morning, Carol saw the condition I was in—out of my head. She was friends with my family doctor and told the nurse to have him take a look at me right away. My doctor was making rounds at the hospital, and he canceled the surgery when he saw me. I found out later that the orthopedic doctor had botched a number of surgeries on wrists and knees—and that his qualifications were questionable. I was lucky that Carol's intervention was at the right time; who knows what the outcome would have been if I'd had the surgery.

I continued therapy on my back, and it got better for a while. In October 1981, I woke up with a terrific backache—and I couldn't get out of bed or stand up. My doctor had anticipated something traumatic happening to the disc in my back and had given me a number to call in an emergency. I called and was carried out of my bedroom on a stretcher, loaded in an ambulance, sent on a painful two-hour ride to Calgary to see a neurologist. Tests showed that I had a prolapsus disci intervertebralis, a herniated spinal disc. Immediate surgery was in order—so I could walk again.

It was seven months before I could get back on my feet. It was a long, depressing, painful recovery. I was restricted to little or no movement. Being unable to sit in a chair, I couldn't sit at the piano. And sex was out of the question—what a boring life. I did a lot of reading and started writing esoteric poetry.

The dependency on strong medication was beginning to get to me. Often I'd have to reread a passage in a book to comprehend its meaning. It was time to stop taking pills. I flushed them down the toilet and went cold turkey. I had become used to the crutch of the pill "high." The return of the full intensity of the pain and anxiety wasn't an easy path, but it was necessary.

St. Valentine Song

Like the remembered gardens of St. Valentine,
Thoughts of the *Thinker* rise like a phantom obelisk,
A great expectation as Don Quixote finds the real illusion—
Those captured childhood memories of survival.
One exists in time and time exists in one like Paleolithic magic,
Maker of images as kaleidoscopic as an erogenous feeling,
Silent graphic chronicles of naive creative accidents.
The silver image is but a reality of the illusion of the mind.
Weathering erosion has weakened sedimentary layers of belief.
Exposed sculptured forms of hardcore perceptions,
Like a Bernini statue, a fossil is frozen for history.
Mediocrity is entombed in the existence of time.
Temporal flesh provides clues for the soul.
The walrus and the carpenter need never have spoken.
Vertical or horizontal, the music is nontemporal.
Language is the prison; metaphor the pardon.

Chapter 16

Road to Recovery

Speeding down an Alberta highway toward Nanton (a little town forty miles south of Calgary), we were preoccupied with fear of another crushing wave of nausea hitting my brother. Bob, Ev, and I had just left the hospital in Calgary for another one of Bob's weekly chemotherapy treatments. A few months earlier, doctors had discovered that my brother had cancer. The big C word scared the hell out of all of us; even though everyone said it was a cancer that was most successfully treated, it didn't diminish our fears. Bob had Hodgkin's lymphoma—and a large tumor behind his heart.

Nanton was a landmark on our medicinal mission; it would signify the beginning of a long week of suffering from the toxic chemicals that were surging through my brother's veins. Around the time we approached Nanton, the nausea and vomiting from the chemotherapy would smash Bob like a tsunami. The toxicity of the treatment destroyed fast-multiplying cells—good and bad.

Bob also suffered an outbreak of herpes zoster (shingles), which left scarring on his back that looked like he'd been hit by a napalm bomb. For a couple of months, we drove to Calgary every week. Bob would just start to recover from the side effects—and he'd have to go for another treatment. For weeks, Ev and I helplessly watched Bob's horrific suffering.

The three of us became a familiar sight at the chemotherapy clinic. Another patient was in the same predicament as Bob. The doctor, talking to the two patients, asked them how they were dealing with their chemotherapy. Bob told him the sickness after the treatment was almost unbearable; at times, the chemo didn't seem worth it.

The other patient had conquered the nausea and vomiting by cooking up a batch of "California Brownies" (brownies made by adding marijuana). Right after the treatment, he'd eat some of the chocolate treats to calm the nausea. The doctor knew of this remedy, but he couldn't prescribe any cannabis since it was against the law. A drug that has been used for more than ten thousand years—and has found to be less harmful and less addictive than smoking tobacco—couldn't be used to ease the suffering of a chemo patient. We have some strange taboos in our so-called civilized society. The cancer didn't kill my brother—and neither did the chemo—but they took years off his life and made life miserable for a while. The good news was that he did go into remission, and the tumor all but disappeared.

The aurora borealis has fascinated me since I first saw them as a boy in North Dakota. The interaction between the magnetosphere and solar winds prompted me to look up all the information I could on the aurora in the two sets of encyclopedias my dad had. The Northern Lights I saw in North Dakota paled in comparison to the ones I saw from Kootenay Lake in British Columbia.

After my back difficulties and Bob's ordeal with Hodgkin's disease, we decided on a week's recovery retreat in the Rocky Mountains. Bob, Ev, and I rented a large houseboat on Kootenay Lake and brought my three children. On one of our adventures, we sailed across the enormous lake to a sandy beach where we anchored, took the dinghy to shore, and set up a little campsite. When it got dark, we watched the most breathtaking display of Northern Lights we'd ever seen. The show was bright and animated—and we could detect an acoustic sound associated with them.

The wonders of nature have always fascinated me. The spectrum of sensory perception that humans possess affords us some of the most amazing experiences of the natural world. I can only imagine what experiences can be found outside the range of human perception; there are probably other dimensions beyond our comprehension.

That vacation was great for all of us; my kids had a great time and connected with their uncle, aunt, and dad. All of us released our worries into the healing arms of Mother Nature.

In 1984, I reached a milestone that grabbed me with authority. The Big Five-O was upon me. Was I supposed to feel older? I didn't. Was I supposed to look older? I didn't. If I do say so myself, I'd weathered those first fifty years on this planet fairly well, considering all of my encounters with ills, chills, bills, spills, and thrills. But it did make me stop and reflect on the realization that my life was more than half over. *Man, I'd better get with it. I've a multitude of subjects to study, distances to travel, people to meet, gigs to play, and stuff to investigate before my expiration date.*

My affirmation that 1984 was an important date came about in a peculiar way. I was reading George Orwell's *Nineteen Eighty-Four* when I was about twenty five, and I realized that I would be fifty in 1984. I made myself a promise that I would reread the book in 1984, which I had enjoyed immensely along with Aldous Huxley's *Brave New World*. I was fortunate to attend a thought-provoking lecture by Huxley when I was at UCSB.

Both of these science-fiction novels presented visions of the future that, in some instances, have or are turning fiction to fact. The formation of a totalitarian society, where the slogan is "Big Brother is watching you," and the concept of "doublethink," where having the allegiance to a government to believe black is white when it is demanded, are upon us.

My fiftieth birthday party was one of those events I filed in the front of the top drawer of my memories. Colleagues, neighbors, friends, relatives, students, and strangers all showed up at my house, yard, deck, and spa to celebrate the day (and the night and the next day). The well-organized bash was orchestrated by my brother and sister-in law and featured a tasty roast pig on a spit, pots of beans, kegs of beer, and a jam session on the deck with musicians from near and far. Even though Alberta's weather at the end of May can be iffy at best, the rain and cold disappeared by noon and said, "Party time!"

I was playing more gigs, and Bob was back to playing his bass again—after a six-year hiatus. His bass was in bad shape and needed a lot of adjustments to the fingerboard. He contacted a violin repair shop in Edmonton, and we took his bass to the shop when we delivered some of our artwork to an exhibit in Edmonton. The violin repair shop botched the job on the repair, and the bass was unplayable.

Bob told me there was only one bass violin repair shop that he could trust. It was a little independent bass shop in San Francisco. In a couple weeks, I would be driving to San Luis Obispo to pick up Allan, Janine, and Joanne's dog. Joanne was living in Lethbridge with me and had just started school at the university. Allan and Janine were moving back to Canada to be with me too. I was delighted to have all my children back home again. I told Bob his bass could hitch a ride in my station wagon; I would drop it off at the shop and pick it up on my way home.

After a week in San Luis Obispo Allan, Janine, and I (and a feisty little cocker spaniel) were ready to hit the road. With bicycles on top of the station wagon, the dog in a kennel in the backseat, and towing a loaded U-Haul trailer, we headed north on Highway 101 to pick up Bob's bass. At the bass shop, the repair man showed me the beautiful new ebony fingerboard he had carved and secured to Bob's bass. Bob would be thrilled with the sound and feel of his "new" bass.

The road to Alberta was long and hot, but we took a relaxing stop at Circus Circus in Las Vegas. I got a massage for my aching back, and the kids were overjoyed by the fact that the hotel accommodated children by having a circus midway and games while I spent a few dollars on the slots. The kids tried tossing a small ring around the neck of a bottle, but no one was successful at it—except Janine. She had a knack for it; every few tosses, she would ring a bottle. This was a hard feat, and the reward was a huge stuffed teddy. After winning a few of these prizes, she attracted a crowd. When she kept winning more stuffed animals, the person running the game looked at his watch and said it was time for his break. He began folding down the sides of the booth and closing the game while Allan and I helped Janine collect all her prizes. I guess the game operator had been told to evacuate when he was losing.

At the border, we did all the necessary paper work to readmit Janine and Allan to Canada. When they asked about all the huge stuffed toys, I told the border officials our Las Vegas story. I guess they thought we had contraband hidden in the stuffing because they prodded every one of them. Thankfully our bodies didn't get the same treatment.

In 1986, my three children, my mom, my brother, my sister-in law, and I spent the Christmas holidays together in Lethbridge. We brought Mom from Williston on the train. She was in poor health; diabetes was taking its toll. We had to shorten her stay with us because her health was deteriorating. Bob took her on the train back to Williston to be cared for by her doctor—and to help her move into a nursing home.

It was hard for Mom to leave her home after more than sixty years. The empathy I felt for my mother's distress was tinged with anger; I wondered why she had to suffer. The last few years of her life were dreadful; her vision and hearing deteriorated, her joints ached, and she felt emotional stress about Dad's death. Reading her diaries gave me a clue about how much pain and stress she had endured in her final years. All her life, she had worked hard for family, relatives, and friends. She was a loving wife and a caring mother and had paid so many dues—for what reward? Mom passed away on April 27, 1987.

I started playing a number of dance gigs with a variety of different groups, including the Lethbridge Big Band. My favorite gigs were playing trio or quartet gigs of standard tunes in a jazz style. Bob and I enjoyed a number of gigs with Paul Walker. Paul was determined to learn every instrument—and he did. He gigged on everything from percussion, reeds, brass, bass, and keyboards. He also wrote arrangements for the Lethbridge Big Band and became its director. Paul played for a number of years with the Lethbridge and Calgary Symphonies. I became good friends with Paul and his wife. Nancy plays alto in the Lethbridge Big Band and is the financial manager of the group.

I was playing vibraphone and piano at the time, but my visual art interests had taken a new direction toward computer art. On a sabbatical in 1984, I attended a seminar on Electronic Arts in Petaluma, California. I spent some time at the San Francisco Art Institute and the Art Department at University of California, Berkeley. This research culminated in a number of computer art exhibits in the United States and Canada.

Bruce Redstone played a fiery alto and taught music in the Lethbridge area. He taught saxophone at the university, and Allan studied tenor with him during high school.

Pheasant hunting trips with Bruce, Bob, and Allan supplied some delicious dinners, which were always accompanied by interesting discussions and humorous anecdotes. We had many midnight jam sessions at my house. We enjoyed many great Mexican dinners cooked by Ev and washed them down with a generous supply of tequila.

Bruce, Bob, Dale Ketcheson, and I began playing gigs together. Our jazz quartet was very well received at a new club in Lethbridge. The owner, a jazz fan from Calgary, was pleased that we were bringing in customers. He went back to Calgary to run a business and left the club to be managed by one of the barmaids. She had a following of bar patrons who wanted their buddies, who had a rock band, to take over our gig at the club. Our popularity began to turn around when the club was overtaken by rock fans—and we lost our jazz clientele.

Before we lost the gig, we did get an interesting offer from a patron. She introduced herself as a production assistant for United Artists Movie Company, and she wanted to hire us for a party. I didn't believe it because her card had a local phone number handwritten on it. As it turned out, she was who she said she was. We ended up playing a barbecue celebration for the movie crew and Hollywood actors who had been shooting a film nearby. *Betrayed*—starring Debra Winger, Tom Berenger, and John Heard—was filmed near Lethbridge and Fort McCloud.

The annual Canadian Music Fest was held in Toronto in 1989, and the Catholic Central High School Jazz Band of Lethbridge earned the right to compete after having excellent results provincially. Allan was a senior in the jazz band that year, and I was asked to act as director of the band when it competed in Toronto. Mike Richey, the band director, was committed to playing a lead in a musical theater production in Lethbridge. He had played trumpet and sang with Chameleon. I was honored to take this group of twenty fine young musicians to the competition. The band won a silver medal, and Allan was named to the honor band for his tenor sax solo. My son and all the kids in the band had made me proud. What a difference in music education since my high school days!

I've covered numerous highway miles in my travels to and from gigs, and one highway where I racked up the odometer clicks was Alberta Highway 3 from Lethbridge to Medicine Hat. Bob and I enjoyed playing gigs in the "Hat" with the Lyle Rebbeck Quartet. Lyle was a fine tenor player, a music instructor at the Medicine Hat College, and the producer of the Medicine Hat Jazz Festival.

When I think about how many hours I've spent making that two-hundred-mile roundtrip to play gigs, teach art classes at the Medicine Hat College, and dig for fossils near the Saskatchewan border, I'm amazed and thankful that I never had an accident on that highway. Death from road accidents is very common for traveling musicians. Considering the weather conditions when traveling that highway spring, summer, fall, and winter—day and night—I count myself very lucky to still be driving.

One of the last hunting trips with my faithful dog was with my brother and Janine. The four of us had taken off on a cold gray November day. A wet snow was falling. The earth was warm enough to turn the unfrozen ground into a bog of gummy mud, making roads slick as axle grease. Walking in this quagmire was a real chore; every step in the mud mixed with the field's chaff and attached to your boot bottoms like an adobe brick mixture. We became heavier and taller with every step.

We had driven my old GMC three-quarter-ton truck off a gravel country road onto a side road beside a stubble field. The irrigation ditch that ran parallel to the field had a lot of good cover for pheasants. Having hunted these parts of southern Alberta before, we knew there were always a number of big old roosters hiding in the thick wild rose cover.

Driving down this little muddy road, the gravel topping begins to thin out, and I decided that it was time to get out and beat the brush. Before the three of us got out of the truck, I started to back up to get onto a more graveled part of the road. We moved a couple of feet—and then we didn't move. The wheels just spun and dug deeper in the mud. It was the same result in forward. We were up to our hubs in muck. We spent about an hour trying to get out, but there was no way that mire would release its hold on the truck. Without tire chains and a shovel, we were beaten. Willie was in the bed of the truck in his carrying kennel and was beginning to whine. He wanted to get out and back to hunting. Janine and I decided to walk to a phone and ask Ev to come rescue us. Bob and the dog would stay with the truck.

It was about a two-mile walk to a farmhouse. When Janine and I knocked on the door, we hoped that someone would be home—and that they had a phone. They were home; we removed our muddy boots and were invited inside. I called Ev and told her that we were about fifty miles from town. Growing up in that country, Ev knew by my description and county road numbers exactly where we were. She would drive out to meet us at a bridge on that road not far from the farmhouse. Janine and I made our way back to the bridge and waited for Ev to arrive.

Ev picked us up, and we drove to the truck in its muddy trap. I walked down the slick road while Janine and Ev waited in the VW. Bob and Willie were happy to see me, and Bob held up a large rooster he'd shot while I was gone.

Shortly after we'd left, Bob decided that he and Willie would hunt the area. He got his shotgun from the gun rack in the truck, loaded it, and let Willie out of his kennel. As soon as Willie jumped from the bed of the truck, he went on point about ten feet from the vehicle. Walking over to the dog, Bob was ready for anything—even a skunk. A large Chinese ring-necked pheasant flew out of the brush. Its long, long tail feathers would make a fine addition to our collection. Bob's quick reaction and marksmanship downed the bird, and we had pheasant for dinner that night.

The next day Bob and I grabbed shovels and tire chains and drove out to rescue my truck.

Times in fields or streams—enjoying great camaraderie, the beauty of nature, and great food—are among my treasured memories. I do not intend to get into the debate of hunter versus nonhunter, but I am against trophy hunting and game butchering beyond bag limits. I see absolutely no reason to kill anything for sport. In the sport of hunting, the emphasis is on the hunting—not the killing.

The late 1990s were some of the last days of hunting for me. The wildlife habitat was being destroyed, and I had been diagnosed as a diabetic. My eyesight was changing rapidly, which was a good excuse for not being able to hit a flying pheasant. The wildlife habitat was being eradicated by large farm co-operations that drained the marshes, flattened and graded brush cover, and cleared the ditches and irrigation canals of any shelter. Human encroachment on natural habitats and land mismanagement took a toll on the environment. Wildlife environmentalists and hunters' organizations formed conservation programs like Ducks Unlimited and Pheasants Forever to battle large corporate lobbyists and the government's poor land-management programs. The disappearance of wildlife bird hunting is often blamed on hunters, but this is a myth. Law-abiding hunters, which most are, help protect the wildlife by only harvesting a few game (according to hunting limits), protect the females of the species for next year's reproduction, and contribute money to wildlife conservation. At one time, this concept didn't exist, but with the responsible hunter of today, we hope to avoid the senseless slaughter of wildlife on a grand scale as we've experienced with the buffalo and the passenger pigeon.

On one of our last hunting trips, Bob and I found that most of the wildlife habitat had been eradicated by plowing the area and seeding it. With the massive earthmoving equipment that some large farms have today, this is a fairly easy task. As the pheasant population began to dwindle, the government—in its wisdom—decided to treat the symptom (declining population of pheasants) rather than treat the cause (lack of habitat).

The government raised penned peasants to be released in the fall for hunting. Bob and I came upon some of these released birds when we hunted in a field by a sheltered ravine that was too big to be plowed under. A dozen or so of these bleached-out roosters were feeding on grain at the edge of the field. We tramped toward the birds—making noises, hollering, and whooping to flush them to pick our shots. Some of the birds took off running; a few would jump and fly a few feet from us, and others would just keep on pecking. These were not the wild pheasants we had hunted since our teens. These were domesticated pen-raised pheasants that were as tame as farmyard chickens. I put down my gun, picked up a couple of dirt lumps, and threw them at the birds. Hitting one in the tail feathers, it took off and glided down into the coulee. I told Bob I wondered if those pen-raised roosters tasted anything like their distant cousins. I'll never know because I didn't shoot any of those scrawny birds. We turned around and headed home empty-handed.

Hunting trips always stirred my primitive instincts, and my trips into nature have justified my being, giving meaning to "I am, therefore I am." Taking a trip into nature puts things in perspective, cutting through all the bullshit I've packed around on my life's journey. Those unforgettable moments come with such straightforwardness as I perform the simplest of tasks. They awaken my senses to a point where I'm totally aware, feeling more alive than ever. I take a step on my trek into nature, void of the media pollution and fixation with commercial smoke and mirror pitches that proclaim their products are necessary for you to be a better human being. I'm not leading or following; I'm just doing. Each step is unassuming, cautious yet confident, ready for anything. My being is consumed as a part of the whole, the whole of nature, the marvelous wonder of being alive.

After hunting for a number of years, I realized that the *experience* of the hunt is the prize—not the killing of the game. The thrill of the hunt no longer meant the sacrifice of a wild creature's life. I'd made a vow not to kill with two exceptions: in self-defense or for food in need of subsistence. I vowed no more hunting for sport, although the urge was still present. Sometimes that urge has been satisfied by shooting photographs rather than shooting bullets. The adventure of fishing still continues, albeit a catch-and-release venture today. The catch-and-release concept is impossible with firearms, but it is possible to capture wildlife without taking a life by replacing the gun with a camera.

Fly fishing the Alberta Rocky Mountain trout streams was one of my favorite getaways; when Allan was a teenager, he became hooked on fly fishing. He was tutored in the art of fly fishing by his Uncle Bob. In the eighties, Bob also introduced Allan to fly tying.

Allan was using one of the first flies he'd tied, and I watched him cast his fly line. Unfurling it in a graceful motion through the warm August air, he gently deposited his artificial bug on the surface of a large deep pool in the Crowsnest River. Just as the fly began floating downstream, a trout suddenly surfaced and grabbed the imitation insect. With a slight upward pull on the rod, Allan had set the hook in the fish's jaw. The adrenaline rush was obvious as the contest began.

I proudly watched my young son skillfully handle his fly rod like a veteran angler. He played the fish like he played his tenor sax—with feeling and skill. The acrobatic trout showed Allan its finest moves, trying to shake the hook. The challenge was in favor of the fisherman; my son had control with the right tension on the line whenever the fish twisted, turned, jumped, dove, or crisscrossed the length and width of the pool. After a long and lively ballet between predator and prey, the drama played out—and Allan landed the trout. This wasn't the first fish he'd caught, but it was one of the first on his tied flies. It was a significant occasion in his career as a fisherman. The beautiful rainbow trout was nineteen inches long, and we decided to have a taxidermy mount of the fish to commemorate that milestone. It hangs proudly in his home in Seattle, where he and his wife, Shana, live and work—and fish.

In the nineties, my kids went off to college. Joanne received a BA degree in social psychology from the University of Lethbridge and a MS degree in psychology and human development from Cal Poly University. Receiving her Board of Behavioral Science California license in marriage and family therapy, she is now employed as a clinical administrator for Family Care Network in San Luis Obispo.

Allan studied music at Chabot College in Hayward, California, and then went to Humboldt State University in Arcata, California, where he obtained a BS degree in fisheries. He received an MS degree in statistics from the University of Idaho and his PhD in fisheries from the University of Washington. While doing his doctorate studies, he worked summers in New Zealand for the National Institute of Water and Atmospheric Research. He is employed by the National Oceanic and Atmospheric Administration at the Northwest Fishery Science Center in Seattle.

Janine attended Cuesta College in San Luis Obispo and received her associate degree in nursing, then received her registered nurse license. She was an RN at French Hospital in San Luis Obispo on the surgical floor and worked as a telemetry nurse in a cardiac unit at Alvarado Hospital in San Diego. Later she worked as a maternity nurse at Sierra Vista Hospital in SLO and works with hospice services as a dedicated nurse for the terminally ill.

I'm immensely proud of the scholastic and professional achievements of my children. The vocations they have chosen have me covered (psychology, nursing, and fishing/musician), and they serve as custodians for any of my emotional angst, physical troubles, and need for recreational activities.

In September 1992, I was married for the third time. Barbara was from a Mormon family and had been married a few times before (how many I was never sure). My impetuous nature overtook me and we ran off to Coeur d'Alene, Idaho, where we could get married in one day. One more time up to bat. But it's three strikes and you're out. Five years later, after an emotional roller-coaster ride, I went through another divorce. When Barbara was good, she was very good—but when she was bad, she was very bad. I met her on the upswing of her good cycle, but the downside came when she continued to drink excessively. I was fifty-eight and didn't need—and couldn't deal with—the stressful situation. In 1997, we parted ways.

Entering my sixties, there were times when I really couldn't believe I'd made it that far. A lot of water had flowed under the bridge, carrying a quantity of debris that made paddling the stream of life precarious, yet interesting. Alterations to my lifestyle in the nineties were provoked by a number of physical and psychological events. My health issues included diabetes, arthritis, severe joint and muscle aches, loss of energy and stamina, and difficulty concentrating.

Most of these negative attributes, I believe, were the consequences of diabetes. This insidious disease, causing so much damage to one's well-being, was not easy to manage. The plus side of my life in the nineties was my enjoyment in teaching at the university. I was nominated for the "Best Teacher Award," and although I didn't win the competition, it was an honor to have been nominated. After almost thirty years of teaching at the university, I retired in 1995 with professor emeritus status.

One of my colleagues said, "Hi, Herbie."

"What is this Herbie bit?" I asked.

"You haven't seen the cover of the latest issue of *Lethbridge Magazine*?"

"No. Why?"

"There's a copy on the table by the secretary's desk."

On the table, among a number of other publications, was the magazine. There was a cover photo of me beside my grand piano. The caption read, "Herbie Hicks Lives the Artist's Dream."

I had done an interview for the fall 1994 issue of the magazine—and a photo session with the photographer—but I never implied that I was called Herbie. The lead of the article said, "Herbie Hicks, one of the lions of the University of Lethbridge Fine Arts Program, was encouraged to pursue his own style in life and now encourages others to do the same."

The design and printing of the magazine was done in Vancouver; whoever wrote the captions decided to call me Herbie—even though the article with the interviewer always referred to me as Herb or Hicks. This was a case of making a subjective judgmental decision before gathering objective information.

Ernie Block and I were asked to play with a seven-piece swing band made up of musicians from a number of towns just south of Calgary. On one occasion, I was booked to play with the band in Nanton and was traveling to the gig in my new Ford Explorer. Carrying my electric piano and equipment, I had room to spare. The December sun had just set, and an early darkness had clothed the landscape. I was hauling ass, but I felt secure in my new vehicle on my first trip down the open highway. It felt like flying a fighter jet. *Bam, Bam!* My fantasy ride was attacked; my Ford Explorer had hit two young deer. With the many road miles I've racked up, I'd hit a number of wild animals before—but never two at the same time. The front end of my new vehicle was now used (but drivable). I chalked up my double deer impact as a "double-Bambi" collision.

A Nanton High School gig was like a journey back in time. A tradition was honored by having a Senior High School Queen's Ball, which included tuxedos, ballroom gowns, and a grand march with the crowning of a queen and her court. My band took over this annual gig from the seven-piece swing band. The band we replaced didn't have a vocalist, so we had an added plus for the event. Our vocalist, George Gallant, was a very fine singer and the vocalist with the Lethbridge Big Band. George, Paul Walker (tenor sax, flute, and drums), Ernie Block (trumpet and alto sax), Dale Ketcheson (drums and guitar), Bob Hicks (bass), and me (piano) played this gig for years. My first gig, almost fifty years earlier, had been similar to this formal event. I felt as though I had come full circle. I realized that the interest I had as a teenager was a continuing passion that was an important thread in the fabric of my existence.

Life is a beautiful, changing gig.

Chapter 17

New Millennium of Discoveries and Losses

When I was young, I loved exploring the prairies and coulees of North Dakota. These explorations initiated my interest in archaeology and paleontology. I've carried this interest with me for years; when I settled in Canada, I learned that more dinosaur fossils have been found in Alberta than in any other Cretaceous fossil site in the world. Bob became involved in the fossil ammonite business in the seventies. After I retired from teaching, I joined Bob and Ev in a fascinating new vocation.

Bob was a master jewelry designer, gold and silversmith, and stonecutter of various gems including his specialties, opal and ammonite stones. I had neither the background nor the skill for stone cutting, but I had the enthusiasm and patience for collecting fossils and restoring them. Bob showed me the techniques for fossil collecting, restoration, and preservation, and I joined him and Ev in the International Fossil Ammonite Company (IFAC).

Ammolite, Alberta's and Lethbridge's official gemstone, is cut, polished, and fashioned from the shell of the sixty-five-million-year-old fossil. Triple-A quality gemstone ammonites are only found in abundance in Alberta. Ammonites were invertebrate mollusks related to the present-day chambered nautilus, squid, and octopus. Millions of these shelled mollusks lived in the shallow sea that covered most of North America at the end of the Cretaceous period. The name ammonite was given to these fossil mollusks because their form resembled the shape of the ram-like horns of the Egyptian god of life, Ammon.

As the seaways receded, the end of the Cretaceous period was marked by an enormous meteorite crashing into earth where we now know as the Yucatan Peninsula of Mexico. This great catastrophic event abruptly caused mass extinction of ammonites, dinosaurs, and many other creatures. The impact of that meteorite left a layer of ash around the globe that was rich in iridium, which is rare in the earth's crust but common in meteorites. Above this thin, grayish geological layer of dirt known as the K-T boundary (Cretaceous-Tertiary), there are no fossils of ammonites or dinosaurs. Whenever we would expose this layer, we'd know that we would have to dig deeper for ammonite fossils. Ammonites were buried and preserved in the marine Bearpaw formation deposited at the bottom of the inland sea. As these ammonites began their fossilization process over millions of years, three components of the Bearpaw Shale in Alberta made unique fossils. The heat, pressure, and minerals of the shale acted on the ammonite shell to give it a multicolored gem quality.

Doing restoration of ammonite fossils was the biggest part of my activities at IFAC. Bob was cutting ammonite gemstones and creating beautiful jewelry with the help of Ev. She would also do some of the lapidary work. I was finishing whole ammonite fossils. It was hard on the hands, and I began to notice the effect it had on my piano-playing fingers. My brother kept warning me of the trauma a grinding tool can have on your hands after hours of vibration. I, being a bullheaded Taurus, ignored his warnings and would become so engrossed with fossil preparation that I'd go for hours chipping, grinding, hammering, and sanding. I paid the price. I developed arthritis and a condition known as Dupuytren's contracture (formation of scar tissue in the tendons of the hand) usually found as a side effect of diabetes.

The fossil mining claim that Bob and Ev had in southern Alberta was located on a vast desolate landscape that we traversed in my Explorer. Those field trips excavating fossils were exciting adventures. We would be scorched by the hot prairie summer sun, covered with dirt from the howling winds kicking up dust from our digging sites, caught in sudden summer thundershowers, and bugged by billions of bloodsucking mosquitoes.

On one fossil dig, the mosquitoes infiltrated the landscape like a horde of barbarians on a conquest. Those mini vampires were exceptionally ruthless and persistent. They have inhabited this planet for millions of years; a mosquito similar to today's insect was found in a seventy-nine-million-year-old piece of amber tree resin. They have been around as long as the fossils we were digging.

Bob and I hoped for some wind to keep the little pests from flying, but Alberta gave us an unusual, perfectly calm day. We had prepared ourselves for the blitz we knew we would encounter with those aggressive insects. Our defense included insect repellent and clothing that had bands around the wrists and ankles, gloves, and a hat with netting that fit over our heads, necks, and shoulders.

Cautiously walking across the simmering landscape, perspiring profusely in our insect paraphernalia—with backpacks and digging tools strapped to us—I told Bob we looked like astronauts exploring some alien planet. I began to jump, hop, and run with exaggerated gestures as though I was in a gravitational environment other than earth. Laughing, Bob followed suit; for a few minutes, the space travelers outran their bloodsucking alien adversaries.

We began digging and chipping at outcroppings, looking for concretions that might contain fossils. Our protection against the determined pests was futile. With dogged enthusiasm, we worked on our outcroppings, but the mosquitoes infiltrated our "spacesuits." We felt bugs in our noses, mouths, and ears.

Bob was gyrating like an exotic dancer, waving his arms, and jumping around. A cloud of flying insects surrounded him like an aura. The tiny creatures had beaten us with sheer numbers, and we retreated to the safety of our vehicle.

I asked, "Why did God create such pesky little buggers to sting us?" Bob had no answer.

Chipping open a concretion to find a fossil that had been hidden for sixty-five million years was an ecstatic moment. Knowing that your hands and eyes were the first to come in contact with this prehistoric object made it hard to wrap your mind around in terms of time and geological history. Unearthing these fossils would take my mind on flights of imagined scenes from millions of years ago. That very spot had a completely different set of conditions millions and millions of years ago, yet holding a fossil in my hand brought a mystical connection between that prehistoric past and the present. This transcendental sensation with a fossil was even more pronounced than the feelings I'd had viewing ancient Egyptian relics.

Baculites, like ammonites, were from the extinct order of Ammonoidea and class Cephalopoda, but the structure in their pear-shaped shell form was a straight, slightly tapered shaft rather than a whorl-coiled shell. The mining claim we collected fossils from produced many baculites.

Baculites were interesting only as a fossil but not as a fossil gemstone. They didn't have the iridescent gem-quality shell of a beautiful ammonite. Bob began experimenting with cutting the fossil in cross-sections and found that some baculite fossils contained intricate patterns formed by the mineralization of calcite in the chambers, displaying a number of beautiful earth colors.

Bob subjected the sliced cross-sections to a lapidary process to produce a beautiful pear-shaped gemstone. Because of their resemblance to African decorative shields, these gemstones were trademarked as Shieldstone by Bob. The September 1994 lapidary journal *New Gem Emerges from Ancient Seas* featured an article about Bob and his Shieldstone enterprise. Bob's new gemstone made its market debut at the September 1994 gem, mineral, and fossil show in Denver.

A valued possession of mine is a ring Bob made for me in 1999. The ring is gold with a beautiful Shieldstone. The setting is flanked by three diamonds (one for each of my children). He gave it to me on my sixty-fifth birthday (fitting that I should receive a sixty-five-million-year-old fossil on my sixty-fifth birthday).

Our quintet started 2000 by playing a New Year's dance in a little town south of Lethbridge. The party marked the beginning of a new millennium—and umpteen New Year's gigs I've played over the years. Even though the gig was in a small town, with a lot of boozing going on, it was nowhere the hostility of the New Year's gig I'd played years earlier in Row. This gig was fun; our vocalist—radio and TV personality Mark Campbell—did an impressive impersonation of Elvis Presley. The new millennium looked promising; my big plans included painting, music, fossil exploration/restoration, and fishing trips.

When I was flying to San Luis Obispo for Joanne's wedding, my thoughts turned to my firstborn daughter and how incredible it was that my little girl was getting married. It seemed like I had just been pushing her in a stroller to get an ice cream cone in Santa Barbara. In a couple of days, I'd be walking her down the aisle to "give her away."

I never *gave away* my daughters—or my son for that matter. "Giving the bride away" implies ownership—as though the bride was an object to be bartered over. I know the saying comes from an old tradition when women didn't have many rights and were treated as property to be sold in marriage for monetary and/or social gain. I feel that my responsibility as a father was not relinquished when my children were married, but I gained a son-in-law or daughter-in-law who supported my position as a father. There are still some cultures that support the practice of treating women like property—the ultimate in male chauvinism.

When the plane landed in San Luis Obispo, I began to feel nauseous. Thinking that it was due to the plane rides and not getting proper nourishment, I tried to shrug off the sensation. My future son-in-law, Michael, picked me up at the airport. On the drive to Paso Robles, where I would be staying, the nausea came back. Feeling tired and dizzy, I retired early that evening.

The next morning, I was awakened by a terrific headache, fever, nausea, and vomiting. My condition worsened in the afternoon. "Nurse Janine" went into emergency mode and took me to the hospital in SLO where she worked. It was only three days before Joanne's wedding, and I was worried I wouldn't make the date.

With some gentle urging from Janine, the doctors were very thorough in their investigating. They did numerous tests to try to find what was ailing me—but no answers. The doctor wanted to do a spinal tap, but he needed me to sign a waiver. I had vivid memories of painful contacts with needles to my spine when I had back surgery and said I wouldn't let them do the spinal tap. Signing a waiver before having any medical tests done was a red flag for me.

My illness was becoming worse. Janine said I needed to have the procedure done to make sure they had checked out every possibility for why I was so ill. Her firm and calm assurance swayed me. She shoved the waiver in front of me, promising that the doctor would be gentle, and that he was the best. I signed the paper.

In the wheelchair on the way to the examination room where the lumbar puncture would take place, my mind raced through the memories of my spinal tests in Lethbridge and Calgary. I was haunted by the bedside manners of the doctors who poked, prodded, and hung me upside down to inject my spinal column with needles loaded with a barium sulfate dye.

My anxiety was calmed by the mild manner of the doctor. He explained every move he made as he searched my lower back for an injection site. He told me I would feel a little pinprick, and he injected a painkiller where he would inject the larger needle to extract the spinal fluid.

The doctor said, "Now we'll inject the needle for the fluid sample."

I waited with anticipation for a terrific, painful, stabbing sensation. The doctor told a nurse to get him a small bandage. "Okay, that's it."

"What do you mean? That's it."

"We're through. We got what we needed."

I was wheeled back to my room. Janine's smiling face and her questions about how it went made me grin with embarrassment. I felt like a fool for being so doubting and childish and wished I and my grin could disappear like the Cheshire Cat.

The day before the wedding, I was out of the hospital and on the mend. The doctors couldn't find the cause of my torment but theorized that I could have picked up some kind of bug on the plane. Before I left Canada, I had taken out travel health insurance; without it, I would have been ill again when I saw my American hospital bill.

Joanne was married in a beautiful garden setting in Cambria, California, in September 2000. She and Michael took up residence in Paso Robles. For her wedding present, I did a painting that was a composite of some of Joanne's favorite locations in the Rocky Mountains of Montana and Alberta. I composed a bossa nova tune I called *Joanne Marie*, which I performed with the band that played at her wedding party.

A little over a year later, I was in San Diego for Janine's wedding. She married Ken Marion on May 5, 2001 in the renowned Mission Basilica San Diego de Alcala.

The historic San Diego Mission, known as the Mother of Missions, was the first of twenty-one missions established in California. It was founded by the Spanish on July 16, 1769. The missions were built along the El Camino Real (the King's Highway), which begins in San Diego and ends six hundred miles north at Mission San Francisco Solano in Sonoma. The missions were built so one could walk from one mission to the next in one day.

The beautiful San Diego mission and the gardens surrounding it prompted me to do a painting. Without seeing the mission in person until the day of the wedding, I did the painting based on photographs of California's first church. I gave it to Janine and Ken as a wedding present. The magnificence of this historic setting was matched by the splendor of their wedding ceremony. Ken and Janine worked in the health care profession in San Diego; they later moved to San Luis Obispo and continue their professions as dedicated health care workers.

I realized that the new millennium was upon me—and the passage of time was marching by, taking my youth and leaving my children grown. Like me, when I was their age, they had looked for, found, and established their own set of statuses. The cycle of life was parading in front of me with a fanfare that made me take note. My daughters were about to start families, and my son was working on a doctorate degree and traveling around the world. I was beginning to look forward to my golden years. I realized they were more like the *tarnished* years—albeit with hints of glitter shining through.

In May 2001, Allan was working for a fisheries company in Wellington, New Zealand. He sent me photos of large rainbow trout he'd caught in the Tongariro River. I wanted to make a trip to New Zealand, but I kept getting too busy with some project—or I would have some health problem. Putting things on hold and waiting for the right time, place, space, and conditions had become an issue I'd fought with myself about. Somewhere along the way, I went from throwing caution to the wind to an overcautious behavior that had become so inhibiting that I missed several opportunities. I began to realize that finding the right combination of reserved and spontaneous behaviors for the appropriate occasion was necessary for a coherent, meaningful life.

I watched the horror of the events of September 11, 2001 on TV. My first reaction was disbelief. I, like millions of other TV viewers, had been primed with images of violence by the entertainment media, and I half-expected to see Bruce Willis wave from a window to signal all was well or Spiderman to rescue the people trapped in the buildings. I was numbed by the fact that what I saw on television was real—in real time—and not some Hollywood special effects spectacular. When the Twin Towers crashed down, I was horrified. Almost three thousand innocent lives were lost in those terrorists attacks. What kind of fiends would orchestrate such a cruel, inhumane act?

Al-Qaeda, Muslim radical Islamists, had declared a global jihad (a religious war against unbelievers in the mission of Muhammad). Osama bin Laden, the self-styled leader of the Islamic terrorist group, issued a fatwa (mandatory religious order) in 1996, declaring war against the United States and its allies. It stated that it was the individual duty of every Muslim to kill Americans and their allies—civilians and military—wherever and whenever they could.

What is so ironic about this religious war is that it mirrors historical events of the Crusades in the twelfth and thirteenth centuries. This mission for a religious war, blessed by Pope Urban II, was an order from the Catholic Church for Christians to retake Palestine from Muslim rule. The Crusaders' motto for the massacre of civilians, the destruction of cities, and countless atrocities was "It is the will of God." The Christian Crusaders who died in the war would be granted, by the Catholic Church, a remission of all sins and immediate entry into heaven. The Crusades are analogous to the acts of terrorists today. Man's inhumanity to man is repeated throughout history.

On that fearful morning, a friend of my children was driving to the Pentagon with her husband who worked for the Secretary of Defense. They witnessed the explosion of the plane hitting the southwest side of the Pentagon. If they had arrived minutes earlier, they might have met with the disaster of that explosion. Good fortune was on their side, and they were not injured. Knowing someone who witnessed this attack in person brings the horror of the event closer to home.

With this catastrophic event lingering in my mind, I fully understood my father's reaction when our family listened to the radio in December 1941 about the Japanese attack on Pearl Harbor. I was only seven, but my father made it quite clear that the attack was an outrageous deed—and the nation was in for dreadful times.

In his inaugural address, President Franklin D. Roosevelt said, "The only thing we have to fear is fear itself." The 9/11 attack, sixty-nine years later, did what FDR had feared; it put the fear of fear in our society. This irrational fear that blankets America today was not only perpetrated by the terrorists in their horrendous attack—it was also aided by George W. Bush's Patriot Act, which gives the government unprecedented power to encroach upon citizen privacy, violating the Fourth Amendment of the Bill of Rights. Bush bestowed upon himself the power to label anyone an "enemy combatant," a person with no legal rights whatsoever, contravening the basic principles of what America stands for.

All air travel in the United States was forbidden for days following 9/11. All, that is, except for members of the bin Laden family and members of the Saudi royal family in the United States who were permitted to fly home to Saudi Arabia while the air travel restriction was still in effect. Fifteen of the nineteen hijackers were Saudis. I would think the president of the United States might have wanted to detain this group of people to find out if they had any information regarding the attack. But then, one wants to show some hospitality to friends who are friends of your oil company friends. Let's get them safely back home; by the way, let's put the fear of fear in *our* citizens—and take away some of their Bill of Rights.

The paranoia generated by this fear of fears is quite apparent when going through an airport security screening line or crossing an international border today. We do have the Homeland Security Program, and I appreciate the necessary screening of photo IDs and the personal inspection of my luggage, my shoes, and my body to make sure I'm not carrying a fingernail clipper or too many ounces of foot lotion—but in some deviant way, it makes me feel criminal and cynical. Does it give me security? Not really—not the freedom from "terror-ism" and "fear-ism" or the freedom I knew in the days before 9/11.

I enjoyed gigs with trios, quartets, and quintets. Brother Bob (bass), Paul Walker (drums, sax, and flute), Don Robb (trumpet), Dale Ketcheson (guitar and drums), Greg or Randy Paskuski (bass), Ernie Block (drums or bass), Jerry Rogers (trombone) and Neil Sheets (drums) were a few of the musicians who made each gig interesting.

Dale Ketcheson introduced Bob and me to Sheena Lawson, a vocalist who had a natural talent for singing in tune and phrasing songs with a jazz feeling. She played a few gigs with our trio. People dug that quartet combination with vocals. Playing jazz with a vocalist is one way to get the music across to audiences since there are words to hang the sounds on. For music-illiterate audiences, instrumental jazz sounds can sometimes be too abstract.

When Mocha Cabana opened in Lethbridge, they had a policy of letting local talent perform on weekends. It was soon discovered there were some top-notch local performers. With the support of Mocha Cabana's managers, Karen Ohno and Lynn Pearson, hiring live local music has made their weekend entertainment series a success. Bob, Neil Sheets, and I started playing the gig with our jazz trio. As time went on, we had a number of different combinations of duos, trios, quartets, and quintets. I finally settled on a quartet with Sheena, Neil, and Bob. This group seemed to click with the audience—and with the sound we wanted. We continued with this group until a shocking event in 2005 changed the combination of our combo.

In October 2002, Joanne and Michael became the proud parents of Alyssa Lynn Myers, my first grandchild. In August 2003, my second grandchild, Luke Allan Marion, arrived to the delight of Janine and Ken. I began my proud role as "Grandpa Herbie" to a beautiful granddaughter and a handsome grandson.

The new millennium was rolling along with delightful events. I had no idea about the grave future occurrence the new millennium had in store for me.

February 27, 2005, was an unusually warm winter day in Lethbridge. The western Chinook winds had blown the snow and winter blues over to Saskatchewan or someplace east. But the blues were to return tenfold. Bob and Ev had gone for a walk in the Research Station Park across the road from our place. When I looked out the window, Bob was sitting outside my studio; he had returned from his walk before Ev. I had been working on some fossils in the studio and was glad to see Bob had returned from his walk since I had some questions to ask him about fossil restoration. When I approached Bob, he nodded with a despondent look. He said he didn't feel well and thought he'd go home to lie down for a while.

Helping him out of the chair, I told him I'd go with him. We walked over to his house, which was located right behind my place. As he staggered up the front steps, I told him I could call an ambulance to get him to the emergency room—or I could drive him there.

"No," he said. "I'll wait till Ev gets back from her walk. Right now, I'll lie down."

We went into the bedroom and sat on the edge of the bed for a minute. He put his head on the pillow, looked at me, and said, "Herb, I think I'm going to pass out."

Those were the last words he ever spoke. His eyes rolled back in his head.

I grabbed him and started pushing and pounding on his chest. I yelled, "Bob. Bob!" I ran to the next room, grabbed a phone, and dashed back into the bedroom while dialing 911.

The emergency operator kept telling me to stay calm and stay on the phone. She told me the ambulance was on its way and asked me if Bob was breathing.

He wasn't; he had taken his last breath while I held him.

The operator, still telling me to stay calm, asked again for directions to Bob's residence. I realized how hard it would be for the ambulance driver to see the house from the county road I had described. Still holding the phone, I ran across the lane to tell the neighbor to go down to the corner to direct the ambulance to Bob's house.

As I was crossing back over the road, Ev walked down the lane.

The ambulance turned onto our road.

The operator said, "What are you doing? Stay calm. Have you seen or heard the ambulance yet?"

"Yes, they are here now."

I held the door open for the EMS guys and thought about what I could do.

It must have been loud enough for the paramedics to hear.

They said, "Just wait here. Stay calm—and let us do our job."

Stay calm? I was in a complete state of shock and panic. I felt as though I'd been turned inside out. My mind was flipping back and forth between negative feelings of hopelessness and positive visions of hopefulness, but I knew that my brother had passed on. Could I have saved him by doing *something* in that last moment I'd held him? Guilt overtook me when I thought I might have revived him if I had known CPR. But he died. My brother left this life like he lived it—with quiet dignity.

At sixty-four, Bob was too young to die. He had too many plans and unfinished projects to leave the world. How God (or whomever) would not let him complete some of his works and retire to do some fishing, gigging, and digging was beyond my comprehension. I had no answers.

Bob's memorial service was attended by family, friends, colleagues, students, and musicians. As I sat deep in thought at the celebration of my brother's life, I reflected on my association with him. I was family, friend, colleague, student, and partner with my brother. And now he was gone, leaving only the memory of his existence—but what a beautiful memory.

The memorial service included musical tributes from Lethbridge's music scene and other musicians, friends, and relatives. Janine and Luke from California, Tom and Helen Carey from Montana, Tony and Pam Cappiello from Seattle, Bruce Redstone from Toronto, and Allan from New Zealand were a few who traveled miles to honor this admirable man I called *brother*.

My brother had an enormous amount of compassion with his students, his fellow musicians and artists, his partners, his customers, his relatives and friends, and everyone he met.

Our cousin, Jim Greutman, said, "Bob had such a positive effect on everyone; we feel his presence every day."

Bob's death hit me with the shocking reality of how fragile life is. In life's twists and turns, there is only a moment between existence and nonexistence. I have tried to value every moment of my existence since then.

In the following months and years, I paid homage to my brother in a number of ways. Two notable tributes were a series of paintings and the production of a music CD.

The Herb Hicks Quartet continued to gig at Mocha Cabana. Ernie Block replaced Bob on bass. Paul Walker sometimes played tenor sax and flute to expand the quartet into a jazz quintet.

Marathon Man, Triathlon Man, and Ironman—my son earned these titles the authentic way—by completing the events. In my youth, I had loved to swim, bike, and run. Although I never did any competitive racing, my lean frame and long legs loved to pump adrenaline though my system and feel that runners' euphoric high, but that was many years ago. I can hardly remember the sensation; today such exertive physical activities, sadly, only exist in my mind.

Allan trained long and hard for his first Ironman race, one of the hardest endurance events in the world, in New Zealand. On March 3, 2007, Allan and his buddy Ryan Leong (Hawaiian Ryan) ran the race together. All of Allan's family and friends would be able to watch the live broadcast online—except for Joanne. She was fortunate enough to get a front-row seat; she went to New Zealand to watch her brother and cheer him on.

The race started at 7:00 a.m. on March 3 in New Zealand, which was 11:00 a.m. on March 2 in Alberta. While tracking Allan's progress, I thought about the time difference and wondered if I was seeing into the future. When the event was being photographed, was my viewing of the digital photographic images on my computer in real-time—or was it a case of Einstein's time dilation theory? I decided those time-space continuum theories are best left to people like Stephen Hawking. I dropped my curiosity about past-future relativity and told my little inner voice to get lost so I could enjoy the present.

Throughout the day, I checked my computer to see how Ironman New Zealand #539 was doing. After twelve hours of swimming, biking, and running, he was getting close to the finish line. I focused on the computer screen as Allan began his run down the finish chute. In the upper corner of my monitor, a little sign kept flashing—*low battery, low battery*—and then the screen went black. I lost the video image, but there was audio.

The announcer said, "From Seattle, USA, #539, Allan Hicks."

I cursed the stupid cameraman who had let the batteries run dead, making me miss Allan crossing the finish line. No one was able to see Allan finish the race on the online broadcast. Later we did receive some great still photos of Allan breaking the finish-line tape with his arms raised high above his exhausted body in triumph and a smile on his tanned, perspiring face. Since that race, Allan has done numerous other marathons and triathlons—and he has encouraged his two sisters and his wife to participate in this "maniac marathon madness."

In May 2007, Ryan and Allan were off again to do the Honu Half Ironman race in Hawaii. It's only half the distance, but the heat on the Big Island would be a factor.

Ryan said, "Allan, it will be brutal—you'll love it."

After hearing that statement, Joanne commented on her brother's running obsession via e-mail. "Yes, I have come to the conclusion you are definitely crazy! 'It's brutal . . . you'll love it!' What kind of crazy man thinks like that? It's only half the distance . . . yeah, whatever."

> *After showering, eating steak, and drinking one beer for dinner, we went back to the finish line to watch the final competitors come in. It pumped me right back up and was very exciting to watch people finish in the sixteen-hour range. What determination to go for that long. One finisher has two artificial legs, and I remember passing him on the run when he was looking very tired. It is that kind of determination, to never stop, that makes an Ironman.*
>
> *I learned some valuable lessons: I am capable of much more than I believe, and my friends and family are more valuable than anything else.*
>
> —Allan Hicks (from his NZ Ironman post-race notes)

Chapter 18

Frightening, Surprising, Thrilling

The first time I thought I was having a heart attack was in January 2009. I called 911 for an ambulance. The hospital did a number of tests after which the ER doctor concluded that I *probably* had a gallbladder infection. I was scheduled for an appointment to have an ultrasound exam, given some medication, and sent home to wait a few days until the appointment. My diagnosis left me somewhat relieved to hear that it was probably my gallbladder rather than my heart. But, I had an eerie feeling that my ticker was being messed with. I had a premonition that this was about things to come.

At the ultrasound appointment, the technician told me the results of the tests looked negative. He didn't see any evidence of gallbladder trouble, but it wasn't his place to say—it was my doctor's. My family doctor concurred with the ultrasound results; the gallbladder was not my worry.

I had a number of gigs booked in February, and I didn't feel up to par during any gig. By that March, I was feeling exhausted. Early Wednesday morning, March 4, a pain in my chest woke me. The pain would come and go, and I thought that if I sat in my favorite comfortable chair, I could get some relief from this acid reflux (which had worked before). Maybe if I waited awhile and took it easy, the pain would go away. I thought I could make myself healthy with the greatest of all healers: time. I was in denial. One of the hardest lessons I've had to learn is that ignoring a problem does not make it go away.

Finally, facing the reality of the situation, I dialed 911 and told the operator I thought I was having a heart attack.

Being wheeled into the ER on a gurney, my thoughts were about close friends and relatives who had died of heart attacks: my father, my brother, Gary Jorgensen, and a host of others came to mind. Was it my turn? I was worried that some doctor would tell me it was only my gallbladder and send me home with some medication. I knew it was more than that.

Hours later, after all the testing, a doctor said, "Mr. Hicks, you've had a heart attack."

No kidding, really? I was relieved to know what my problem was—or at least part of my problem. Without an intelligent diagnosis, there cannot be a significant treatment. The doctor said I would be going into the intensive care unit right away. To me, it meant there was something seriously wrong with me to be placed on twenty-four-hour watch with monitors, IV bags, and oxygen being fed into my body. My moments of relief were followed by worry, depression, and finally sleep.

Ev called my children in the States to inform them about my situation. I watched nurses come and go, disturbing me from resting to take pills, have my blood glucose tested, and draw blood for more tests. A cardiologist told me I'd have to go to the Calgary Foothills Hospital to have an angiogram.

The doc said, "I'll put you on the waiting list."

There is always a waiting list for socialized medicine. I'd be kept in the hospital in Lethbridge for a few days until an appointment was available. Then I'd be flown to Calgary in an air ambulance. With that bit of information, I couldn't decide if I should be delighted that more tests would be done or depressed at the thought of finding more things wrong. Those thoughts swirled around my mind.

The doctor said, "We'll make your stay here as comfortable as possible. For now, try to get some rest. I hope it won't be too long before we send you to Calgary."

In my distressed state, I thought he said Calvary. *Oh my god—I'm going to be crucified.* I drifted off to sleep and dreamed unimaginable scenes of torment and gloom. As I fought my way toward illumination, I slowly opened my eyes and saw an angel standing at the foot of my bed. Awaking from my slumbering stupor, I recognized the angel was Janine.

Part of Janine's experience as a nurse was working in a hospital heart trauma unit in San Diego. When she received word of my heart attack, she got on a plane from California to Canada. Seeing her was the best medicine I could have received. My depression left, and I was so filled with joy I would have jumped out of bed and hugged her—if it were not for all the tubes and lines draped over me like the restraints on Gulliver.

Four days later, another patient and I were waiting for an ambulance to take us to the airport for the airlift to Calgary. It was 7:30 a.m. The ambulance was to be there at eight. I was anxious to get this ordeal going and over with. I'd prepared myself for the event in Calgary by getting my head straightened around to take a positive attitude and shaving pubic hair from part of my groin where they would insert a tube and thread it up toward my heart to do the angiogram. Janine was driving to Calgary that morning to meet me at the hospital.

At nine, no ambulance. At ten, no ambulance. At eleven, two medics came rushing into the room with wheelchairs to whisk us off to the ambulance and airport. It seems the ambulance dispatcher had neglected to get the message to the driver to pick us up at eight. It was definitely a communication SNAFU.

With lights flashing, siren wailing, and tires screeching, we sped onto the tarmac at the airfield. The pilot and attendant waved for us to hurry. Scrambling to be loaded into the small plane, the pilot told us we might not make the appointment time in Calgary—but he'd try. That would mean rescheduling—and another waiting list. Getting buckled in and taxiing down the runway to get airborne, the four of us were like characters from some bizarre scene of *M*A*S*H*. My partner patient (who was not so very patient) said he needed a cigarette and asked if it was okay if he smoked. Three resounding no's went up loud and clear.

The pilot made good time, and the ambulance ride to the Foothills Hospital was just like flying. Still moving at a fast pace, I was wheeled into the hospital for an elevator ride to the appropriate floor. In the hallway, there was a long line of gurneys and patients. I was wheeled to the end of the line.

A cheery nurse with glasses on the end of her nose, a clipboard in one hand, and a pencil in the other asked if I was Herb Hicks.

You would have thought I ran all the way from Lethbridge to get there. I was out of breath after my whirlwind ride. I nodded and mumbled, "Yeah."

Nurse Cheerful said, "You just made it."

Janine said, "Hi, Dad. Where you been?" She had driven to Calgary before I could fly there.

I explained our situation and told her how glad I was to see her. I was beginning to feel overtaken by anxiety, and Janine could always calm me.

In the operating room, I couldn't help but notice all the TV monitors and a large glass control room that looked like a recording studio. After receiving a relaxant to relieve my anxieties, a doctor explained exactly what the procedure would involve. He made me feel very relaxed—and the medication started taking effect—and I was one happy camper. He told me I could watch the procedure on a TV monitor over my head if I wanted to see my blood vessels and heart at work.

Hey, why not? I've seen my face on TV, why not my heart?

Numbing the site in my groin, the doctor inserted a tube in my femoral artery. A catheter was pushed through the tube and guided through the blood vessel toward the arteries in my heart. The doctor told me I would feel a warm rush throughout my body as they injected a dye through the catheter. With moving x-rays, he could see on the TV monitors what blockages were visible in the vessels, valves, and heart chambers. I saw my heart and blood vessels on the monitor. I was viewing the inside of my chest, which was scary and wonderful. What marvelous organic contraptions humans are. Although I had an eerie, uneasy feeling about my vulnerability and my own mortality, I couldn't keep my eyes off the monitor and the image of my beating heart that has faithfully served me since 1934.

The doctor was talking over the intercom with a technician in the control room.

Janine was standing beside me and talked with the doctor. "Good news, Dad," she said. "They don't have to do a bypass surgery—just put in a stent in an artery." An angioplasty is much less dangerous than cardiac surgery. This was good news, but I had to take a number on the waiting list again.

Patients on gurneys were crowding the hallways like vehicles backed-up on a freeway at rush hour. The nurses told me it would be three or four hours before I would have the angioplasty performed. They moved me upstairs to a recovery ward and put a plug in the hole in my groin. They would push the stent up the same path they had used before—into my artery—to hold the blockage open. Janine, always at my side, gave me a blow-by-blow account of what was happening. I was supposed to remain flat on my back with my legs straight so I did not to disturb the groin injection site. She also told me what I could expect when they did the angioplasty.

Three hours later, I was back in the OR. I was surrounded by familiar sights and sounds, but I was with the stent team. I had opted not to watch the monitors while they positioned the stent in my artery. I listened to the conversation between the doctor and the technician in the control room.

"You'll have to use a longer stent . . . no . . . longer . . . longer . . . that should do it. Okay, that looks good . . . Just a little further . . . further . . . okay . . . there . . . we got it . . . looks good!"

After the angioplasty procedure, I was wheeled back to a ward where I was told to lie flat on my back, keep my legs straight, and keep still. This would challenge my sleeping habits. I always slept on my side and was a roller (so I've been told by sleeping partners). I was exhausted. As I drifted off to sleep, I kept thinking the conversation in the OR was as matter-of-fact as two mechanics repairing an automobile. As well it should be—a skilled surgeon should be as assertive as an expert mechanic. I concluded that I would be good for at least another hundred thousand miles—my stint with my stent would be a long stretch.

I woke in the morning and felt some pain in my chest and groin. Janine walked into the room while a nurse took my blood pressure. She was staying at a motel near the hospital and was back bright and early to check on me.

When the doctor arrived, he told me the pain I was experiencing was normal. The confidence of this doctor, as he examined me, helped ease any fears I had. My distressing emotions were lessened when he told me I should be able to go home that day.

While Janine focused on the road as she drove us back to Lethbridge, I noticed how stark and depressing the countryside looked. The snowy windswept landscape of Alberta in March is lifeless and dreary; the period between the clutches of winter and the arrival of spring has always been a downer for me. I felt a certain joy I had never known before at that time of year.

I realized my joy was a combination of a number of fortunate events—not only within the last few weeks but throughout my life.

I know my despair would have reached an all-time low if it had not been for my loving children. My recovery was speedy and successful because of Joanne, Allan, and Janine. Each of them took two-week turns from their busy schedules to fly to Alberta and nurse me through my recovery. They organized the assortment of medications I had been prescribed so I wouldn't miss a dosage. They drove me to doctor appointments, cleaned my house, cooked, and filled my freezer with healthy, easy-to-prepare meals.

After six weeks, I was getting back into my old routine. My children had taken excellent care of me, and they were back at their homes, attending to their lives after getting my life in order. I was able to drive myself, and I was eager to start playing gigs again.

In April, I played my first gig after the heart attack. A young fine tenor sax player, Andrew Ickakawa, with whom I had played a number of gigs, had a booking for a quartet at a banquet celebrating the opening of a new Buddhist church in town. As I was setting up my piano, a Japanese lady approached me, called my name, and opened her arms for an embrace. It took me a second to recognize her as my old friend and student. Toyo was married to the Buddhist minister who had performed my second marriage ceremony.

I hadn't seen her or her husband for over thirty years because they had moved shortly after my wedding. They were back for the dedication of the new Buddhist church. The three of us had a short reunion before I had to start playing. They told me it looked like I had lost a lot of weight, and I told them about my recent heart problem. A lot of people I knew noticed I had lost a lot of weight. They were right. I reflected on their comment—and how lucky I was to have only lost some weight.

Recovering from my loss of joie de vivre and my loss of weight, I reflected on my upcoming seventy-fifth year. A poem emerged from my contemplations.

Old Spring

Spring is here
I didn't see you in the mirror
But in its place
I saw this old weathered face.
Spring, I once knew you
Then like a butterfly, away you flew
For only a fleeting moment you did stay
Then time took you away.
In your wake, you let summer arrive
Celebrating your growth of being alive
Then the long days of heat and sun
Began to shorten, their time was done.

Cool air and warm colors replaced the green
Autumn a refreshing and beautiful scene
Forecasting colder things in store
Old man winter's knocking at the door.
You may try, but time can't be outdone
Ride the winter through; there's nowhere to run
Just remember there is one sure thing:
There will always be another spring.

My seventy-fifth birthday was coming up on May 7, 2009. My kids were all going to travel to Canada to celebrate the milestone with me. Arranging their schedules so everyone could be there at the same time, they decided on the latter part of June. This would be a good time for everyone to be there since I had my jazz quartet booked at the Mocha Cabana for the weekend of June 19–20. Allan would bring his tenor sax and play the gigs with us. They all arrived a week before the gig.

On Friday, Allan and I went to the Mocha Cabana to set up the band early and meet the rest of our gang for dinner before the gig. It was a warm, sunny, windless day, and we were able to set the band up in the patio, which was like a walled, Spanish-style courtyard. On Friday night, we had a great gig. It was packed to capacity with an appreciative audience.

We planned another family dinner for Saturday. Ev, her sister Janet, brother-in-law Richard, and their two sons, Marty and Jeff, would join us. I told one of the waitresses at the Mocha that I'd like to make dinner reservations for Saturday night. She told me they were not taking any reservations because they were booked. I was perturbed to think that my family and relatives would not be able to get into the Mocha at dinnertime and our first music set. I talked with the owner, and she assured me they would reserve space for us at 5:30.

On Saturday evening, I was getting ready for the gig at my usual snail's pace. Allan and his girlfriend, Shana, said they were going early to make sure we had reservations. They would meet me there.

I said, "Okay. I'll be along shortly."

"Don't be too long, Dad. We want time to have a relaxed meal before the gig."

I vaguely remember when Dad gave the orders and advice to the children, but the protocol had changed. The children were responsible for giving out the guidance. I didn't mind my children giving me instructions and listened to them as much as they had listened to me—and as I had listened to my parents. Everything had come full circle again.

When I arrived at the back door to the café's patio, Allan appeared in the opening. He turned to the people inside and said, "He's here."

I stepped inside and was greeted with a loud cheer and a roaring, "Surprise! Happy Birthday!"

The place was packed with friends and relations. I was overwhelmed. I felt weak in the knees and thought I was about to have another heart attack. How everyone had kept this secret from me was amazing. My kids had been arranging this surprise birthday bash for over a month.

It was a great party. Musicians performed—and people ate, drank, and socialized while I renewed acquaintances I hadn't seen for a long time. The hors d'oeuvres were delicious. I had more than my fair share of jumbo prawns and chicken wings—my favorites—and a large slice of the carrot cake. It was another favorite, which I hadn't had for years because of my diabetes.

What the heck! I was three-quarters-of-a-century old, and I figured one side step from my sugar-free diet wouldn't do me in. My glass of champagne was also a no-no, but it was tolerable on this occasion. I was high on the festivity and felt as though I'd had a magnum of the bubbly stuff (like in the past when I could tolerate such shenanigans). The euphoria I felt reaffirmed my belief that life is a beautiful gig—and my loving family and good friends are among the most important things in life.

August 29, 2010 in Seattle was just slightly overcast, and a slight breeze blew off Lake Union. I was setting up an electronic piano in a dining room on a docked ferryboat, the *MV Skansonia*. Our trio would perform later that evening at Allan's wedding. It was fitting that he would get married on a boat. Allan was marrying the lovely Shana Clary. I felt extremely happy for my son and his bride-to-be. Since meeting Shana more than two years earlier, I had felt as though she was one of my own daughters.

Our trio was called the Spigot Jazz Trio in reference to the trio I had played with at the Spigot forty years earlier. The original trio included Bob on bass and Tony Cappiello on drums. Since Tony and his wife were living in the Seattle area, Allan and I asked him to play drums at the gig. I knew we would miss my brother at the gig; he would have enjoyed playing with Tony again. I had vivid memories of the many gigs Bob, Tony, and I had played together. The chemistry created by our musical feelings and communication enabled us to lock in on a groovy rhythmic circle feeling that took us, as a rhythm section, on a musical flight. It was as though we were one instrument.

We hired a bass player from Seattle who Tony had played with to complete the trio. After so many years, it was a delight to play with Tony again. Allan sat in for a couple of tunes and played his tenor sax to the delight of all the wedding guests. During the wedding ceremony, Allan played a beautiful Sonny Rollins rendition of "My One and Only Love" as Shana was ushered down the aisle.

I did a painting for a wedding present for Allan and Shana. They had met on a canoeing trip on a lake in Washington. The painting depicts a canoe on a beach with their wedding logo of a hummingbird on the bow of the canoe and the numbers 29-8-2010, the date of the wedding. On the side of the canoe is their website name: Shanallan. The canoe is ready to be launched on the lake, and there are snowcapped mountains in the background. A number of symbols express the time, place, and significance of their meeting—flowers, birds, water, rocks, and trees.

Their beautiful home in Edmonds, Washington, is surrounded by fruit trees. It is home to a number of egg-producing chickens and a large boxer dog. Ev and I took a pleasant overnight train ride from Shelby, Montana, to Edmonds in early October 2011 for a quick visit. The four of us flew to California for Joanne's second marriage.

Flying was certainly quicker, but it was not as pleasant as our train ride. Allan (a frequent flyer) had warned me about taking lotions and liquids over 3.4 fluid ounces in my carry-on luggage. I inadvertently had left a tube of foot lotion in my bag that was 5.3 fluid ounces. I was also carrying (if needed) a 0.4 mg spray of nitroglycerin for my heart.

After I declared my nitro, the security guard asked if I had any other liquids in my bag.

Forgetting about my foot lotion, I said, "No. None."

I was asked to remove my shoes and put them and my bag through the scanner. Another security officer told me to take my bag and follow her. We went to a small screening area, and she told me to place my bag on the metal table. She opened my leather carry-on and began rummaging through the contents.

She found my illegal item—the tube of foot lotion was clearly marked "foot lotion."

"What's this?" she asked.

"My foot lotion?" Not wanting to be mistaken for sounding flippant, I quickly added, "I'm a diabetic and need it for my feet."

She snapped, "It's illegal. I'll have to take this. It's over the limit."

During this little charade, Ev was having her own little travesty. She had recently had a hip replacement; as she went through the screening stall, her new hip set off the alarm. A security guard told her the body x-ray machine wasn't working, and she would have to be taken to a room where they could exam her for evidence of a hip implant. While the security officers were looking for hip bombs, I was hopping around and trying to get my shoes back on after being examined for shoe bombs. With no place to sit down, I walked to the main concourse in my stocking feet. Allan and Shana were waiting for us. I was thankful to know that Ev and I weren't terrorist threats. Homeland Security had done their job—which, seriously, I am thankful for—even at a traveler's expense of embarrassment.

After the quick flight to San Francisco, we rented a car and drove to the little beach resort town of Cayucos. Joanne and her fiancé had rented a large home in a beautiful location overlooking the beach and ocean—and a view of Morro Bay. Jon Nibbio and Joanne would be married at this beach location on October 8.

A couple of months earlier, Joanne had asked if I knew a song with the lyrics: "Someday he'll come along, the man I love."

I said, "Yeah, I know that tune. It's 'The Man I Love' by George Gershwin."

She wanted Allan and me to play it at her wedding. Jon is an enchanting person who is the chief operations officer and director of Clinical Services for Family Care Network, Inc. in San Luis Obispo and Santa Barbara Counties. Joanne is a clinical administrator for California Mental Health Services. I joke with them that Jon is the boss at work—and Joanne is the boss at home.

Allan and I were delighted to play at the wedding ceremony. We had made arrangements to pick up an electronic piano in San Luis Obispo to use at the ceremony and the reception. Standing on a little pathway in the yard of the cliff house with Joanne arm in arm, I waited for the cue to walk my daughter toward the preacher and her husband-to-be. The crashing waves, surfers, sounds, sights, and smells of the ocean, and the warm California sun on my face took me back to my beach days in Santa Barbara. Allan began playing "The Man I Love" on his tenor sax. That was my cue to walk my daughter down the path. As soon as we reached Jon, I did a little sidestep, slipped behind the keyboard, and joined Allan in our musical interlude.

Joanne's daughter was included in the wedding ceremony. Alyssa adores her new stepfather, and the feeling is mutual. Allan and I played for a while during the reception, and then we joined the wedding party and guests in some cool drinks and great food. Later, we set the electronic piano up in the living room.

Alyssa was in for a big surprise the next day. Her birthday was coming up on October 27. Ev, Shana, Allan, and I thought we would give her an early birthday present. We had purchased the piano and presented it to Alyssa the day after her mom's wedding. She was thrilled with her present. Every time she'd come to visit her grandpa, she'd head straight for my grand piano and create some little musical ditty. Now that she has her own keyboard, her fingers will find an endless array of new sounds. A year later, I gave my grandson, Luke, a piano for Christmas. Both grandchildren can enjoy the beautiful experience that music has to offer.

We sat on the deck of the beautiful oceanfront home and had lunch and sunned while we took in the magnificent view of the yard, beach, and sea. We watched huge Monarch butterflies gracefully gliding around the yard—and dolphins effortlessly swimming offshore. People on the beach were doing the things I used to do—jumping in and out of the salty surf, looking for shells and sand dollars, and running along the shore like sandpipers.

A wave hit me—a wave of nostalgia. I was drawn back into the past. I had forgotten just how beautiful the coast of California could be—the weather, the sea, the beach, the flora, and especially the carefreeness of people enjoying a temperate climate. I was happy for my children to know they were experiencing those days of sun, surf, and sand that had captivated my being so many years ago. Joanne in Cayucos, Janine in San Luis Obispo, and Allan in Seattle—they are all blessed with environments that are much less harsh than the northern plains.

I wondered why I hadn't moved back to California (a lot of my friends wondered that too). I had found some reasons—medical, financial, acquaintances, amenities, and securities combined with my intrinsic affection of the seasons and the environment.

Life is a frightening, surprising, and thrilling gig.

Afterword

Challenges, Choices, Chances, Changes

*L*ife's journey has led me to discover many paths. Some were planned, designed, and anticipated—and others were found by intuitive awareness that defied any justifiable reasoning. Some were fortunate or unfortunate accidents, and others serendipitously crossed the roads of circumstance. Some paths were delightful and gratifying, and others were cruel and dismal. They all had one thing in common—they were the experiences that life is made of, the good and the bad, the beautiful and the ugly.

The challenges in my life that I met with courage and confidence were usually successful, and the challenges that I met with trepidation and doubt were usually failures. But failures can be instructive, and I've learned important information from my failures. Over the years, the most significant lesson I've learned was that the greatest failure was the fear of failing. The fear of taking a calculated risk—to experience something that may possibly improve me—can be my biggest failure.

Challenges in creating my works of art were met by playing around with observations that were, at first glance, seemingly chaotic—and then embracing associations that, depending upon my abilities and interests—led me by intuition, skill, and intellect toward actions that I hoped became expressive. The final chapter, the last brush stroke, or the last note announced if my work was creative—and if I had given form to chaos or if it failed and was merely surface decoration without depth.

My challenge in finding the courage to bring to a conclusion an artistic work is a joyful and terrifying experience. For me, the delight of creativeness is in the process; for an appreciative audience, the pleasure is in the end result. To play around with an idea and see what happens—where something happens—I keep following my intuition as my work takes off on a life of its own. I no longer singly lead the work; it's a tandem effort. I lead the work as I follow the work. Like an improvised solo, I cannot formulate a structured, predicable design if I want a creative work that surpasses simple ornamentation.

The challenge of finding happiness is not reliant upon how commercially successful I am with my achievement according to an expected and accepted standard—but on my *acceptance* or *rejection* of my achievement. There have been extremely successful people achieving high standards with their objectives who have been unhappy to the point of destroying themselves by ultimate self-criticism: suicide. On the other hand, there are those who are immensely delighted with their accomplishments without any affirmation of celebrity or artistic attainment.

When I was young, the challenges of understanding my world seemed enormous. It was exciting to question the known and confront the unknown. Some of my early childhood challenges were unsubstantiated fears; fear of mistakes, fear of punishment, fear of ridicule, and fear of the unknown were the most prevalent. My greatest challenge, as a child, was overcoming my extreme shyness. Conquering this phobia was no small feat, but with the understanding assistance from my parents, grandparents, and a few dedicated teachers, I suppressed the paranoia. The fear faded as I grew older, although there are still remnants buried deep in the dark recesses of my being. I still have to work at keeping my timorousness at bay, which sounds like a dinosaur from the Jurassic era.

Leaving the security of my childhood home, finding a path, finding knowledge, finding love and companionship, and finding myself were all significant challenges I was confronted with as I approached adulthood. Learning to cope with challenges are the experiences that define my journey. My biggest challenge as an adult is the question of my reality. I've found that existence for me is the same as for others—yet it is different. As my mind identifies in what manner I appear to myself, it is not necessarily the reality of how I exist. How I appear to others is not necessarily how I really exist.

The complexity of human existence has myriad variables based on every physical, emotional, and connected association one experiences. The human brain is the only brain on the planet that allows its possessor to make abstract choices, fantasize, recognize its own mortality, and decide what it wants to do with its existence. My cat doesn't question her existence; I question mine (and hers). It is an awesome power humans have to be able to plan their lives in different ways, according to their copious desires. No other animal has this gift.

The enormous challenge in finding *me* is being able to get in touch with my total experience—not just my conscious observations. A holistic approach to my reality is questioning my social, political, artistic, scientific, and religious beliefs—while obtaining an awareness of my inner emotional world and my observations of the outer corporal world. The vulnerability of public exposure is a challenge I face as an artist. The jeopardy of the real me becoming lost to public opinion of "fitting in" is a challenge. I endeavor to be who I am—not to be who others think I'm supposed to be. My challenge is to find the self-determination to become focused enough about living to let myself, and others, find the real me through my actions.

Choices in education, vocations, hobbies, friends, lovers, and lifestyles all pose questions about which choices are a sure thing and which are a gamble. I cannot predict what life-altering incidents will occur when I make certain choices, but many times they have given meaning to my life. I consider myself very fortunate to have (in most instances) the freedom of choice. It's obvious some choices are restricted by the laws of nature and the laws of man.

Choices I've made were provoked by one of two emotional predispositions—memories of past experiences or expectations of future events. I am who I am because of choices I've made in what I want to do. What I want to do is found out by acting on what I want to do. Choices I've made because of being told or believing "it would be good for me" have led to paths that range from incredibly happy events to disastrous consequences. Making the choices I've made seemed to be, for the most part, a gamble. I was never content to make choices that were of safe foreknown situations; I preferred taking chances with my choices to discover the unknown.

Chances that have transpired by unforeseen events, people, and timing have made a number of unintended alterations in my life's journey—some had significance while others were uninspiring.

I've had some "chance-of-a-lifetime" opportunities. At times, I'd grab the brass ring; other times, I'd miss by a mile. A hunch about something may be as correct as a precisely designed blueprint. Life's journey is a gamble and a blueprint—and every degree in between.

While serving in the air force, my chance encounter with people I'd met in Europe and their interests in the visual arts affected my life significantly. My exposure to art venues in Europe increased my visual awareness to the point that my curiosity led me to take courses in art. I wanted to learn more about why I was so taken by the works of art my European friends had introduced me to.

A chance encounter during a bungled appointment for an interview with an electronics company turned me toward a path to the arts—and chance meetings with people in that field.

Changes I've embraced are events that have restructured my life. How I view my world in my seventies has differences and similarities to my views when I was seventeen. At seventeen (as my memory serves me), I was a bustling, youthful crusader. Sixty years later, I'm more of a serene inquirer. My behavior today is based on changes in my views.

I am a creature of habit, but I am also capable of adapting to major or minor changes (musical pun intended).

As I grow older, the changes in my physical and mental abilities are part of my evolution as an individual—and they have given me insight about who I am. Changes can sometimes be terrifying transformations, but there can be no progressing without change.

Making changes that I've selected have had positive and negative effects on my life; risks are involved. I cannot predict what life-changing incidents will occur when I make changes in education, vocation, lifestyle, environment, relationships, or other behavioral traits. My assumption used to be that changes that had inadvertently happened were, for the most part, detrimental, but experience has shown that most were beneficial. Changes sometimes are a way of reality grabbing our attention toward self-realization.

One significant, unintentional change in my life was my back operation. After the operation, my insistence on returning to work as soon as possible caused my back to be sprained. Ending up flat on my back again for almost a year made me realize that my mind and my body needed some downtime. I was more considerate of how I treated my back, my body, and my mind after that.

My decision to devote a large portion of my time to a new field of study changed the focus of my life. For a while, music and art took a backseat to the study of paleontology. My brother's involvement with the fossil ammonite industry motivated me to take an active part in a field of study that had interested me since my youth. I renovated my painting studio to accommodate the study of fossils, and with my brother, I became occupied with the exploration and restoration of ammonite fossils. This change has given me insight into the evolutionary history of life on earth and the reality of my own being.

A change brought about by my heart attack in 2009 taught me to be more introspective about how I was—or was not—taking care of myself. Controlling my diabetes, high cholesterol, and high blood pressure are major insurance policies on which I try to keep the premiums up to date (along with following the judicious advice from my children). I don't have a hypochondriac's list of nonexistent illnesses, but I do have a number of real health issues that I wish I could make changes to. The most troubling health issue is the arthritic pain in my fingers and wrists when playing the piano, but retiring from playing the piano is not an option. That would be the ultimate change, resulting in retiring from life.

I continue going to and from gigs, meeting the challenges, making the choices, taking the chances, and embracing the changes throughout my life that define my being.

CPSIA information can be obtained at www.ICGtesting.com
Printed in the USA
LVOW13s2050300614

392373LV00001B/25/P